Great Recipes
From The
World's Great Cooks

Books by Peggy Harvey

WHEN THE COOK'S AWAY

SEASON TO TASTE

A BRIDE'S COOKBOOK

GREAT RECIPES FROM THE WORLD'S GREAT COOKS

Great Recipes
From The
World's Great Cooks

FORMERLY THE HORN OF PLENTY

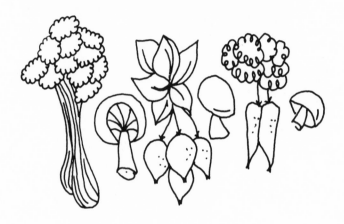

by Peggy Harvey

GRAMERCY PUBLISHING COMPANY • NEW YORK

Library of Congress Catalog Card No: 64-21484

This edition published by Gramercy Publishing Company,
distributed by Crown Publishers, Inc.,
by arrangement with Little, Brown & Company.

Manufactured in the United States of America

ISBN: 0-517-084643

p o n m l k j

For Peter

Mix a little love of adventure with the recipes on a page. That is the way that miracles are performed. This cookbook is a guide, not an oracle, and dishes are made, not born.

Louis P. de Gouy, *The Gold Cook Book*

Preface

IT DID NOT occur to me, at the outset, that in compiling this anthology I would be doing myself a great favor. Within a few months I will have, between the covers of a book, the recipes to which I most often refer and which I often have difficulty finding. No longer will I have to stand before the shelves scratching my head and striving to remember where I saw Fonduta alla Piemontese or in which black notebook I scribbled the directions for a Javanese cocktail tidbit given to me by someone from the UN.

The recipes that comprise the major portion of this collection come from books by my friends and/or competitors and have been chosen for three different reasons. First, there are my favorites, such as Jim Beard's simple Shad Roe en Papillote from *House and Garden's Cook Book*. This is the way I always do the first roe of the season and, simple though it may be, I believe in checking a familiar recipe just to make sure that I haven't forgotten something. Secondly, there are the interesting or challenging dishes that I had always meant to experiment with but had not got around to until I was putting this book together. An outstanding example is Helen Evans Brown's Winter Melon Soup, which, when I made it successfully, gave me a tremendous sense of accomplishment. Thirdly, I have tried to remember and include all the recipes that I have found for people. This statement requires a bit of explanation.

Cookbook writers are constantly being asked for recipes. We are considered to be authorities and, as such, are expected to be able to give, off the cuff, foolproof instructions for any kind of dish from poached eggs to something unpronounceable that someone had in the Himalayas last weekend. Most of us are able to come through some of the time but I defy anyone to be able to do so all of the time. Certainly I cannot.

It is fun to be asked, though; and when I have to give up, I enjoy doing research on the problem for my questioner. At a dinner party not too long ago, someone described an Italian cheese soup with white truffles and croutons and asked me how to make it. I said that I would be happy to find out and promptly went to work. The recipe I came up with was for the Fonduta alla Piemontese mentioned above, which I found in Maria Luisa Taglienti's *Italian Cookbook.* In my search I had come across other recipes for *fonduta* but they were all for the heavier fondue, which is, incidentally, what one ordinarily gets when one orders *fonduta* in Italy. Miss Taglienti's recipe, however, turned out to be just what my dinner partner had in mind. Later I tried it myself, liked it and have included it here.

The second and smaller section of this book is composed of recipes by amateur as well as professional cooks which have not been published heretofore, or at least, not in book form. In getting these together I have reaped another benefit; I have been forced to collect, from all the scraps of paper, letters, backs of envelopes and old notebooks, the recipes I've jotted down from time to time. After separating the wheat from the chaff, I have had to try out the untried and organize the results. It will be wonderful to have them all together, proven and *readable.*

Actually, an anthology of recipes, in order to be worthy of the name, should encompass considerably more material than this one does. Can such a book be complete without mention of Escoffier, Ali Bab, Carème and others of that period? Should there not be something from Madame Prunier's famous fish cookbook? Is it right to slight Mrs. Beaton? Obviously, if all these great names were to be given their deserved space the book would be overpowering in content and size. I comfort myself with the knowledge — and this is not mere rationalization — that these famous pioneers and many others *are* here in essence, since all modern cookery is based on their discoveries, their theories and their genius. It is more difficult to explain why many fine contemporary recipe-makers are not in evidence on these pages. In a few isolated cases, permission to re-print has been refused but, in general, I must plead lack of space. This explanation must also cover the omission of any recipes from quite a number of foreign countries. I have tried, however, to make of the book a reasonably representative collection of provocative culinary formulas, and I hope that having it on your kitchen shelf will make you as happy as I fully expect it to make me.

PEGGY HARVEY

Contents

I

Cookbooks at Their Best

The Gentleman's Companion, an Exotic Cookery Book

CHARLES H. BAKER, JR.

TWENTY-ODD YEARS AGO, two slim volumes — one on exotic cooking and one on exotic drinks — were published under the collective title *The Gentleman's Companion*. In charmingly florid style, the author dealt with food and drink from the four corners of the earth. Since this is a collection of recipes for edibles rather than potables, it is the cookery book that concerns us here. This, as Mr. Baker puts it, is "a company of hand-picked receipts, each one beloved and notable in its place, collected faithfully on three voyages and a quarter million miles around the world, and other journeys." In addition, there are those garnered from "friends and correspondents . . . in odd and intriguing spots of the globe." It was extremely difficult to select a meager two recipes from this fascinating book. Before I present my choices, here is Mr. Baker's "Word to the Wise," which I took to heart many years ago.

EXPLODED OLD WIVES' TALE: THE FALLACY OF
PLUNGING LOBSTERS, OR FOR THAT MATTER
ANY CRUSTACEANS INTO BOILING WATER

We are glad to announce that what we, in our modest fumbling manner, found to be true twenty-five years ago when doing our own cooking on a canoe trip down the east coast of Florida, is now confirmed by none other than the incomparable Henri Charpentier. Never plunge, toss, slide or push lobsters or crawfish into boiling water. Sudden contact of fleshy tissue with this scalding bath sets up an aggravated and permanent case of rigour-mortis. Once-tender muscles toughen; tough muscles become adamant. Rather take a kettle filled with sea or salted water — preferably with slight acidulation of vinegar or lemon juice — and gently lower the victim into it. Lobsters, crawfish, crabs, cannot feel. It is not cruel. The slowly mounting heat lulls them to rest and they emerge rosily, tender as they went in. It's the same as making a stew. Hot or boiling water toughens meat fibers instantly.

[NOTE: The same procedure works equally well with boiled eggs and corn, based on the same theory. Eggs cooked this way are called "coddled," and the whites are delicate rather than rubbery. One thing to bear in mind is that your timing starts when the water comes to a boil, and the crustacean, corn or egg should boil or simmer half as long as when cooked in the ordinary manner, a four-minute egg boiling for two minutes and so forth. — P. H.]

ARROZ CON POLLO (Chicken with Rice)

Cristobal on the Atlantic and Balboa on the Pacific — those are the model towns under Uncle Sam's jurisdiction in the "Zone," and they lie like neat, prim, starched maidens, cheek-by-jowl with the modern evolution of the civilization left by the Conquistadores for better or for worse in Colón and Panama City. There in Old Panama the ruined cathedral tower points up an accusing finger denouncing its sack and burning by Morgan's men. Culture and lotteries, courtly Spanish girls with big gazelle eyes whisk by in shiny motor cars and guarded closely by their duennas; while a block away is the so-called Coconut Grove section with ladies of all nations behind their grilled windows . . .

In the Union Club, perched high on stilts above the huge Pacific tides, is where the cream of Panamanian society gathers. They have a good chef there. His Arroz con Pollo, although basically still the old favorite from Spain, has local and tropical touches. It will nourish from four to six guests.

2 plump chickens of tender years	4 to 5 cups of Spanish rice
6 thin slices dead ripe pineapple	½ cup raisins or currants
2 tbsp lime or lemon juice	4 tbsp tomato paste
½ cup fine bread crumbs	1 orange sliced quite thin
1 tsp, scant, of Tabasco sauce	1 cup butter
Salt and pepper to taste	½ cup sherry wine
2 pinches saffron	½ cup guava jelly for garnish

Cut chickens into pieces, brush with lime juice, season with salt and pepper; let marinate in this lime juice and seasoning bath for 2 hours to seal in flavours. Now fry gently in butter, and when tender add tomato paste, raisins, wine and other seasonings. Stir once, cover tightly and keep warm but do not cook again. . . . On a large hot platter make a ring of Spanish Saffron Rice, and in the center of this pleasant atoll pile the chicken. Turn sauce over chicken also. Meanwhile cut up ripe fresh pineapple slices into 1″ square bits and fry out for 5 minutes with the crumbs — using canned fruit if no really ripe fresh ones are at hand; but discard the juice entirely. Turn this over the chicken, garnish with thin slices of orange, mounting a crimson jewel of guava jelly on each slice. . . . Scarlet pimento also garnishes well.

To Make Spanish Saffron Rice:

Take 1 cup rice; pick out any dark grains or foreign substances, but do not wash. Put 2 tbsp olive oil in the top of a double boiler, place directly on a slow fire and gently fry out 1 finely minced onion with half a bisected garlic clove. When tender, discard garlic, turn in the cup of rice, ¼ tsp saffron, ½ tsp salt. Stir well and add just enough beef or chicken broth to cover. Cook uncovered in a double boiler until tender, adding more broth as needed. Stir gently with a wooden fork to keep from breaking grains. When tender, turn into a shallow pan and dry in a warm — not hot — oven. Rice should be quite dry.

YAMS AUX MARRONS,
FLAMBÉ A LA FORT-DE-FRANCE

Many lovely things come from Martinique, including the Empress Josephine who was born on neighboring Trois Isles. There the aristocratic French planters lived a life of luxury and ease seldom matched. There the school of Creole cookery is toothsome, torrid and more original. The employment of candied chestnuts is a typically French gesture. . . . Choose round, fat yams. Scrub them and parboil until semi-tender. Slice lengthwise slices after peeling, and about ½″ thick. Sauté gently 5 minutes in hot butter, then arrange on a flat pottery or Pyrex oven dish. Dust with sugar, the grated green peel of 3 limes; tee up 2 or 3 big candied marrons on each slice, ring each marron with raisins; and put under the broiler or into a hot oven around 400°. Arrange on a platter, garnish with small brilliant blossoms of any kind. Heat a ladle of cognac brandy and spill 1 tsp or so on each yam slice, serving with lights properly dimmed, flambé. . . . Personally we have found that any medium dark rum seems to marry with the tropical yam and the candied chestnuts, even better than the brandy. Martinique rum is procurable in all cities now. Incidentally this is one of the finest companion dishes to roast guinea hen we have ever come upon; and it also suits wild duck, turkey, and all sorts of game. It is very rich and if served, cut the other vegetables down to perhaps a single partner such as broccoli hollandaise, wild rice or artichokes.

The Esquire Culinary Companion

CHARLES H. BAKER, JR.

THIS MORE RECENT BOOK of Mr. Baker's is a personal report on the best restaurants in a dozen countries and "a compendium of pearls wheedled away from chefs during three years journeying back and forth across Europe on behalf of *Esquire* magazine," where these recipes first appeared.

CREAM-CHICKEN-AVOCADO SOUP

One of the Simplest Yet Most Delicious Soups We've Ever Tasted: a CREAM-CHICKEN-AVOCADO Affair Called SOPE DE AVE E ABACATE, from a Small Restaurant High Above the Town of Funchal in Madeira. When you take the silly little cogwheel railway up 6000-foot Pico Ruivo, which centers this island, you get a magnificent view of the town, the terraced arbors of white Verdello, red Negra Molle and superb golden Malvasia grapes, and all sorts of fruits, vegetables and sugar cane. Part of the way up they'll toss you into a weird hammock slung under a pole, hist the thing on two men's shoulders and rock-&-roll you to the top of the damnedest ride you ever took; then, after lunch at the simple restaurant there, you get into an equally weird sledlike affair and swish down, only instead of on snow, it's on surface of small, round pebbles paving the improbably steep mountain road! Remember, Portugal owns Madeira, and Portugal once owned Brazil, and Brazil has avocados by the ton. Not appreciated at all in Spain, despite the fact they found them good in South and Central America back in the days of the Conquistadores. Simple to do. . . .

The Dish: To serve two, add equal amount cold water to 1 can Campbell's cream of chicken soup, 1 tablespoon scraped onion pulp, a few Julienne slivers scarlet pimento, ½ teaspoon chili powder (cumin, oregano and dried sweet peppers), a little hand-milled black pepper, and ½ teaspoon grated yellow lemon peel. Final gift is 4 tablespoons fine-cubed avocado pulp. Let simmer up slowly, covered for 5 to 6 minutes; stir 5 or 6 times to soften avocado cubes and blend flavors. Serve with thick slices crusty bread, toasted lightly. Dunking in order. Portuguese also know the avocado as *fruta da América tropical.*

BROOK TROUT POACHED IN BUTTER
From Delightful Cramond Inn, 5 Miles Outside Edinburgh, Scotland.

Scarcely fifteen minutes' motoring from town, you'll find this nice 300-year-old tavern with its own village pub, faithfully restored by a wealthy Scotsman named Lindsay Gumler, complete with great low-beamed ceilings of ancient hand-adzed oak and colorful oil paintings. Its situation couldn't be more charming set as it is where the River Almond joins the famous Firth of Forth. Not only is its native Scottish cookery sound, but amazingly enough it boasts some of the nicest French wines, cask-imported and bottled by the owner himself; delicious as his own home-smoked salmon. It is tiny, so reserve a day ahead of time; accommodates two dozen or so guests, total. Ask for specialty of the day, which may include anything from goose, duck, game in season, delicious cold-water lobster, roast joints, even as succulent a Welsh Rabbit as ever passed the lips.

The Trout: Trick about this simple trout dish is to use twice as much butter as you'd usually plan, and heat gradually until hot but in no way smoking. Dry fish carefully, season with nothing but salt and hand-milled pepper; dip in a trifle of flour — shaking off all excess. Then the next trick: Put tail of every fish into hot butter first until covered 1½" or so. Hold thus for a few seconds each, then lay gently in butter and poach. This way the fish do not curl up as usual. Brown over not-too-furious heat. Fish come out tender and moist. A bit of fine-snipped parsley and a wedge of lemon, perhaps, is the sole garnish. No extra flavors to detract from the fish itself, which is correct as can be.

This is a Potato Puff Affair Known as P F L U T T E R S   A L S A C I E N N E
From Restaurant Maison de Têtes, in Colmar, in Alsace.

This justly famous place dates back to 1609 or so, and boasts a vast array of sculptured heads — hence its name; a fine courtyard and steeply gabled roof. A good array of Alsatian wines is offered you in pitchers borne by buxom, appled-cheeked Alsatian gals in native costume, who are vastly happy to be once more under the French flag, this coveted, rich province having been taken back from Germany during the last war, with plenty help from the U. S. Army of liberation. Colmar itself was not badly damaged. Splendid fish and game dishes here; neighboring Strasbourg is world-famous for its matchless *Pâté de Foie Gras,* created from hand-fed, penned-up Alsatian geese.

The Dish: To around 4 cups mashed potatoes add 2 tablespoons flour, first worked smooth in saucepan with same amount of butter, 1 crushed garlic clove, 2 tablespoons fine-snipped parsley, a couple or 3 well-beaten eggs, salt and cayenne to taste; then the crowning gift: just enough ground nutmeg to flavor delicately. Blend diligently, take rounded tablespoonfuls and place in lines on well-buttered oven pan. Cook in preheated slow oven at around 325 degrees, until well set; a trifle over 10 minutes does the trick. Now brush gently with melted butter, and pop under broiler until they're a pale, golden brown. Serve at once with a little melted sweet butter poured over. Makes a fine side dish for fish or game, or poultry of any kind.

A Delicious Dessert Course is a Typically Danish Business Anyone Can Do
Called R O M F L O D E or R U M - C R E A M   C U S T A R D , from
Smart Restaurant Aalborghallens in Aalborg, in Danish Jutland.

This is another one of Denmark's smartest new out-of-Copenhagen restaurants; we lunched here during our inspection of the Akvavit distillery. Their menu is elaborate, in Danish and French; wine list very good; chef dedicated. Furthermore, for a change, this is a custard-type dish the ladies will like to do; most of our European specialties thus far have been more or less pointed at the males. . . .

The Dish: To serve six, dissolve 1½ to 2 tablespoons unflavored gelatine in 3 tablespoons chilled milk. Reserve. Next scald 1½ cups light or heavy cream mixed with 1 cup milk. Meanwhile beat 5 egg yolks with ¼ cup sugar and about ⅓ teaspoon salt. When well-frothed and stiffish, add ¼ cup of the scalded cream-milk; stir until smooth, then add the rest of same. Put into double boiler and stir until well thickened and smooth. Put a couple tablespoons of this hot mixture into the gelatine, stir until dissolved well and add to the rest. At very last add 2 tablespoons Gold Label St. Croix rum, stirring well. Put in pre-wet mold, or small individual jobs. Chill well for 3 hours or so. Serve with mask of whipped cream flavored with a trifle of almond extract, and final garnish of lingonberry conserve, grenadine syrup or melted black currant jelly. Remember, we bought the Virgin Islands from Denmark in '17, and they've always admired rum flavorings.

James Beard's Treasury of Outdoor Cooking

IT IS DIFFICULT to introduce James Beard, which is hardly necessary anyway, without employing the hackneyed phrase which inevitably follows his name whenever it appears, to wit: "America's foremost authority on food and wine." I, however, am going to try another tack: Jim is a big man; he has a big voice, a big appetite, a big reputation, a big heart and, as a result of the last, a big group of friends to which I am proud to belong. His energy is as enormous as everything else about him. There is always a cookbook or a magazine article on the fire, so to speak. He is constantly just leaving on or just back from a trip involving a wine or food tasting, a consultation or a demonstration. Sometimes the trip is just from his house on Tenth Street to the Time and Life Building but almost as often it is to the West Coast, the Orient or somewhere in Europe. Occasionally these junkets force him to miss a Broadway opening or a Saturday afternoon performance at the Metropolitan but not if he can help it. Meanwhile, from October until April, his cooking school thrives, and on the evenings when the Tenth Street kitchen is not filled with students, it is apt to be filled with guests for a cocktail party or a buffet — the jovial host looking as if he had nothing on his mind but the pleasures of the moment. These recipes are from big Jim's biggest and, at this time, most recent book.

ROLLED SPITTED TURKEY

Have the butcher bone a turkey for you. Spread it with butter, sprinkle with chopped shallots or green onions, salt and pepper to taste, and enhance either with thyme, rosemary, tarragon or sage. Roll and tie the bird securely, adjust it on the spit, and roast to an internal temperature of about 165 F. Serve with tiny creamed onions and peas, crisp, buttered toast, and a hearty white wine.

[NOTE: If you wish to cook this turkey in the oven, wrap it in aluminum foil and bake at 350 degrees for 2½-3 hours or until internal temperature is 165 F. Unwrap for the last half hour and brown.

For a more elaborate dish, make 6 cups of broth from the turkey bones, the giblets (except the liver), the usual soup pot vegetables (carrot, onion, celery leaves, etc.) seasonings and 2 quarts cold water.

Make a forcemeat of 2 lbs. finely minced raw veal mixed with 2 beaten eggs, 1 tablespoon chopped parsley, 1 teaspoon salt and freshly ground black pepper. Spread the boned turkey out on a board, skin-side down. Cover with the forcemeat and sprinkle with the turkey liver, coarsely chopped. A chopped truffle or two would not be amiss. Roll the turkey up, as in a jelly roll, tie and bake as above. Serve with a Suprême Sauce made as follows:

Melt 4 tablespoons butter and stir in 4 tablespoons flour. When blended, add gradually 6 cups hot, strained turkey broth. Cook over low heat, stirring frequently, until reduced to two-thirds of its original volume. Add light cream until sauce reaches the desired consistency. Correct seasoning. — P.H.]

CHOUCROUTE GARNIE

3 pounds of loin of pork	2 teaspoons pepper
Bacon or salt pork in thick slices	Juniper berries
4 pounds of sauerkraut	White wine
6 pig's feet or knuckles	Garlic sausages
6 knockwurst	3 cloves garlic
1 large piece of salt pork	9 to 12 potatoes

As you will discover when you try this, it is not only a hearty buffet dish, but can be varied in many interesting ways. Another advantage is that it can be made a day ahead and reheated. As a matter of fact, it is better this way. Line a large kettle with strips of salt pork or bacon. If the sauerkraut is old, wash it in cold water and tear it apart. If it is fairly new it will not require this. Place in the kettle and cover with white wine. Cover kettle and steam for 2 hours. Then add the pork loin, pig's feet or knuckles, the large piece of salt pork, garlic, pepper and juniper. Simmer gently for about 2 hours. Now add the garlic sausage and cook for another 15 minutes. Then add the knockwurst and cook for another twenty minutes. About 30 minutes before the dish has finished, cook your potatoes in their jackets separately. When they are finished, remove the jackets and shake them over a flame to dry them out. Arrange the choucroute in the center of a large platter and surround it with the various meats.

Variations: Substitute beer for the white wine. Or any good stock or bouillon to which you have added a good half-cup or more of dry gin and 7 or 8 crushed juniper berries. You may also make this dish with a smoked pork loin, or chicken and fresh pork, or a piece of feathered game, such as pheasant or duck.

POLENTA

1½ cups of corn meal	1 teaspoon salt
3 cups of water	

Bring the water and salt to a boil in a very heavy saucepan. Very slowly, without letting the boiling cease, pour in the corn meal. Stir with a wooden spoon so that the meal does not lump. Continue cooking and stirring until it is quite thick and smooth. Line a strainer or colander with cloth and pour the mix into it. Place over simmering water, covered, and let steam for 3 hours, or until the corn meal has become a firm loaf. Serve it cut into slices, with plenty of melted butter, salt and pepper, and, if you like, grated Parmesan cheese. This will serve four.

Variations: Polenta is delicious prepared as above and served with any of the many sauces that are used for spaghetti or, if you prefer, a cheese sauce. Any leftover polenta can be allowed to cool, then cut into slices and gently fried in butter or oil. Serve with grated cheese or sauce.

MUSHROOM SALAD

Choose white and very fresh mushrooms. See that the gills have not opened. Wash them briefly and dry well. Pluck the stems out and put the caps into a salad bowl. Cover with a French dressing to which you have added a bit of crushed garlic and a tablespoon of chopped fresh tarragon. If you are using the dried kind, use half that amount. Toss well and let the mushrooms marinate for at least an hour — longer is even better. Each time you pass the bowl in the course of your duties, give the mushrooms a light toss. When you are ready to serve, add Belgian endive — which you have previously rinsed and split into quarters, or stripped into long leaves and kept cold — to the salad and toss well. The salad seems to have a quality of great elegance and subtlety, and, oddly enough, if served outdoors it takes on a robust character.

CUBAN BREAD

1 package or 1 cake of yeast	1 tablespoon of sugar
2 cups of lukewarm water	6 to 9 cups of flour
1¼ tablespoons of salt	

Dissolve the yeast in the warm water and add the salt and sugar. Using a wooden spoon, add the flour a cup at a time, beating it in well. We give you the variable amount of flour since all flour varies in the amount of liquid it will absorb. Use enough to make a smooth, firm dough. Cover with a towel and put in a warm place to rise until it is double in bulk. Turn it out on a table or board that is well-floured and knead for a few minutes, then shape into loaves in any of the following forms: long French, round Italian, or small individual loaves. Sprinkle corn meal liberally on a baking sheet and arrange the loaves on this. Allow to rise for 5 minutes. Cut a slash across the loaves 2 or 3 times or make a long slash down the middle, brush with cold water and place in a cold oven. Set the oven for 400 F. Place a pan of boiling water on the rack below the loaves and bake for about 40 to 45 minutes.

Note: The more you knead the better your result will be.

James Beard's Fish Cookery

J IM CALLS THIS book his "favorite child."

MOUSSE OF LOBSTER

1 pound lobster meat	2 cups heavy cream
2 egg whites	Butter
Ice	24 mushroom caps
Salt, pepper	1 cup white wine
Paprika	Hollandaise sauce

Grind the lobster meat with the fine blade, putting it through the grinder twice. Or you may pound it in a mortar. Gradually work in the egg whites with a wooden spoon. Next put the mixture through a purée machine or a fine sieve. Place a bowl over cracked ice, place the mixture in the bowl and, with a wooden spoon, work in salt, pepper and paprika to taste and the heavy cream.

Butter a ring mold or charlotte mold and decorate it with slices of truffle, if you wish. Fill the mold ¾ full with the lobster mixture. Place in a pan of hot water and cook, either over a low flame or in a moderate oven (350 degrees), until set. This should take about 30 minutes. Unmold on a hot platter and decorate with mushrooms which have been poached briefly in the white wine. Serve with a Hollandaise sauce.

Note: Individual molds of the mousse may be made and served in the same way.

QUENELLES DE BROCHET

These have been great favorites in France for many years. They are not simple to make, and they must be done properly or they are not good.

3 cups soft bread crumbs	¼ teaspoon nutmeg
1 cup boiling milk	1 cup creamed butter
1 pound of pike	2 eggs
1 teaspoon salt	4 or 5 egg yolks
1 grind of fresh pepper	

Pour the boiling milk over the bread crumbs and let the crumbs soak until the milk is completely absorbed. Mix them well with a wooden spoon until they are practically a paste. Place this over the lowest flame on your stove and dry it out, working it all the time with the wooden spoon. Spread it out on a flat pan and let it cool thoroughly. Put the pike through the fine grinder twice. Then work it in a mortar or put it in a heavy bowl and work it with a wooden spoon. Add salt, pepper and nutmeg and blend thoroughly. Turn it out on a board, combine it with the crumb mixture and mix well with your hands. Return it to the mortar or bowl, add the creamed butter and continue blending until it is smooth and thoroughly mixed. Gradually work in 2 whole eggs and 4 or 5 additional egg yolks. Put the mixture through a fine sieve or a food mill and work it again with a wooden spoon until it has a smooth and silky texture.

Form into oval cakes about the size of an egg or a little larger, and arrange them in a buttered skillet so that they barely touch one another. Cover them with boiling salted water and poach gently for about 10 minutes. Remove the cooked quenelles to absorbent paper. Serve them with a rich cream sauce.

COLD TROUT IN JELLY

6 trout	1½ envelopes gelatin
White wine court bouillon (see below)	Green onions, leek, chives, tarragon leaves, hard-cooked eggs
White of egg and egg shells	

Poach the trout in the bouillon and remove them to a platter. Reduce the bouillon to 3 cups and clarify [See Note below—P. H.]. Soak the gelatin in ½ cup of water and combine it with the boiling broth. Chill until it is thick and syrupy.

The fish may be decorated as elaborately as you choose. Or you may prefer to serve them plain, simply masked with the jelly. If you want a spectacular dish, remove about half of the skin from the chilled, cooked trout. Then make a flower design on the flesh. Use the green stems of the onions, leek, or chives, green tarragon leaves and make tiny flowers out of hard-cooked eggs.

Pour enough of the jelly over the decorated (or plain) trout to mask it thoroughly. Put the platter with the fish and a bowl of the rest of the jelly in the refrigerator to chill. Just before serving, chop the rest of the jelly very fine and garnish the fish platter with it. Serve with mayonnaise or a rémoulade sauce.

Variation: Reduce the broth to 1 cup and add 1 cup of red wine or port wine. Add 1 envelope of gelatin to make a jelly.

[NOTE: To clarify: Beat lightly with a fork the white and crushed shell of 1 egg. Add, stirring, to the boiling bouillon. Stop stirring and simmer for 3 minutes. Turn off heat and let stand for 15 minutes before straining. — P. H.]

Rich White Wine Court Bouillon for Aspics

1 pound fish bones and heads	2 carrots, diced
1 quart water	2 cloves garlic
1 quart dry white wine	1 bay leaf
1 teaspoon dried thyme	Salt, pepper
2 onions stuck with cloves	

Cook the fish bones and heads in the water for 30 minutes. Strain through fine cloth. You should have about a quart of bouillon. Add all the other ingredients, bring to a boil and simmer for 20 minutes before adding the fish. For aspic, reduce the bouillon over a brisk flame after the fish is removed.

CURRIED SOFT-SHELLED CRABS

The smaller the soft-shelled crab and the earlier it is caught in the molting process, the tenderer and better flavored it will be. Usually soft-shelled crab is bought already cleaned at the market but here is the process in case you must do it yourself: With the aid of a small, sharp-pointed knife, fold back the covering at the points of the back, and remove all the spongy bits you find there. Turn the crab over and remove the small apron on the front.

4 onions, finely chopped	1 cup white wine (or more)
5 tablespoons butter	½ cup ground almonds mixed with
1 unpeeled apple, coarsely chopped	1 cup heavy cream
2 tomatoes, coarsely chopped	Salt, pepper
2 tablespoons curry powder	

Sauté the chopped onions in butter until they are just creamy colored. Add the apple and the tomatoes. Cover and simmer for 1 hour or more. Put through a purée or a coarse sieve. Add the curry powder and the white wine. Return to the stove and cook for 10 minutes. Then add the almonds and cream and let it all come to a boil. Taste for seasoning.

12 soft-shelled crabs (prepared for cooking)	6 tablespoons butter
	Flour

Dip the crabs in flour and brown quickly in butter. Add them to the sauce and let them cook for 10 minutes.

Serve with rice. Serves 4 to 6.

BOUILLABAISSE

This is the recipe of Jean Suprenat, who owns the restaurant La Méditerranée in Paris.

Certain Mediterranean fish, not available in this country, are traditional in the bouillabaisse, but excellent substitutes can be found. A good selection for an American bouillabaisse is haddock or bass for the hearty fish; then lemon sole, whiting, red snapper, flounder — practically any other fish you want. And always eel. For shellfish, use lobster, mussels, sea urchins. For a large bouillabaisse:

3 pounds fish
  1 pound eel
  1 pound haddock or sea bass
  1 pound red snapper
    (Or you may use a larger variety
    of fish — ½ pound each of 6
    different kinds)
3 pounds lobster
3 dozen mussels
3 leeks
2 large onions, chopped

3 cloves garlic
3 tomatoes
⅓ cup olive oil
Bouquet garni (thyme, bay leaf, pars-
  ley, celery, rosemary)
Pinch of saffron
Water or fish broth
Salt, pepper
Cayenne
Croutons fried in garlic-flavored olive
  oil

Cut the fish into small serving-size pieces. Keep the richer, heavier fish — eel, haddock, cod, bass — separate from the more delicate types. Cut the live lobster into pieces. Wash and clean the mussels.

Cut the white part of the leeks into small pieces. Chop the onion and the garlic. Peel and seed the tomatoes.

Heat the olive oil in a large kettle. Add the vegetables and let them cook well together. Add the bouquet garni and the heavier fish. Let this cook about 7 or 8 minutes. Add the lighter fish, the lobster and a good pinch of saffron. Cover with water or fish broth. Cook for 15 minutes. Add the mussels and cook until they open. Place the fish in a deep serving dish and pour the hot liquid over it. Serve garlic-flavored croutons separately.

Variations: 1. Boil heads and bones of fish with water and white wine — 3 quarts of liquid to 3 pounds of heads and bones — for ½ hour. Then simmer until the liquid is reduced to 1½ quarts. Strain, clarify and use as liquid for the bouillabaisse.

2. Substitute ½ cup of butter for the olive oil. The result is a more delicate dish.

POACHED WHITEFISH

This delicate fish takes very well to poaching. Be careful not to overcook it, and remove it from the boiler very gently. The old method of wrapping fish in cheesecloth is excellent; it's a good idea to leave long ends of the cloth that you can use as handles when you lift the fish. Of course, a real fish boiler with a rack solves the problem.

[NOTE: I paraphrase, here, Jim Beard's directions for poaching a whole fish: Scale the fish but leave the head and tail intact. A mixture of milk and water, half and half, is the perfect poaching liquid for this type of fish. Bring the liquid to a boil, reduce the heat and put in the fish. The liquid must never boil, never bubble but just simmer without any visible movement. Cook about 8 minutes to the pound. — P. H.]

There is a wide variety of sauces to use with poached whitefish. Personally, I like an oyster or shrimp sauce, but Hollandaise and Béarnaise go well with it, too. Serve plain boiled potatoes and a purée of spinach mixed with a little grated garlic, grated Parmesan cheese, and butter.

THREE RECIPES FROM

The James Beard Cookbook

THESE RECIPES constitute a very slight, but I hope intriguing, sampling from a sizable basic cookbook.

LONDON BROIL (Serves 4)

3-pound flank steak   **Pepper**
Salt

Many people insist that flank steak must be cooked by a long slow process. This well-known dish calls for *broiling* flank steak and is delicious if properly served. The secret is in the carving.

This is the one exception to the rule that you must always cook meat at room temperature. Flank steak should be at refrigerator temperature, so take it out at the last minute. Remove the tough membrane on the outside. You will need the help of a sharp knife for this.

Broil it quickly by gas, electricity or charcoal, allowing about 5 minutes on each side. Season to taste with salt and pepper and remove it to a hot platter or carving board. Now comes the tricky part. With a very sharp knife held at an angle, almost flat to the top of the meat, slice diagonally through to the bottom. This cuts across the tough fibers of the flank. The slices should be very thin and the meat should be rare inside. Otherwise it will be tough.

Serve the hot slices of steak on hot toasted and buttered French bread.

Suggested accompaniments: French-fried onion rings and plain potatoes in their jackets.

Variation: Orientale — Combine ½ cup of soy sauce with ¾ cup of dry vermouth or red wine, a 1-inch piece of fresh ginger grated (or candied ginger finely chopped), 3 cloves of garlic chopped and a handful of chopped parsley. Pour this mixture into the bottom of a deep platter or dish large enough to hold the steak. Marinate the steak in this sauce for several hours, turning it occasionally. Then broil as above, brushing it during the cooking with the marinade. Do not season the steak after cooking.

Suggested accompaniments: Buttered rice and spinach.

PILAFF (Serves 4)

1 cup of uncooked rice	Stock, broth or bouillon (about 2
4 tablespoons of butter	cups)
1 large onion, sliced	

Wash the rice thoroughly in a pan of cold water. Pour off the water and repeat. Continue washing in fresh water until the water runs clear. This is to rid the rice of excess starch. Brown the sliced onion lightly in the butter and add the rice. Cook it in the butter over low heat for about 4 to 5 minutes, stirring it often to let it brown evenly. It should be just lightly colored. Heat the liquid to the boiling point and pour it over the rice until it is a good 1½ inches above. Cover the pan tightly and bake in a 350 degree oven for 25 to 30 minutes, or until all the liquid is absorbed. Serve with plenty of butter.

Note: This can be cooked on top of the stove over very low heat.

Variations: With mushrooms: Sauté ½ pound of sliced mushrooms with the sliced onion and cook them with the rice.

With green pepper: Sauté 1 green pepper cut in strips with the onion and cook with the rice.

With herbs: Add a pinch of thyme or oregano to the broth.

Saffron rice: Add a pinch of saffron to the broth in which the rice is cooked.

Pilaff Moghul: Puff 1 cup raisins by cooking them in a little stock or wine. Drain and add three-quarters of the amount to Saffron Rice. Also add ¼ cup toasted, slivered almonds and/or peanuts. Arrange the rice on a platter, sprinkle with the rest of the raisins and another ¼ cup nuts. Surround with French-fried onions. Serve with broiled chicken that has been basted with a curry-flavored butter.

COUNTRY-FRIED CABBAGE (Serves 4)

2- to 3-pound head of cabbage	3 to 4 tablespoons of bacon fat
1 tablespoon of vinegar	4 tablespoons of heavy cream

Remove any outer wilted leaves and trim off stalk end of cabbage. With a sharp knife, cut through the head in thin slices, shredding it as you would for cole slaw. Soak for 20 to 30 minutes in cold water to which you have added 1 teaspoon of salt.

In a large skillet melt the bacon fat. Add the well-drained cabbage and brown it in the hot fat, turning with a spatula to be sure it cooks evenly. When browned, cover with a tight lid and continue cooking until tender. Taste for seasoning. If the bacon fat is not salty enough, add salt to taste. Sprinkle with the vinegar and heavy cream, and continue cooking just until the cream is hot through.

Mastering the Art of French Cooking

BECK, BERTHOLLE AND CHILD

SIMONE BECK, thoroughly French, Louisette Bertholle, half French and half American, and California-born Julia Child have several things in common: love of French food, expertise in cooking gained at the Cordon Bleu and from private lessons from distinguished chefs, their own cooking school in Paris, and now this big, authoritative book. Their primary purpose, both at the school and in the book, is to teach people how to cook so that they can understand the basic techniques and gradually divorce themselves from a dependence on recipes. This is a new, and I believe an excellent approach. The sound theory is that all recipes stem from, and are variations of, "Master Recipes." Each "Master Recipe," in turn, is a member of one family of fundamental techniques. It follows that, once the student has conquered (or "mastered") the latter, he or she is equipped to cope with any variation and, eventually, fly solo, so to speak. While the book is arranged so that the veriest tyro, if studiously inclined, can cook successfully while learning from scratch, each recipe stands on its own for the benefit of the casual and more knowledgeable cookbook user.

At present, Mesdames Bertholle and Beck are managing L'École des Trois Gourmandes, the school in Paris, and Mrs. Child is demonstrating the art of mastering French cooking on television from Cambridge, Massachusetts. where she now makes her home.

PURÉE DE POMMES DE TERRE À L'AIL
(Garlic Mashed Potatoes)

[With some trepidation, I produced these potatoes as an accompaniment to Christmas goose when my guests included a garlic hater (rabid), an I-get-sick-if-it's-there-even-if-I-can't-taste-it type and two people who ordinarily shun potatoes in any form. (As for myself, I am ordinarily against garlic except for the most delicate soupçon, lurking unostentatiously in snails, salads or lamb.) There were two helpings of potatoes all around, no one felt (or smelt) ill effects and when the secret finally came out, a week later, jaws dropped. Incidentally, my goose boasted a skin as crisp as a potato chip due to my basting it, as instructed by these ladies, with boiling water. After a 20-minute searing, the heat was lowered and, at 15-minute intervals, excess fat was removed and 3 tablespoons of boiling water splattered over the bird. All that was necessary was a bulb baster, kitchen mittens, a long reach and a little nerve. The end result was worth it all. — P. H.]

Two whole heads of garlic will seem like a horrifying amount if you have not made this type of recipe before. But if less is used, you will regret it, for the long cooking of the garlic removes all of its harsh strength, leaving just a pleasant flavor. Garlic mashed potatoes go with roast lamb, pork, goose or sausages. Although both garlic sauce and potatoes may be cooked in advance, they should be combined only at the last minute; the completed purée loses its nice consistency if it sits too long over heat, or if it is cooked and then reheated.

For 6 to 8 people:

2 heads garlic, about 30 cloves

Separate the garlic cloves. Drop into boiling water, and boil 2 minutes. Drain. Peel.

A 3- to 4-cup heavy-bottomed saucepan with cover
4 Tb butter

Cook the garlic slowly with the butter in the covered saucepan for about 20 minutes or until very tender but not browned.

2 Tb flour
1 cup boiling milk
¼ tsp salt
Pinch of pepper

Blend in the flour and stir over low heat until it froths with the butter for 2 minutes without browning. Off heat, beat in the boiling milk and seasonings. Boil, stir-

'n spoon, or an elec-

ring for 1 minute. Rub the sauce through a sieve or purée it in the electric blender. Simmer for 2 minutes more.

May be done ahead of time. Dot top of sauce with bits of butter to keep a skin from forming. Reheat when needed.

2½ lbs. baking potatoes
A potato ricer
A 2½ quart enameled saucepan
A wooden spatula or spoon
4 Tb softened butter
Salt and white pepper

Peel and quarter the potatoes. Drop in boiling salted water to cover, and boil until tender. Drain immediately and put through a potato ricer. Place the hot purée in the saucepan and beat with the spatula or spoon for several minutes over moderate heat to evaporate moisture. As soon as the purée begins to form a film in the bottom of the pan, remove from heat and beat in the butter a tablespoon at a time. Beat in salt and pepper to taste.

If not used immediately, set aside uncovered. To reheat, cover and set over boiling water, beating frequently.

3 to 4 Tb whipping cream
4 Tb minced parsley
A hot, lightly buttered vegetable dish

Shortly before serving, beat the hot garlic sauce vigorously into the hot potatoes. Beat in the cream by spoonfuls but do not thin out the purée too much. Beat in the parsley. Correct seasoning. Turn into hot vegetable dish.

FILETS DE POISSON EN SOUFFLÉ
(Fish Soufflé Baked on a Platter)

[I have had several experiences with this dish. All of them proved that it was impressive to behold and delicious to taste while two of them indicated how easy it is to make. I first encountered it at Madame Beck's charming flat in Neuilly where I recently had the good fortune to dine. During the cheese course, as we sipped a velvety claret from our host's own vineyard in the South of France, I learned that the soufflé was a specialty at the Café des Artistes in Montmartre. It was there that I tasted it for the second time, equally beautiful, equally delicious. Next, back at home, I watched Julia Child as she deftly put it together on television and finally I made it myself — quickly, easily and with great success. I highly recommend it. — P. H.]

For 6 people:

Preheat oven to 350 degrees.

½ lb. skinless flounder filets
½ cup dry white wine or dry white
   vermouth
½ tsp. salt
Pinch of pepper
1 Tb minced shallots or green onions

Measure out ingredients. Poach the fish filets for 8 to 10 minutes in wine, seasonings, and shallots. Drain all the cooking liquor and boil it down in an enameled saucepan until it has reduced to ¼ cup.

Set it aside for your sauce Mousseline Sabayon. Turn oven up to 425 degrees.

2½ Tb butter
3 Tb flour
A 2½ quart saucepan
1 cup boiling milk
½ tsp salt
Pinch of pepper
Pinch of nutmeg
1 egg yolk

Cook the butter and flour slowly in the saucepan for 2 minutes without coloring. Off heat, beat in the boiling milk and seasonings. Boil, stirring for 1 minute. Off heat, beat in the egg yolk. Check seasoning.

4 or 5 egg whites
Pinch of salt
½ cup (2 ounces) coarsely grated
   Swiss cheese

Beat the egg whites and salt until stiff. Stir one-fourth of them into the soufflé base. Stir in all but 2 tablespoons of the cheese. Delicately fold in the rest of the egg whites.

A buttered oval fireproof platter
   about 16 inches long

Spread a ¼-inch layer of soufflé in the bottom of the platter. Flake the poached fish filets and divide into 6 portions on the platter. Heap the rest of the soufflé mixture over the fish, making 6 mounds. Sprinkle with the remaining cheese and set on a rack in upper third of preheated 425-degree oven. Bake for 15 to 18 minutes or until soufflé has puffed and browned on top.

Meanwhile, prepare the sauce as follows:

Sauce Mousseline Sabayon (1½ cups)

3 egg yolks
½ cup whipping cream
The ¼ cup concentrated fish liquor
A 4-cup enameled saucepan and a
   wire whip

Beat the egg yolks, cream and fish liquor over low heat until they gradually thicken into a light cream that coats the wires of the whip (165 degrees). Do not overheat or the egg yolks will scramble.

6 ounces (1½ sticks) softened butter divided into 10 pieces

Off heat, beat in the butter a piece at a time, beating until each is almost absorbed before adding another. The sauce will thicken like a hollandaise.

Salt and pepper
Lemon juice if necessary

Taste carefully for seasoning, and add drops of lemon juice if you feel they are needed. Keep sauce over tepid — not hot — water, and when the soufflé is done, pour the sauce into a warm sauceboat to accompany the soufflé.

HOMARD AUX AROMATES
(Lobster Steamed in Wine with Herb Sauce)

[Paul and Julia Child recently returned from Oslo, where Paul had been U. S. Cultural Attaché for several years. They bought a big, old house in Cambridge and set about remodeling it. The huge kitchen, a bedroom and a living room were attended to in that order and, before any of them were fully completed, a small group of us feasted on this splendid dish. As we sat around the waxed birch table in the kitchen and nibbled at melon and prosciutto, the lobsters steamed aromatically on the hotel-size gas stove. A dry white Burgundy, hot French bread, a green salad and cheese rounded out the menu. It was a memorable evening. — P. H.]

For 6 people:
A covered, enameled or stainless steel kettle with a tight-fitting cover
3 cups dry white wine (or 2 cups dry white vermouth) and 2 cups water
A large onion, a medium carrot and a celery stalk, all thinly sliced
6 parsley sprigs
1 bay leaf
¼ teaspoon thyme
6 peppercorns
1 tablespoon fresh or dried tarragon
3 live lobsters, 2 lbs. each

Simmer wine, water, vegetables, herbs and seasonings in the kettle for 15 minutes. Then bring to a rolling boil and add the live lobsters. Cover and boil for about 20 minutes. The lobsters are done when they are bright red and the long head-feelers can be pulled from the sockets fairly easily. Remove the lobsters. Rapidly boil down their cooking liquid until it has reduced to 2 cups. The sliced carrot and onion need not be removed.

1½ tablespoons flour blended to a paste with 1½ tablespoons softened butter
About 1 cup whipping cream

Off heat, beat in the flour and butter paste. Then bring to the boil for 15 seconds. Reduce to the simmer and stir in the cream by tablespoons until the sauce

3 to 4 tablespoons fresh, minced green herbs: parsley, chervil and tarragon or parsley only

is the consistency of a light cream soup. Correct the seasoning and stir in the herbs.

Split the lobsters in two, lengthwise. Remove stomach sacks in heads and intestinal tubes. Arrange the lobsters in a serving dish and pour the sauce over them.

SUPRÊMES DE VOLAILLE À BLANC
(Breast of Chicken with Cream)

Serve these with buttered asparagus tips, green peas, artichoke hearts, or creamed spinach, a good risotto cooked in chicken stock, and a bottle of chilled white Burgundy or Traminer.

For 4 people:

Preheat oven to 400 degrees.

4 suprêmes (boned breasts from two fryers)
½ tsp lemon juice
¼ tsp salt
Big pinch white pepper
A heavy, covered, fireproof casserole about 10″ in dia.
A round waxed paper 10″ in dia. and buttered on 1 side
4 Tb butter

Rub the suprêmes with drops of lemon juice and sprinkle lightly with salt and pepper. Heat the butter in the casserole until it is foaming.

Quickly roll the suprêmes in the butter, lay the buttered paper over them, cover the casserole and place in hot oven. After 6 minutes, press top of suprêmes with your finger. If still soft, return to oven for a moment or two. When the meat is springy, it is done. Remove the suprêmes to a warm platter and cover while making the sauce (2 to 3 minutes).

For the sauce:
¼ cup white or brown stock or canned beef bouillon
¼ cup port, Madeira, or dry white vermouth
1 cup whipping cream
Salt and pepper
Lemon juice as needed
2 Tb fresh minced parsley

Pour the stock or bouillon and wine into the casserole with the cooking butter and boil down quickly over high heat until liquid is syrupy. Stir in cream and boil down again until cream has thickened slightly. Off heat, taste carefully for seasoning, and add drops of lemon juice to taste. Pour the sauce over the suprêmes, sprinkle with parsley and serve at once.

CRÈME FRAÎCHE

French cream is matured cream, that is, lactic acids and natural ferments have been allowed to work in it until the cream has thickened and taken on a nutty flavor. It is not sour. Commercially made sour cream with a butterfat content of only 18 to 20 per cent is no substitute; furthermore, it cannot be boiled without curdling. French cream has a butterfat content of at least 30 per cent. American whipping cream with its comparable butterfat content may be used in any French recipe for crème fraîche. If it is allowed to thicken with a little buttermilk, it will taste quite a bit like French cream, can be boiled without curdling, and will keep for 10 days or more under refrigeration; use it on fruits or desserts or in cooking.

1 tsp commercial buttermilk **1 cup whipping cream**	Stir the buttermilk into the cream and heat to luke-warm — not over 83 degrees. Pour the mixture into a loosely covered jar and let it stand at a temperature of not over 85 degrees nor under 60 degrees until it has thickened. This will take 5 to 8 hours on a hot day, 24 to 36 hours at low temperature. Stir, cover and refrigerate.

[NOTE: Crème Fraîche is the perfect accompaniment or topping for hot or cold fruit tarts and is lovely poured over lightly sweetened fresh fruit. It may be flavored and colored by mixing it with a purée of strawberries or raspberries which has been sweetened to taste. When these berries are in season, a silver bowl of pink Crème Fraîche is always in evidence at the Restaurant Fabien in Paris and is offered with almost every dessert on the menu. — P. H.]

HARICOTS VERTS BLANCHIS
(Blanched Green Beans — Preliminary Cooking)

Whatever recipe you choose for your beans, always give them a preliminary blanching in a very large kettle of rapidly boiling salted water. Depending on what you plan to do to them later, boil them either until tender or until almost tender, and drain immediately. This essential step in the French art of bean cookery always produces a fine, fresh bean of perfect texture and flavor.

Preparation for cooking:

Snap the tip of one end of a bean with your fingers and draw it down the length of one side of the bean to remove any possible string. Do the same thing with the other end, pulling it down the other side of the bean.

Beans of not much more than ¼ inch in diameter are cooked whole, and retain their maximum flavor. If they are large in circumference, you may slice them on the bias to make several 2½-inch lengths per bean; this or machine slicing is usually called Frenched beans though it is rarely done in France as it is seldom necessary. Sliced beans never have the flavor of whole beans.

For 6 to 8 people:

3 lbs. green beans, trimmed and washed

A large kettle containing at least 7 to 8 quarts of rapidly boiling water

1½ tsp salt per quart of water

A handful at a time, drop the beans into the rapidly boiling salted water. Bring the water back to the boil as quickly as possible, and boil the beans slowly, uncovered, for 10 to 15 minutes; test the beans frequently after 8 minutes by eating one. A well-cooked bean should be tender, but still retain the slightest suggestion of crunchiness. Drain the beans as soon as they are done.

For Immediate Serving:

Turn the beans into a large, heavy-bottomed saucepan and toss them gently over moderately high heat by flipping the pan, not by stirring them. This will evaporate their moisture in 2 to 3 minutes.

For Later Serving or to Serve Cold:

Run cold water over the beans for 3 to 4 minutes. This will stop the cooking immediately and the beans will retain color, taste and texture. Drain, spread them out on a clean towel, and pat dry. The beans may then be set aside in a colander, or put in a covered bowl in the refrigerator where they will keep perfectly for 24 hours.

To Reheat: Depending on your recipe, either drop the beans in a large kettle of rapidly boiling salted water, bring gently again to the boil, then drain immediately, or toss the beans in a tablespoon or two of hot butter or oil, season them, cover the pan and let them warm thoroughly for 3 to 4 minutes over moderate heat. Then proceed with any recipe.

The Talisman Italian Cook Book

ADA BONI, TRANSLATED AND EDITED BY
MATILDE LA ROSA

ADA BONI'S monumental *Talismano della Felicitá*, of which this volume is a condensed translation and adaptation, is universally recognized in Italy as the standard national cookbook. About half the two thousand or more recipes in it are non-Italian in origin but these have been excluded from the American edition, as have those containing ingredients totally unavailable in this country. The remaining recipes, which are for dishes regularly eaten throughout the length and breadth of the peninsula, constitute a true Italian cookbook. Some go back to the Renaissance, when Italian cookery was internationally renowned and French chefs went there to learn their art. Others are comparatively modern. All are good.

LOIN OF PORK WITH MILK

4 lbs. boned loin of pork	1 quart milk
2 tablespoons butter	1 small white truffle (optional)

Have pork boned and trim off excess fat. Dust with salt and pepper and let stand a few hours. Place meat in Dutch oven and brown in butter on top of stove until meat is golden brown on all sides. Add milk, cover pan, and cook slowly over moderate fire about 1 hour and 45 minutes until meat is thoroughly done. The milk sauce will be creamy and thick and slightly brown in color.

Remove meat from pan, slice and place in serving dish. If you desire, add thinly sliced truffle to milk sauce and cook a few minutes. Pour sauce over meat. Serves 6.

FRESH HAM WITH CAPERS

2 pounds fresh ham	½ teaspoon thyme
½ teaspoon salt	1 teaspoon chopped parsley
½ teaspoon pepper	2 cups dry red wine
½ medium onion, chopped	¼ cup butter
½ carrot, sliced	½ tablespoon flour
½ clove garlic, chopped	2 cups stock or water
½ bay leaf	2 tablespoons capers

Make a marinade of salt, pepper, onion, carrot, garlic, bay leaf, thyme, parsley and wine and let meat stand in this bath 10 hours, turning occasionally.

When ready to cook, melt butter in large pan, remove meat from marinade, dry it and brown thoroughly in hot butter. Remove meat from pan when brown, add flour to fat in pan, blend in well and add strained marinade liquid. Bring to boiling point, stirring well. Return meat to pan, add stock or water, cover pan, lower flame and cook 2 hours. Add capers [I suggest ¼ cup — P. H.] just before serving. Slice meat and serve with gravy. Serves 6.

The Best of Boulestin

ALMOST ALL of the dozen cookbooks written by Marcel Boulestin are out of print or are extremely difficult to find. Fortunately this volume, which is a compilation of recipes, bits of philosophy and invaluable cooking maxims culled from all his works, is available. It was published in 1952 by Heinemann, the English firm that brought out, in 1918, his first cookbook, *Simple French Cooking for English Homes.* As a young man, Boulestin "adopted" England and, after serving in the French Army during the war, returned to settle in London and devote himself to educating the English in French cuisine and in what Montaigne called "the policy of the table." His first cookbook was his first step. This was followed by a catering service, a cooking school, more books and many articles and finally in 1925 the establishment of the famous restaurant which still bears his name.

Boulestin's philosophy of cooking may be summed up in four words: "No absolutes, only compromises." He cooked and taught people to cook by tasting, feeling with the fingers and pricking with a fork rather than by precise instructions. Stoves vary, as do vegetables and fruits in size, chickens in age, fish in freshness and meats in tenderness; therefore, one cannot cook by strict rules, according to M. Boulestin. The three examples which follow show how he points one in the direction of a perfect, finished dish; how he indi-

---

Reprinted by permission of A. D. Peters, London. William Heinemann Ltd., Publishers.

cates which turns to take along the way and how he leaves much of the actual journey to one's own discretion. Cooking with Boulestin is something of a challenge, but I think you will find it, as I do, stimulating and edifying and fun.

GALANTINE

Take 2 pounds of veal, one pound of streaky pork [well-marbled with fat — P. H.], a quarter of a pound of liver and mince it fairly fine together, but keep a few nice thin pieces of veal apart. Mix the mince well on the board, add one shallot and a little parsley chopped, spices and a good deal of salt and pepper. Butter a deep pie dish, put in a layer of minced meat, a rasher of bacon, a slice of veal sprinkled with seasoning, another rasher, more minced meat and so on until the terrine is full. Cover with buttered paper and cook in a moderate oven for an hour and a quarter. Put a weight over it and let it grow cold. It will be better if made twenty-four hours before it is to be eaten. It can also be made with hare or rabbit instead of veal. Serve in the dish. [Serves perhaps 8. — P. H.]

CHICKEN SAUTÉ WITH CAPERS

Make a white roux (about one ounce of butter and same quantity of flour). Stir it while cooking, but be careful the flour does not brown. Put in a tender chicken cut in five pieces, wings, legs and breast, cook them for two minutes, seeing that they are well coated with roux.

Then add little by little veal or chicken stock, just enough to cover the pieces of chicken. As the sauce will thicken during the cooking, the sauce at the beginning should be quite liquid. Add more stock if you see that it becomes too thick. Add salt, pepper and a tablespoon of vinegar. Cook slowly, with the lid on, in a moderate oven, say for about half an hour for a young chicken. Meanwhile, prepare a binding with two yolks of eggs diluted with a tablespoon of cream, a little lemon juice and capers. Add this to the chicken when ready. Mix well with the sauce. See that it is really hot, but do not let it reach the boiling point. Add chopped tarragon. [Serves 3-4. — P. H.]

STUFFED CUCUMBERS

Choose some rather fat cucumbers, peel them and cut them in pieces about three inches long, and scoop out some of the flesh to make a cavity large enough to hold a certain amount of stuffing.

For the stuffing: Fry in butter one onion, finely chopped, together with one rasher of streaky bacon [a combination of lean and fat — P. H.] cut in very small pieces; add a few mushrooms and tomatoes, some of the cucumber flesh and parsley, also finely chopped; cook a few minutes in butter and stir in a few white breadcrumbs, then stuff the pieces of cucumber.

Put these in a flat saucepan on a bed of bacon rind, pieces of onions, of carrots, of tomatoes and a little consommé. Cook on a moderate fire and finish browning in the oven. Serve with the gravy poured over through a strainer. Some people parboil the pieces of cucumber first.

Brennan's New Orleans Cookbook

ALTHOUGH FROM NOW on I may have to visit Antoine's or Galatoire's incognito, I must state in no uncertain terms that Brennan's is my favorite restaurant in New Orleans. I like its looks: its blush-pink stucco exterior, the spacious, ell-shaped dining room opening on the garden courtyard and the cool, arched entrance hall with its tiled floor. I like the drinks, which are served in the patio among banana palms and magnolia trees. I like the Clan Brennan, as the proprietary family is known, and last, but hardly least, I like the food (and that is a glaring understatement).

The restaurant was opened in 1956. This was not the first "Brennan's," but for that fascinating story you must read Hermann B. Deutsch's detailed account of the doings of the Clan Brennan from 1840 to today, which comprises the opening section of this handsome cookbook.

Although "Breakfast at Brennan's" is an unforgettable experience and the high spot of a Sunday in New Orleans, the recipes I have selected are not from the breakfast section. They are, however, typical of Brennan's, which is to say typical of New Orleans cooking at its very best.

CRAYFISH BISQUE

Stuffing:

½ cup butter	1 cup bread crumbs
1 cup chopped shallots	1 tablespoon flour
½ teaspoon salt	½ teaspoon pepper
1 can tomatoes	

Soup:

10 lbs. crayfish	½ cup flour
1 cup butter	5 cups fish stock
1 cup coarsely chopped onion	1 cup whole tomatoes
½ teaspoon minced garlic	1 tablespoon paprika
1 cup chopped celery	4 bay leaves
1 cup chopped green onion	1 teaspoon salt
2 carrots sliced coarse	½ teaspoon cayenne

Soak the 10 lbs. of crayfish ½ hour in cold water with 6 tablespoons of salt.

Sauté onions, celery, carrots and garlic in a cup of butter. Add flour, then tomatoes and a tablespoon paprika. Add bay leaves and fish stock. Put all but 20 of the crayfish in a baking pan and crush as much as possible with a wooden mallet. Bake in 350-degree oven 15-20 minutes. Add to soup. Boil slowly for 25 minutes. Remove from heat and strain through coarse sieve and return to heat. Boil again 5 minutes. Strain again through fine sieve. If necessary add more water. Simmer while stuffing heads.

Stuffing:

Take remaining 20 large crayfish and boil 5 minutes. Remove shells of heads and save. Take out all of the meat. Melt butter. Sauté shallots; add flour, tomatoes and bread crumbs, and finely chopped crayfish tails. Salt and pepper to taste. Stuff into shells of heads. Add to soup and simmer 5 minutes.

Serves 6-8.

CREOLE GUMBO

1 cup butter	3 dozen oysters
1 cup finely chopped white onion	1 dozen crabs*
1 cup finely chopped celery	2 cups raw shrimp, peeled and veined
½ cup flour	3 cups okra, sliced thin
4 cups liquid (add water to oyster water to make 1 qt.)	4 teaspoons salt
	¾ teaspoon white pepper
2 cups whole canned tomatoes	Dash cayenne
3-4 bay leaves	

Melt butter in a 4-quart saucepan over medium heat. Add celery and onion and sauté until lightly browned. Stir in flour and cook to golden

---

* Scald live crabs. Clean, remove hard shell and legs, split crabs in half and crack claws.

brown. Blend in liquid and tomatoes and simmer about 5 minutes. Add bay leaves, crabs, oysters, shrimp, okra, salt and pepper and continue cooking on low heat for 20 minutes. Serve with hot fluffy rice. Yield: about 2 quarts.

POMPANO PONTCHARTRAIN AMANDINE

1½ pounds pompano with head
1 buster*
1 egg
1 cup milk
½ cup butter

⅓ cup slivered almonds
Juice of 2 lemons
2 tablespoons Worcestershire sauce
1 tablespoon chopped parsley

Thoroughly wash and dry the fish and the buster. Make a batter of the egg and milk. Dip both the fish and the buster in this batter and drain. Dredge in seasoned flour. In a large skillet, melt butter and sauté the fish and the buster until tender and golden brown. Remove first the fish to a warm serving platter and then the buster, which must be placed across the head of the fish on a diagonal. Add almonds to skillet and brown. Add lemon juice, Worcestershire sauce and parsley, heat through and pour over fish. 1 serving.

HAMBURGER BRENNAN

2 pounds ground beef
¼ cup minced shallots
¼ cup minced white onion
½ cup toasted Holland rusk crumbs
1½ teaspoons salt

½ teaspoon pepper
2 tablespoons Worcestershire sauce
1 tablespoon chopped parsley
2 eggs
Dash nutmeg

Combine all ingredients together thoroughly and shape into 6 patties (oval in shape) and grill.

Sauce Maison

¼ lb. butter
¾ cup *jus* (from meat)
[or beef stock — P. H.]

1 tablespoon Worcestershire sauce
Pinch chopped parsley

---

* Or substitute 3 boiled shrimp and 3 scalded oysters, if busters are not available. ⸢Busters are an indigenous Louisiana crab — P. H.]

Melt butter until golden brown. Add Worcestershire sauce and *jus* and cook 1 minute. Add parsley and serve with meat.

OYSTER SALAD

⅓ cup finely chopped celery
¼ cup minced parsley
2 tablespoons finely chopped pimiento

¼ teaspoon white pepper
¼ teaspoon salt
⅓ cup thick French dressing*
4 cups chopped poached oysters**

Thoroughly mix first six ingredients; chill. Poach oysters in boiling water. Drain, chop and chill. Add oysters to dressing and mix lightly. Serve in mounds on bed of greens. Garnish with tomato slices or wedges. Serves 4.

PRALINE PARFAIT SAUCE

2 cups dark corn syrup
⅓ cup sugar
⅓ cup boiling water

1 cup chopped pecans (or small halves)

Combine all ingredients in a saucepan and bring to boil over medium heat. As soon as mixture reaches a boiling stage, remove from heat immediately. Cool and store in a covered jar.

To make a Praline Parfait spoon alternate layers of vanilla ice cream and Praline Parfait Sauce into a tall parfait glass, ending with a layer of sauce. Top with whipped cream. Garnish with pecan halves.

---

* Thicken French dessing by beating it.
** Poaching differs from boiling in that very little water is used, barely to cover. You may add wine vinegar or lemon juice.

Chafing Dish Book

HELEN EVANS BROWN

HELEN EVANS BROWN is in the enviable position of having achieved eminence in her chosen field (writing about food) while living in her favorite part of the country (Southern California) with a husband (Philip S. Brown) who not only shares her interests but aids and abets her in her work. Together they experiment in a superbly equipped kitchen, on occasion he co-authors her books, and, through his work as a partner of Yale and Brown, Booksellers, he has collected a library of over 10,000 cookbooks for their mutual research. The small volume from which the following recipes have been selected is, however, a solo venture. It was written because Helen Brown believes that "there is no greater gesture . . . of true hospitality — than to allow the guests to watch the cooking."

STUFFED SHRIMP

Select a pound of jumbo shrimp or prawns for this. Remove the shells and split them two-thirds of the way through the back, removing their sand veins in the process. Insert half an anchovy in each split and put the shrimp in the blazer with ⅛ pound of butter and a crushed clove of garlic and juice of half a lemon. Cook, stirring, for 3 or 4 minutes, then sprinkle with salt and pepper, cover and continue cooking until the shellfish are bright pink and have lost any transparent look. Serve them on pieces of well-buttered pumpernickel bread. Unless you want the guests to skip their dinner, you'd better not be too generous with these delicacies.

CELESTIAL SHRIMP WITH WALNUTS

This is a Chinese recipe, so it calls for rice as an accompaniment. Cook 2 pounds of green shrimp, remove shells and sand veins. Put ½ pound of walnut halves in a 450-degree oven for 6 minutes, then rub off the brown skins — a stiff brush will help in this operation. Cut 6 green onions into thin diagonal slices and cook them in the blazer for a minute along with 2 tablespoons of butter. Pour on 2 cups of hot chicken stock, bring to a boil, add 3 tablespoons of cornstarch which has been mixed with 3 tablespoons of soy sauce, and cook until thickened and clear. Add the shrimps and the walnuts, heat for the merest minute, and serve. Blanched almonds may be used instead of the walnuts, lobster meat instead of the shrimp.

GRENADINE OF BEEF WITH OYSTERS

Have 4 slices, ½ inch thick or a little less, cut from the center of the beef tenderloin. Heat 2 tablespoons of butter in the blazer, add the beef, cook quickly on both sides, remove to a hot platter. Add a cup of small oysters to the pan, cover and heat until the oysters plump. Pour them around the grenadines, sprinkle with minced parsley and salt and serve.

A variation: Omit oysters, add ½ cup of sliced chicken livers and ¼ cup each of Madeira and consommé to the pan; cook 5 minutes before pouring over the grenadines.

CHINESE SPINACH

When barbecued spareribs, cooked at the charcoal grill, are the pièce de résistance, this vegetable dish may be made in the patio in the time it takes to toss off a final martini. The spinach, a couple of pounds of it, will have to have been washed and blanched — the latter to reduce its bulk. (Simply plunge in boiling water for a few seconds, then drain.) Now to the chafing dish: Crush a large clove of garlic and heat in the blazer with 2 tablespoons of bland oil. Remove garlic, add well-drained spinach, and cook, turning, until the spinach is bright green and wilted. Pour in — believe it or not — a jigger of bourbon whisky and 2 tablespoons soy sauce. Heat another few seconds and serve.

HASH BROWN POTATOES WITH SESAME

Melt 4 tablespoons of butter in the blazer and add a tablespoon of minced shallots. When wilted, add ¼ cup of sesame seeds and cook them until delicately colored, then add 4 large baked potatoes that have been cut into minute — and neat — cubes. Sprinkle with a teaspoon of salt, a grinding or two of fresh white pepper, and ¼ cup of heavy cream. Cook, stirring now and then, until the potatoes are a golden brown. Superb!

TRIPE AND OYSTERS

Tripe is often available "prepared" or pre-boiled. If not, cook it from 4 to 5 hours in acidulated water.

Cut a pound of prepared tripe into cubes and scald a pint of drained oysters by pouring boiling water over them. Heat ¼ cup of butter in the blazer and in it cook 3 tablespoons of chopped onion until wilted. Add ¼ cup of flour, cook, stirring, for 2 or 3 minutes, add ½ teaspoon of Spice Islands Thyme Seasoning Powder and 2 cups of thin cream, as well as the juice drained from the oysters. Heat until smooth, season with salt and pepper, then add the tripe. Cook until it is well heated, then add the oysters and serve as soon as they are plump.

Helen Brown's West Coast Cook Book

JAMES BEARD, self-styled "food-minded native son of the Northwest," says that in this book Helen Evans Brown "has captured, with complete success, the unique qualities of Western cooking and has given us one of the most delectable books of regional cooking, in its true sense, that I have ever read." Need I say more?

WINTER MELON SOUP

This is, to me, one of the most fascinating of soups. It is Chinese, but I can see no reason why it shouldn't be served at any meal — it's that good. It's a spectacular soup, as the melon itself plays the role of soup tureen!

Purchase a large Winter melon at a Chinese market. Wash it, cut a slice from the top, and scoop out the seeds. Put the melon on a rack in a large kettle, but not so large a one that the melon won't stand upright. Pour some hot water around the outside of the melon and fill the inside with a soup made by simmering ½ cup of Chinese dried shrimps in 3 cups of water for an hour, then combining with 3 cups of chicken stock. (If this doesn't fill the melon, add more chicken stock.)

Cover the pot and let the whole thing steam for an hour, or until the melon is tender. Don't overcook though — if you do the whole beautiful thing will collapse. Lift the melon, soup and all, into a bowl that will hold it right side up. The Chinese handle it in a cradle or sling made of string. Add ¼ cup of watercress leaves and ladle into individual bowls, scooping a little of the melon into each serving. This tastes better, somehow, if eaten

Chinese soup spoons made of porcelain and served from Chinese soup bowls. Serves 8 to 12.

1 large Winter melon	¼ cup watercress leaves
½ cup Chinese dried shrimp	3 cups water
3 cups chicken stock (or more)	

Note: This may be made with any clear soup, though it should really have a Chinese character. A soup made by adding tiny dice of ham and water chestnuts to chicken soup would be good, or a duck soup with a few raw green peas.

LEEKS WITH BACON

The craze for Vichyssoise, which hit the West too, seemed to revive our interest in leeks. We now serve them frequently as a vegetable, and a darned good one, too!

Split a bunch of leeks, cut off the tough top part and wash very thoroughly, being sure to ferret out the sand that will be hiding in the tender heart. Cook 4 slices of bacon until crisp, remove and save, and cook the leeks, cut side down, in the bacon fat until brown. Add ¼ cup of stock and cover, continuing to cook until tender. Sprinkle the leeks with the crumbled bacon and serve hot with veal chops and spinach. Serves 4.

1 bunch leeks	4 slices bacon
¼ cup stock	

Note: Braised leeks with olives are good, particularly when served with duck. Prepare as above, but use butter instead of bacon fat and substitute green olives, chopped, for bacon, using ½ cup for each bunch.

Note: Cold leeks boiled, then thoroughly drained and gently pressed to remove excess moisture, are delicious when served as a salad with French dressing.

ASPARAGUS SAN FERNANDO

This is a very new way of cooking asparagus, and, I think, a perfect one. Any size of stalks may be used, and they need not be uniform, which means that "field-run" asparagus may be used. All that matters is that it be fresh.

Snap off the tough ends where the snapping is easy. Wash and remove all the scales, then slice the asparagus in very thin diagonal slices. Make the cuts at a very oblique angle, so that they are several times longer than the diameter of the stalks. Get it? Put the asparagus in a frying basket and have the deep frying pan filled with boiling salted water. Just before eating, plunge the basket into the boiling water, cook 2 minutes, drain, and serve with melted butter, salt and pepper. And please don't reject this recipe without giving it a try. This is a good way to do asparagus for salad, too, rinsing it in cold water after draining so that it won't cook any longer.

CHINESE SQUAB WITH ASPARAGUS

Not surprisingly, there were few squab recipes in early cook books, and they weren't mentioned in the hotel menus of the last century, at least in those which have come to my attention. The Hotel del Coronado, in 1896, has a "squab à la casserole," and a recipe for "squab en casserole" appears in a book of the '90s but doesn't seem worth perpetuating. Not so, the Chinese recipes for squab. They cook it exquisitely.

Cut 3 squabs into 2-inch pieces without removing their bones. (Do this with a heavy sharp knife, or a pair of poultry shears.) Brown them in ⅓ cup of oil until tender. Add a cup of sliced mushrooms, a cup of sliced water chestnuts, and a cup of asparagus, sliced diagonally; also a cup of chicken stock, cover, and cook 4 minutes, then remove squab and vegetables to a hot serving dish. Make a sauce in the same pan by adding enough stock to make 1½ cups, ¼ cup of sherry, 2 tablespoons of soy sauce, and 2 tablespoons of cornstarch. Pour over squab and vegetables. Serves 3 to 6.

3 squabs	1 cup chicken stock (and more as
⅓ cup oil	needed)
1 cup sliced mushrooms	¼ cup Sherry
1 cup sliced water chestnuts	2 tablespoons soy sauce
1 cup sliced asparagus	2 tablespoons cornstarch

CHINESE PRESSED DUCK

Have a duckling split down the back, and boil it in water to cover, but don't drown it. When tender, remove the bones very carefully, flatten the meat out on a pan, put another pan on top, and weigh it down with an iron or something else that's good and heavy. Let stand until very cold, then dust with flour and brown in oil. Make a sauce with ½ cup of the duck stock, ¼ cup of sherry, and 2 tablespoons of soy sauce, and thicken it with a tablespoon of cornstarch and ½ teaspoon of almond extract. Cut the duck in neat-as-can-be squares, paint with the sauce, and sprinkle very thickly with coarsely chopped toasted almonds. Serves 6.

1 duckling	2 tablespoons soy sauce
Oil	1 tablespoon cornstarch
½ cup duck stock	½ teaspoon almond extract
¼ cup sherry	Chopped toasted almonds

Note: Another Oriental way with duck is to skin and bone it (or just skin it if that suits you better), cut it in serving pieces (right through the bone), and marinate in ½ cup of California sherry, 2 tablespoons of soy sauce, and 2 tablespoons of honey. Cook, covered, until tender, then uncover and finish in a moderate oven until brown.

ORANGE MARMALADE SOUFFLÉ

This is a soufflé that can wait and wait, so cooks adore it. So do guests.

Allow 1 egg for each guest. For 6, beat 6 egg whites stiff, fold in ⅓ cup of sugar and ⅓ cup of bitter marmalade. Grease the top of a double boiler and pour in the pudding. Steam for 1 hour. If dinner is delayed, don't remove the cover, but let the soufflé stand over hot water until needed. The rum sauce is made by beating 4 egg yolks with 2 tablespoons of sugar, and adding to 1½ cups of milk. Cook in a double boiler until thick, and flavor to taste with Jamaica rum. Serves 6.

Soufflé

6 egg whites	⅓ cup bitter marmalade
⅓ cup sugar	

Rum Sauce

4 egg yolks	1½ cups milk
2 tablespoons sugar	Jamaica rum to taste

SEVEN RECIPES FROM

Game Cookery in America and Europe
RAYMOND R. CAMP

IT IS MR. CAMP'S contention that more crimes against the palate are committed in the field of game cooking than in any other form of culinary activity. He feels that, particularly in this country, game is apt to arrive in the kitchen without proper care and to emerge minus the flavor and texture it should possess. His aim, in this book, is to correct the situation, and he does so, simply and authoritatively. The recipes, collected on his travels, come from farm kitchens in the Dakotas, inns in France, hunting lodges in Austria, clubs in the Bahamas and cabins in Alaska.

QUAIL GALLO

[I must rephrase Mr. Camp's introduction to this recipe since, as originally written, it refers to material which is not included here. This method of preparation, the author says, stems from one Eugenio Gallo of Naples. Mr. Gallo took Mr. Camp on his first Italian quail shoot, which was extremely successful, and then prepared the quail in this manner — P. H.]

Requirements:
- 8 quail
- 8 small artichoke hearts in oil
- 8 large pitted olives
- 1 cup browned breadcrumbs
- 1½ cups of dry white wine (Lacrima Christi)
- 8 small pinches of oregano
- 1 clove garlic
- ½ cup olive oil
- Salt
- Pepper

Drain the oil from eight small artichoke hearts and save the oil. In a saucepan place 1½ cups of dry white wine and the 8 artichoke hearts. Bring to a boil and immediately remove from heat. Remove and cool the hearts of artichoke. Rub the inside of 8 quail with salt and pepper, push 1 large pitted olive into the stomach cavity of each bird, follow this with an artichoke heart, and plug with browned breadcrumbs slightly moistened with the dry white wine. Rub the birds outside, thoroughly, with the oil from the artichoke hearts supplemented by ½ cup of olive oil, place in a roasting pan, put a pinch of oregano over each breast, split a clove of garlic and put it in the bottom of the roasting pan, and put in a 450-degree oven for five minutes.

Meanwhile add the remainder of the olive oil to the saucepan with the white wine. After five minutes reduce the oven to 300 degrees and, basting frequently with the wine-oil mixture, cook for another 15 minutes, or until quail is tender. Remove to serving platter and eat immediately, along with saffron rice, baked zucchini squash, and a tossed green salad. The rest of the bottle of dry white wine should accompany it, if the cook has not finished it off. After the breasts have been sliced, quail, like the leaves of the artichoke and the fingers of asparagus, should be eaten with the fingers. The artichoke and olive does something — don't ask me what. But try it.

GROUSE CASSEROLE MICHIGAN

2 grouse	1 dash of Tabasco sauce
⅙ pound butter	1 tablespoon minced parsley
1 clove of garlic	¼ pound thinly sliced ham (Pros-
4 shallots	ciutto)
¼ teaspoon of basil	Salt
1 cup of button mushrooms	Freshly ground black pepper
2 cups dry white wine	1 cup sour cream
½ cup of flour	

Disjoint 2 grouse and rub the sections with salt and pepper, then lightly dust with flour. In a large skillet melt ⅙ pound of butter and when hot add the grouse sections along with the diced livers, hearts and gizzards. Sauté until light brown, then remove. Line the bottom and sides of an earthenware casserole with paper-thin slices of Italian ham. Arrange the grouse sections in the bottom of the casserole. In the skillet, with the hearts, livers, and gizzards, add four shallots diced fine, one clove of garlic minced, and sauté for 2 or 3 minutes. Then add 1 cup of dry white wine, 1 cup of button mushrooms, 1 tablespoon of minced parsley, ¼ teaspoon of basil, and a dash of Tabasco sauce. Bring to a boil and pour over the grouse in the casserole. Add another cup of dry white wine and place cover on the casserole. Cook for 1½ hours in a 350-degree oven. Stir in, carefully, one cup of sour cream, return to the oven for 5 minutes, then remove and serve.

SPITTED GROUSE (or Pheasant)

This is my favorite method of preparing either grouse or pheasant, but unfortunately it is within the reach of only those who happen to be in possession of a grill and spit. No other method, in my opinion, can produce a finished product as juicy, tender and full of flavor. The spit and grill, because of the increased interest in this form of cookery, can be obtained at a very reasonable cost today, and should be an integral part of every household in which good cooking is considered important. I cannot even recall where I obtained the requirements for this recipe but I have found it to be excellent (varying only in quantity) for all game birds, as well as chickens and turkeys. Anyway, here it is.

Requirements:

3 grouse or 2 pheasant	1 teaspoon of tarragon
¼ pound butter	1 dash Tabasco sauce
1 lemon	2 tablespoons Worcestershire sauce
2 cups dry white wine	Salt
12 sprigs of parsley	Freshly ground black pepper
1 small onion	

Rub three grouse inside and out with salt and pepper. In a saucepan melt ¼ pound of butter and add 1 minced onion. When onion is browned, add 2 cups of dry white wine, 1 teaspoon of tarragon, 1 dash of Tabasco sauce, 2 tablespoons of Worcestershire sauce, salt and pepper. Place a cover on the saucepan and simmer slowly for 15 minutes. Strain and add the juice of 1 lemon. With a small stick and string, make a brush of 12 sprigs of parsley. Place grouse on spit and baste liberally with the basting fluid before putting on turnspit. Place drip pan under spit, and baste grouse frequently while turning, using brush of parsley and drippings when basting fluid is gone.

Turn until golden brown and tender, and serve. I prefer this served with
baked macaroni-and-cheese, lima beans in cream, a lettuce salad with a
very tart dressing, and a chilled bottle of Tavel. Herb rolls also would be
included, as long as I'm wishing.

PHEASANT WITH DUMPLINGS, VAN MEER

This recipe has a strong flavor of Pennsylvania Dutch, which is not surprising in view of the fact that its donor, who prepared it for me, comes
from a farmhouse not much more than a long musket shot from Lancaster.
The farmhouse kitchen had an ancient coal range, but it lacked nothing
in the way of spices and herbs, and was redolent of the secret ingredients
that go to make up the inevitable seven sweets and seven sours. Food was
prepared slowly and carefully, yet with complete ease.

Requirements:

2 pheasants	1 cup of beer (drink the rest of the
3 medium-sized onions	bottle)
3 cups of chicken stock	¼ pound butter
¼ teaspoon of powdered ginger	3 eggs
½ teaspoon rosemary	1¼ cups sifted flour
1 cup of mashed sweet potato	½ teaspoon salt
1 cup of bread crumbs	1½ teaspoons baking powder
½ cup of heavy cream	3½ stalks celery

In a saucepan place 1 tablespoon of butter (from the ¼ pound) and
over a moderate flame sauté one minced onion and half a stalk of celery
finely diced. Soak one cup of breadcrumbs in a half-cup of heavy cream,
place in a mixing bowl and stir in one cup of mashed sweet potato, ½
teaspoon of rosemary and the contents of the saucepan. Rub 2 pheasants
inside and out with salt and pepper, then stuff with the dressing and sew
opening carefully. In a large earthenware pot place 3 cups of chicken stock,
¼ teaspoon of powdered ginger, 3 stalks of celery, 1 cup of beer, 2 medium-
sized onions minced fine; place cover on pot and bring to a boil, then remove cover, add the 2 stuffed pheasants and reduce heat to a simmer. Allow
to simmer for 2 hours. Meanwhile place remainder of ¼ pound of butter
in a mixing bowl and work with a spoon until soft and creamy, work in
three eggs, beating the mixture thoroughly after each egg is added. Beat in
½ teaspoon of salt, then add 1¼ cup of flour which has been blended

with 1½ teaspoons of baking powder. Mix thoroughly, then shape into a long roll about 1 inch in diameter and allow to set for at least twenty minutes. When pheasants are tender (2 hours should be adequate) remove them to a serving casserole and place in a warming oven. Break off one-inch chunks of the dough and drop, one at a time, in the pheasant stock, which has been brought to a low boil. Remove the dumplings shortly after they rise to the top, and place in the casserole with the pheasants. Strain the stock, pour it on the pheasant and dumplings and serve. The pheasants should be carved at the table. With them Mrs. Van Meer serves spiced stewed tomatoes, green beans, cabbage slaw with a sweet-sour dressing, and a wide assortment of traditional sweets and sours.

VENISON BLUHNBACH

A few years ago I was fortunate enough to be invited for ten days of shooting at Bluhnbach, the amazing hunting lodge of Alfred Krupp in the heart of the Austrian Alps. The hunting was superb and the food, because of a wealth of game coupled with culinary art, was — well a gourmet would have stowed away in the huge old castle. I came away with a number of choice recipes, involving various forms of venison, rebok and chamois. I will simplify the names of these recipes, for the combined Austrian-French-German terms are somewhat involved.

Fillet Marinade Bluhnbach

Requirements:

One 8 to 10 lb. venison fillet (or equivalent)	2 cloves garlic
1 pint of dry red wine	2 bay leaves
1 wineglass Calvados (or applejack)	½ pound of salt pork
4 peppercorns	2 cups of sour cream
2 tablespoons tarragon	Salt
	Freshly ground black pepper

With an awl or ice pick, insert thin slivers of garlic (two cloves) in the fillet. In an earthenware crock prepare the following marinade: 1 pint of red wine, one cup of water, 4 peppercorns, 2 bay leaves, 2 tablespoons of tarragon, 1 tablespoon of salt, 1 level teaspoon of freshly ground black pepper. Stir thoroughly and then place fillet in marinade in a cool place (not refrigerator) for 24 hours, turning 3 or 4 times and making certain it is covered by marinade. Remove from the marinade, place in a shallow roasting pan and cover with thin slices of salt pork. Place in an oven preheated to 450 degrees and roast for 2 to 2½ hours, basting frequently with drippings. Remove from oven, remove salt pork and place fillet on a platter and in warming oven. Pour off half the drippings, place roasting pan over a light flame and add 1 cup of strained marinade and 1 wine glass of Calvados. Stir briskly and slowly and add 2 cups of sour cream. Pour over fillet on platter and serve. Carve in slices, across the grain, ½ inch thick.

VENISON PAPRIKA BLUHNBACH

Requirements:

3 pounds of venison steak	2 tablespoons of paprika
⅙ lb. of butter	1 cup of sour cream
4 medium onions (size of a golf ball)	½ cup of flour
2 cloves of garlic	Salt
1 teaspoon marjoram	Freshly ground black pepper
1 wineglass of dry sherry	1 cup diced tomatoes

Cut steaks into one-inch cubes. In a brown paper bag place ½ cup flour, salt and pepper. Shake up cubes of steak until dusted. In a large skillet melt ⅙ lb. of butter. When hot, add cubes of steak and lightly brown them. Remove steak and to pan add 4 medium onions diced fine, 2 cloves of garlic minced, 1 teaspoon of marjoram, 1 cup of diced tomatoes, 1 wineglass of dry sherry, 2 tablespoons of paprika, and cook slowly, with lid on the skillet, for 15 minutes. Add the cube steak, replace lid on skillet and cook slowly until steak is tender (45 minutes to 1 hour). Stir in 1 cup of sour cream and serve.

RABBIT NORMANDY

A friend of mine who made an interesting tour of France after entering the country at a point known to history as Omaha Beach was unable to make up his mind whether he liked the cooking of northern France better than that of the south, but he insists that there is no group of people better versed in the preparation of rabbit and hare than the Normans. "I never realized there were as many means of preparing one kind of meat," he explained, "but if you want to try a really different method, cook up some Rabbit Normandy." I can vouch for the truth of this.

Requirements:

2 rabbits	**1 shallot**
¾ cup of bacon grease	**1 cup of cider**
½ cup of flour	**1 cup of Calvados (or applejack)**
½ cup of cornmeal	**Salt**
½ cup of milk	**Pepper**
2 eggs	

Beat up 2 eggs and ½ cup of milk in a bowl and put in a shallow dish. Place ½ cup of flour in a pie tin, and ½ cup of cornmeal in another pie tin. Dip the sections of rabbit in the milk-egg mixture, then in the flour, then in the milk-egg mixture, then in the cornmeal. Sprinkle the sections with salt and pepper and put them to one side for 10 to 15 minutes. In a large skillet melt ¾ cup of bacon grease and over a low flame brown one shallot sliced in 3 or 4 pieces. Remove the shallot and throw it away. Sauté the rabbit in the bacon grease until well browned, reduce the flame and pour 1 cup of cider and 1 cup of Calvados (or applejack) over the rabbit, place a lid on the skillet and simmer very slowly until the liquid has been absorbed or evaporated. Incidentally, if you don't happen to consume it all at one sitting, which is doubtful, it is also delicious cold. After my first trial I made twice as much, just to insure that there would be some to eat cold.

NINE RECIPES FROM

Bouquet de France

SAMUEL CHAMBERLAIN

WHEN A MAN POSSESSES several talents he is seldom equally gifted in each field. Samuel Chamberlain, I think everyone will agree, is an exception. He is a superb draughtsman, excellent at drypoint, a brilliant photographer and an eloquent and skillful writer. When one adds to all this a knowledge and appreciation of good food and wine, it is hardly surprising that his combination cook-and-guide books are, by all standards, the best and most beautiful of their kind. It seems hardly fair that, to cap the climax, Mr. Chamberlain has a wife, Narcissa, who is a painter, a Cordon Bleu graduate and a cookbook writer. She translates, adapts and edits the recipes that she and her husband collect on their travels. A third member of this fabulous family will receive her encomiums a little later on.

POTAGE CRÈME À LA NIVERNAISE
(Cream of Carrot Soup Nivernaise)

Cook 5 carrots, peeled and thinly sliced, on a low fire in a covered heavy pan with 2 tablespoons butter, 1 teaspoon sugar, ½ teaspoon salt and 4 tablespoons water for 20 to 25 minutes. Reserve a few cooked carrot slices and dice them. Make a Béchamel with 2 tablespoons butter, 2 tablespoons flour, ½ teaspoon salt, a little pepper, and 2¼ cups milk. Add this to the carrots and cook for ¾ hour in a double boiler. Pass the mixture through a fine sieve — or, better still, whip to smoothness in an electric blender. Add ½ cup cream and the diced carrots, heat and serve.

Serves 4.

MOUSSE AUX CHOUX-FLEURS
(Cauliflower Mousse)

This is a Burgundian dish.

Cook a cauliflower weighing about 1 pound in boiling salted water until tender, drain and pass it through a fine sieve to make a purée. To the purée add a thick white sauce made with 1 tablespoon butter, 1 tablespoon flour, ½ cup milk, and 3 well-beaten eggs. Season with salt and pepper and pour the mixture into a buttered soufflé mold. Place the mold in water and bake in a moderate oven (350 degrees F.) about 45 minutes.

Unmold the mousse on a platter and serve with a sauce Béchamel, made with cream.

Serves 4.

DODINE DE CANARD
(Cold Stuffed Duck)

This recipe appears through the generosity of Monsieur Bony of the Hôtel de la Poste in Saint-Seine l'Abbaye near Dijon.

Bone a duck, beginning by slitting the skin down the back. Remove the meat from the bones with a sharp boning knife, keeping it as whole as possible and leaving the skin and legs intact. Season the inside surface with salt, freshly ground pepper, and brandy and keep the duck in the refrigerator for 24 hours.

Make a stuffing of 1 pound each of finely ground veal and lean pork, ½ pound of bacon or salt pork, chopped, 1 egg, 4 or 5 chopped chicken or duck livers, 2 truffles, chopped, salt, pepper, and brandy. Add a pinch each of nutmeg, cinnamon and clove, 1 beaten egg and mix well. Stuff the duck with this forcemeat and reshape it, sewing it up and tying it with string to give a rounded form. Roast the duck in a moderate oven (350 degrees F.) for about 1½ hours, cool, and chill in the refrigerator. Arrange slices of the dodine on a chilled platter and decorate with chicken aspic.

FONDS D'ARTICHAUTS AU FOIE GRAS
(Artichoke Bottoms with Foie Gras)

A fundamental recipe from Perigord.

Use the bases of large cooked artichokes or canned fonds d'artichauts. Sprinkle each with lemon juice and salt and place on it a generous slice of foie gras. Pour 1 tablespoonful Madeira on each. Make a sauce Béchamel with 1 generous tablespoon butter, ½ tablespoon flour, salt and pepper, 1 cup heavy cream, and 2 tablespoons grated Swiss cheese. The sauce should be plentiful. Pour the sauce over the artichoke fonds, sprinkle with grated Swiss cheese and glaze in a hot oven.

TARTE À L'OIGNON ALSACIENNE
(Alsatian Onion Tart)

Make enough rich pie dough for a single-crust, 9-inch pie and line a pie plate with it. Slice enough young onions with some of the green or small white onions to make 2 cups. Sauté the onions in 2 heaping tablespoons butter until they are soft and pale yellow. Beat 3 eggs and add to them 1 cup cream, salt and pepper, and the onions. Stir well and pour the mixture into the lined pie plate. Sprinkle with 1 slice of bacon cut into tiny squares and bake in a hot oven (400 degrees F.) for about ½ hour. Serve at once.

Serves four as an entrée; six as a first course.

ENDIVE À LA PARISIENNE

Wash 2 pounds of endive and place the heads side by side in a well-buttered shallow baking dish. Salt them and dot them with butter. Cover them with a buttered paper and cook in a very slow oven (250 degrees F.). In about half an hour turn the endive over and cover them with heavy cream mixed with 5 tablespoons concentrated veal stock or juices from a roast. When the endive are soft and tender and coated with the sauce, place them on a serving dish and pour over them the sauce, to which you may add 1 cup Hollandaise sauce.

Serves 4.

SALADE CAUCHOISE
(Potato Salad with Cream)

An interesting salad is made in the Pays de Caux and the Rouen district by combining diced boiled potatoes with diced celery and ham cut in tiny strips. Season with salt, pepper, vinegar and lemon juice, moisten with heavy cream and toss lightly.

POIRES SAVOIE
(Caramel Pears)

Peel 6 handsome pears of the Anjou species or a similar type. The pears must not be too ripe or they will break up in cooking. Cut them into quarters, remove the cores, and place the pieces rather closely together in a shallow baking dish. Sprinkle them very plentifully with a layer of granulated sugar and put a piece of butter, about 1 teaspoon, on each pear quarter. Preheat the oven to its very highest point and place the dish of pears in this little furnace until the sugar is burned a good brown, basting once or twice with the juice that comes out of the fruit. When the sugar is well caramelized, pour in ¾ to 1 cup heavy cream, blend it with the sugar and serve hot. The result is an exquisite caramel cream.

Serves 6.

TARTE DES DEMOISELLES TATIN
(Upside-down Apple Tart)

Coat the inside of a round pie or baking dish a little over 2 inches deep with a thick layer of softened butter. Cover the butter with ¼-inch layer of granulated sugar. Fill the dish with sliced tart apples. Sprinkle with a little more sugar and dot with butter. Cap the whole with a covering of your favorite pie dough. Bake in a moderate oven (375 degrees F.) for about

30 minutes. Test by gingerly lifting the crust and peeking discreetly to see if the apples are golden and if the sugar is beginning to caramelize. When the dish has reached this point, loosen the crust and cover the dish with an ample serving platter. Turn the whole thing over with an expert gesture and serve hot with whipped cream sweetened and flavored to taste.

This may be made with peaches instead of apples. In either case, *"Vous m'en direz des nouvelles."* And that's good.

[NOTE: to serve 8 people, use 4 lbs. apples and a 10-inch Pyrex baking dish. Instead of whipped cream, you could serve Crème Fraîche (see index for recipe). — P. H.]

Clémentine in the Kitchen

PHINEAS BECK (SAMUEL CHAMBERLAIN)

I FIRST ENCOUNTERED "Clémentine," as did thousands of other food fanciers, in the pages of *Gourmet* magazine during the first two years of its existence, 1941-1942. To those of us who knew, loved, and were mourning for France, it was a joy to be able to escape from grim reality once a month and revel in the exploits of this little Burgundian *cuisinière*. The book came out in 1943 and by the time its twentieth-anniversary edition appeared, slightly enlarged by Narcissa G. Chamberlain, it had sold well over 75,000 copies. One of the first of these was mine and I shall always treasure it. Its stained cover and well-thumbed pages attest to its having been much used and often read. It is a small classic of gastronomical literature.

PÂTÉ EN CROÛTE
(Mixed Meats)

Cut 1½ cups (¾ pound) cooked ham into dice and mix it with ¾ pound each of finely ground veal and fresh pork. Season with 1 teaspoon of finely chopped parsley, a little thyme, a finely crushed bay leaf, a little tarragon, salt and pepper, 2 tablespoons of Madeira wine and 1 tablespoon of brandy. Add 1 chopped truffle if possible, or 2 chopped mushrooms. Form into a loaf which should be placed in the center of the pastry.

Roll the pie pastry out about ¼ inch thick and cut in the form of a wide cross whose center section is the width and length of your loaf. Roll the 4 sides of the cross thinner than the center section and fold these 4 flaps up over your loaf. Place another thin rectangle on top and pinch the edges together all around the 4 sides. Make a row of slits in the top with a knife. Bake this in a moderately hot oven until the crust is golden brown. Place it on a baking sheet, and cover at first with oiled paper; toward the end, remove the paper to brown the pastry properly. Serve hot and cut in thick delicious smoking slices.

FOIE DE VEAU MÉNAGÈRE (LIVER)

Cook in butter 4 thin slices of calf's liver, salted and peppered, until lightly browned but still exuding pink juice when pricked. (Clémentine says that to cook them longer renders them inedible.) Remove and keep them hot and add to the juice in the pan ½ cup of dry white wine, ¼ cup of Madeira, and ¼ cup of consommé. Allow this to reduce by half, then add 1 teaspoon each of chopped parsley, and chervil, and a few leaves of basil. Simmer all together for 2 minutes. Place the slices of liver on a hot platter, a thin slice of cooked ham on each, and pour the sauce over all. Serve with steamed potatoes. Serves two.

L'ESTOUFFAT LAMANDÉ
(Pot Roasted Beef Lamandé)

Clémentine used the fragrant Beaujolais for a sublimated pot roast which I exhort you to try. Beaujolais is not essential to its success, however. A good California red will do handsomely. Here is the recipe, translated from Clémentine's faded notebook. It begins magnificently:

A morsel of beef, massive and tender (4 or 5 pounds)	Two fresh pig's feet
	One fresh sweet red pepper
A pound and a quarter of tender fresh carrots	A light farce of truffles, garlic and bread crumbs
One half pound peeled fresh mushrooms	One quart Beaujolais wine
	Salt, pepper and a bouquet garni
One quarter pound green olives without pits	

Place the beef, after searing slightly, in a large earthen casserole, whose cover can be hermetically sealed. Apply the stuffing of chopped garlic, truf-

fles and bread crumbs to the top of the meat. Surround it with sliced carrots, mushrooms, olives, pepper and pig's feet. Pour in the wine. Salt and
pepper your morsel and add the bouquet garni. With a long strip of dough
seal the cover of the earthen casserole and cook for six or seven hours in a
slow heat. Serve in the casserole.

This symphonic dish used to gurgle gently in our oven from noon until
seven, making a soft sound like a bubbling of a spring. The fragrance of the
truffle and the garlic seeped down through the meat as the wine reduced
slowly. When the casserole came on the table and the crust was broken for
the first time, the aroma which escaped perfumed the whole house for
hours. And the morsel of beef, massive and tender, crowned by its light
farce, could be eaten with a teaspoon. Serves 6 to 8.

HADDOCK AU VIN BLANC

Place the cleaned fish in a flat baking dish (porcelain, glass or earthenware) with butter, thinly sliced mushrooms and a few small onions. Add
salt, pepper, a bay leaf and a sprig of thyme. Sprinkle with bread crumbs
and dot with butter. Pour a generous glass of dry white wine in the baking
dish and cook in a medium oven until tender, basting now and then. Serve
with steamed potatoes and a trickle of lemon juice.

The French cook dorade, pike, sole, flounder and many another fish in
this way. An utterly simple recipe, it lends itself to many of our own fish,
from fresh and salt waters, and it has the potential power to improve con-
jugal harmony in American households by at least 3 per cent, especially
if the fish is served with a worthy dry white wine. Allow ¾ pound per serving.

FOUR RECIPES FROM

The Flavor of France

Narcissa G. Chamberlain and Narcisse Chamberlain

NOW WE COME TO the third member of the Chamberlain family, daughter Narcisse, who has been working with her parents for several years on their annual "Chamberlain Calendars of Cooking" also published by Hastings House. *The Flavor of France* is a collection of recipes culled from the "Calendars" and is therefore the work of all three Chamberlains, but Narcisse did the job, this time, of planning and editing. In her introduction, she calls the book an abbreviated profile of France, designed to "make new friends for the *cuisine bourgeoise*" which is the traditional, day-to-day fare of the French country people. This is the missing link in the average epicure's experience of French cooking because it is not often encountered in restaurants. Modest though it is, however, it constitutes the solid foundation upon which the *haute cuisine* of France is built.

JAMBON À LA CRÈME NIVERNAISE
(Ham in Cream Nivernaise)

(Ham, unsalted butter, white wine, chicken consommé, cream)

In a heavy skillet heat 8 slices of cooked ham in 2 tablespoons of unsalted butter. Cook the ham on both sides but do not let it brown. Add 1 cup of dry white wine and let the liquid in the pan reduce to a very small quantity. Put the slices of ham on a warm platter and keep it hot. Blend a teaspoon of flour into the pan juices, stir in 1 cup of chicken consommé and simmer the sauce for about 5 minutes. Then add ½ cup of heavy cream and pour the sauce over the ham. Serves 4.

TURBOT AU FOUR A LA CREME
(Halibut Baked in Cream)

(Halibut, mushrooms, onions, bay leaf, garlic, white wine, cream, new potatoes)

Wipe a 3-pound piece of turbot or halibut with a cloth and rub it with a little flour seasoned with salt and pepper. Put the fish in a generously buttered baking dish and dot it with 4 tablespoons of butter. Bake the fish in a 350-degree oven for 20 minutes and baste it often. Then add ½ pound of whole button mushrooms, ¾ cup of thinly sliced white onions, 1 bay leaf, 1 cut clove of garlic and 1 cup of dry white wine. Cover the baking dish with a piece of buttered brown paper to keep the fish from drying and bake it for another 20 minutes, still basting it frequently. Transfer the fish, mushrooms and onions to a heated platter and discard the bay leaf and garlic. To the liquid left in the baking dish add 1 cup of warm heavy cream. Heat the sauce to the boiling point, taste it for seasoning and pour it over the fish. Finish the platter with boiled new potatoes and several decorative sprigs of parsley. Serves six.

ÉPINARDS AU MADÈRE À LA GERMAINE
(Spinach Creamed with Madeira, Germaine)

(Spinach, mushrooms, cream, Madeira, croutons)

Epinards au Madère is no ordinary vegetable; it deserves to be eaten as a separate course.

Cook 2 pounds of spinach, covered, with ¼ cup of water for about 10 minutes, or until it is just soft. Drain it thoroughly and put it through the finest blade of the meat grinder. Drain the spinach again, add 1 tablespoon of butter, a dash of nutmeg, salt and pepper, and ¼ cup of heavy cream. Sauté ¼ pound of sliced mushrooms in 1 tablespoon of butter for 4 or 5 minutes, add them to the spinach and stir in 2 tablespoons of Madeira. Sauté 1 cup of diced white bread in 2 tablespoons of butter until the croutons are crisp and golden brown. Reheat the spinach and sprinkle it with the croutons. Serves four.

MOUSSE DE POMMES
(Hot Apple Mousse)

(Apples, butter, sugar, egg whites, apricot jam, kirsch)

Peel, quarter and core 2 pounds of tart apples. Bake them, covered with a piece of heavily buttered paper, buttered side down, in a 350-degree oven for 45 minutes, stirring them occasionally. Force the apples through a sieve, add ⅓ cup of sugar, simmer them until they are thick and jamlike, stirring often, and let them cool. Meanwhile, in a saucepan over medium heat melt ½ cup of sugar and heat it, stirring constantly, until it turns golden brown. Coat the inside of a 1½ quart soufflé mold with this caramel and let it harden. Beat 6 egg whites stiff with 3 tablespoons of sugar and fold them into the applesauce. Spoon the apple mousse into the mold and bake it in a pan of hot water, on a low rack in a 350-degree oven, for 1¼ hours. Let it cool for 15 minutes, then unmold it onto a platter. Serve warm, with a hot sauce made of 1½ cups of apricot jam puréed in an electric blender, thinned with a little water if necessary, and flavored with 2 teaspoons of kirsch. Serves six.

FOUR RECIPES FROM

The Pleasures of Cooking with Wine

EMILY CHASE

THIS IS NOT, as one might expect from the title, a volume devoted to *haute cuisine*. What Miss Chase advocates is the enhancement of everyday food by the subtle and judicious use of wine in cooking. During her six years as foods consultant to the Home Advisory Board of the Wine Institute, she originated and collected and tested over a thousand recipes. Her book contains the best and most provocative of these, and in them, wine is used tastefully in both senses of the word, as is evidenced in the following recipes:

STUFFED PORK CHOPS IN ORANGE SAUCE

4 pork chops, cut about 1¼ inches thick
2 cups (firmly packed) grated crumbs
2 tablespoons grated onion
6 tablespoons melted butter
Salt and pepper to taste

3 tablespoons flour
1 cup orange juice
½ cup dry white table wine
¼ cup water
¼ cup brown sugar
2 tablespoons grated orange peel
1 teaspoon grated lemon peel

Have chops slit from fat side to bone to form a pocket. Mix bread crumbs, onion and 3 tablespoons of the melted butter; season with salt and pepper. Fill pockets of pork chops with this stuffing; fasten openings securely with skewers or toothpicks. Heat a large heavy skillet; grease it with a bit of fat trimmed from the chops; brown chops slowly on both sides. Pour off fat from skillet. In a saucepan blend remaining 3 tablespoons melted butter with the flour; add orange juice, wine and water; cook, stirring, until mixture boils and thickens. Add brown sugar, orange peel, lemon peel, and salt to taste; pour sauce over browned chops. Cover and simmer gently about 1¼ hours, or until chops are tender. Turn and baste chops occasionally, and add a little additional water if gravy becomes too thick.

Serves four. Fluffy mashed sweet potatoes and a spinach ring filled with buttered whole-kernel corn are perfect with these.

SAVORY SPARERIBS

4 pounds meaty spareribs, cut in pieces for serving
1 cup chili sauce
½ cup dry vermouth
½ cup water

¼ cup chopped onion
Bit of chopped or pressed garlic (if you like)
1 teaspoon Worcestershire sauce
Salt and pepper to taste

Arrange spareribs in a single layer in a large, shallow baking pan. Mix remaining ingredients; pour over ribs. Bake, uncovered, in a moderate oven (350 F.) for 1¾ to 2 hours, turning and basting the ribs frequently. Serves 4 or 5. Good with mashed potatoes and buttered green beans to which a generous sprinkling of celery seed has been added.

CRUSTY BAKED FISH FILLETS

1 pound fish fillets
1 cup dry white table wine or dry Vermouth
2 teaspoons salt
1 cup very fine, dry bread crumbs

(toast dry bread and roll your own, or use packaged crumbs)
2 or 3 tablespoons melted butter or salad oil
Paprika

Arrange fish fillets in a single layer in a shallow pan or baking dish. Mix wine and salt; pour over fish; let stand 30 minutes or so. Remove fillets from wine and roll in bread crumbs, turning until well coated. Place fillets on a well-greased baking sheet or shallow baking pan. Drizzle melted butter evenly over them; dust with paprika. Bake in a very hot oven (500 degrees F.) for 10 to 12 minutes or until tender and nicely browned. Serve at once with tartar sauce or cucumber sauce. Serves two if you enjoy fish as much as we do, three if your appetites are more modest.

Note: Fresh or frozen sole, sea bass, cod, halibut, perch or salmon may be used. Frozen fillets should be thawed and separated before cooking.

BRAISED SHOULDER OF LAMB

4 to 5 pounds lamb shoulder, boned and rolled
Flour
Salt and pepper
2 tablespoons butter or bacon drippings
1 large onion, chopped
1 clove garlic, chopped

1 cup dry red table wine
1 cup boiling water
1 bay leaf
3 or 4 peppercorns
Pinch of thyme
2 tablespoons chopped parsley
1 to 2 tablespoons dry or medium sherry

Dredge lamb with flour seasoned with salt and pepper. Heat butter in a Dutch oven or other heavy kettle; brown lamb slowly on all sides. Add onion, garlic, wine, water, bay leaf, peppercorns, thyme, parsley and salt to taste. Cover tightly and simmer gently for 2 to 2½ hours, or until meat is tender, turning meat occasionally. Place lamb on a heated platter.

THREE RECIPES FROM

The Burger Cookbook

RUTH ELLEN CHURCH

NO MATTER WHAT paper you read, you cannot live in Chicago for any length of time without hearing often of Mary Meade, food editor of the Chicago *Tribune*. For most of the years I lived there, however, I was never quite sure that such a person actually existed; I thought that Mary Meade was probably a fictional female like the one whose eternally young face graces the advertisements of a well-known milling company and that *Tribune* food editors came and went under the familiar pseudonym. That such was — and is — not the case I learned when Ruth Ellen Church traveled with our party on the trip to Avery Island which is mentioned elsewhere in this book. Not only does this charming lady exist but she has held down the tremendous job of being Mary Meade for over twenty years and has found time besides to raise two boys and write four books. While most of "The Burger Cookbook" is as down-to-earth American as its title suggests, culinary sophistication is apparent in many of the recipes, such as the three presented here.

BEEF STRUDEL (8-10 servings)

It may take a little practice to stretch the dough paper-thin. It's worth working at.

1¼ cups unsifted flour	2 tablespoons oil
½ teaspoon salt	1½ pounds ground beef
3 tablespoons oil	¼ cup chopped parsley
⅓ cup water	2 teaspoons salt
2 large onions, diced	½ teaspoon pepper

Mix first 4 ingredients in a bowl until well blended. Let stand 10 minutes. Meanwhile sauté onions in 2 tablespoons oil until golden. Add beef and cook until browned. Add parsley and seasonings; cool. Roll and stretch the dough paper-thin into a circle on a floured pastry cloth. Spread cooled filling on dough and roll up like a jelly roll. Oil a large, heavy skillet or Dutch oven and coil the roll in it. Cover tight and cook over low heat 30 minutes. Turn with care and cook 30 minutes more. Cut and serve very hot.

FRENCH CANADIAN PORK PIE (6 servings)

"Tourtière" is the name of this dish north of the border; it is a popular favorite in French-speaking Canada.

1 small clove garlic	Few grains cayenne
1 teaspoon salt	1 tablespoon cornstarch
¼ teaspoon pepper	1 cup water
¼ teaspoon nutmeg	1 pound ground lean pork
⅛ teaspoon mace	Pastry for 2-crust pie

Mash garlic with the salt and mix with seasonings and cornstarch. Add water and blend. Add to meat in heavy saucepan, heat to boiling, then cover and simmer gently for 30 minutes. Line an 8-inch pie pan with pastry. Pour in filling; top with a pastry round in which you've cut steam vents. Bake at 425 degrees F. for 30 minutes.

SWEDISH CABBAGE ROLLS (6 or more servings)

1 medium head cabbage	¼ cup minced onion
½ pound ground beef	Milk or stock to moisten filling
¼ pound ground veal	Butter for browning
1 cup cooked rice	1 cup stock or bouillon
1 teaspoon salt	¼ teaspoon pepper
1 teaspoon sugar	

Core cabbage and cook in boiling water or steam until wilted. Separate the leaves and trim the midrib in each for easy rolling.

Mix beef, veal, rice, seasonings, and milk or stock enough to moisten. Put a tablespoonful of the mixture at the base of each cabbage leaf, fold in the sides and roll into a neat package. Skewer each with a toothpick or metal skewer, or tie with string. Brown rolls on all sides in butter, then pour stock over them and cover; simmer about 1 hour. Remove strings or skewers before serving.

Cream is added to the stock to make a sauce in some recipes. Ham might be used as part or all of the meat. One might also use some ground pork.

The New York Times Cook Book

EDITED BY CRAIG CLAIBORNE

CRAIG CLAIBORNE, who will probably always look, as he does today, half his actual age, holds two degrees. One is in journalism from the University of Mississippi and the other is in professional cooking and hotel keeping from the École Hotelière in Lausanne, Switzerland. It took a long time, however, some of it spent in the Navy and the rest in the field of public relations, before he landed in the perfect job for someone with his training and interests. As Food Editor of the New York *Times*, his writing ability and his culinary knowledge make his column and Sunday pieces both readable and authoritative. Mr. Claiborne gives credit to many others for the quality of the big *New York Times Cook Book*, but his was the ultimate responsibility and to him go the laurels for a fine achievement.

BILLI BI (4 servings)

This may well be the most elegant and delicious soup ever created. It may be served hot or cold. This is the recipe of Pierre Franey, one of the nation's greatest chefs.

2 pounds mussels	1 cup dry white wine
2 shallots, coarsely chopped	2 tablespoons butter
2 small onions, quartered	½ bay leaf
2 stalks of parsley	½ teaspoon thyme
Salt	2 cups heavy cream
Freshly ground black pepper	1 egg yolk, lightly beaten
Pinch of cayenne pepper	

1. Scrub the mussels well to remove all exterior sand and dirt. Place them in a large kettle with the shallots, onions, parsley, salt, black pepper, cayenne, wine, butter, bay leaf and thyme. Cover and bring to a boil. Simmer 5 to 10 minutes or until the mussels have opened. Discard any mussels that do not open.

2. Strain the liquid through a double thickness of cheesecloth. Reserve the mussels for another use or remove them from the shells and use them as a garnish for the soup.

3. Bring the liquid in the saucepan to a boil and add the cream. Return to the boil and remove from the heat. Add the beaten egg yolk and return to the heat long enough for the soup to thicken slightly. Do not boil. Serve hot or cold.

PORK CHOPS ZINGARA (4 servings)

4 loin pork chops
1 small white onion, chopped
¼ pound mushrooms, cut in thin strips julienne style
1 cup tomato sauce
2 tablespoons julienne-cut cooked ham
2 tablespoons julienne-cut cooked tongue
3 tablespoons dry sherry
Salt and freshly ground black pepper to taste

1. In a lightly greased skillet brown the chops on both sides over brisk heat. Cover, reduce the heat and cook slowly until the chops are almost tender, about 20 minutes.

2. Add the onion and mushrooms and cook slowly, covered, until the chops are tender and the onion is soft, about 5 minutes.

3. Add the tomato sauce, heat to simmering and add the remaining ingredients.

Note: If desired, finish off by adding bits of butter to the sauce just before serving and swirling it in to give the sauce a gloss.

CASSOULET (8 to 10 servings)

4 cups (2 pounds) small dried pea beans
2 quarts of water
1½ pounds lean pork, cubed
1 pound boneless lamb, cubed
2 Bermuda onions, chopped

1 tablespoon salt
2 cloves garlic, minced
2 carrots, quartered
2 onions each studded with 3 whole cloves
1 bouquet garni (parsley, celery, bay leaf and thyme tied in cheesecloth)
½ cup diced salt pork
3 tablespoons duck drippings or cooking oil

1 cup chopped shallots
1 cup thinly sliced celery
1 can (8 ounces) tomato sauce
1 cup dry white wine
1 garlic or Polish sausage
1 roasted duck removed from the bone and cut into bite-sized pieces (or canned preserved goose)

1. Combine the beans, water and salt in a large kettle, and let stand overnight; or boil 2 minutes and let soak one hour.

2. Add the garlic, carrots, onions studded with cloves, bouquet garni and salt pork. Bring to a boil. Reduce the heat and cook gently one hour. Skim the foam from the surface.

3. Heat the duck drippings or oil in a skillet. Add the meats and sauté until browned. Transfer to the bean mixture.

4. Sauté the onion, shallots and celery in the remaining drippings until tender. Add the tomato sauce and wine and simmer five minutes. Add to the beans. Add the garlic sausage, cover and simmer until the meats and beans are tender, about 1 hour, adding water if necessary to cover the beans. Skim off the excess fat. Discard the bouquet garni.

5. Transfer the mixture to a large earthenware casserole. Add the pieces of roasted duck or preserved goose. Bake, uncovered, in a preheated moderate oven (350 degrees F.) 35 minutes.

SWEDISH LAMB (6 to 8 servings)

1 tablespoon salt
1 tablespoon freshly ground black pepper
1 five-pound leg of lamb
3 onions, sliced

3 carrots, sliced
1 cup hot beef broth
1½ cups hot strong coffee
½ cup heavy cream
1 tablespoon sugar

1. Preheat oven to hot (425 degrees F.).

2. Rub the salt and pepper into the lamb and place the meat on a rack in a roasting pan surrounded with the onions and carrots. Roast 30 minutes, then skim off the fat.

3. Reduce the oven temperature to moderate (350 degrees F.) and add

the broth, coffee, cream and sugar. Continue roasting, basting frequently, 40 minutes to 1 hour, depending on the desired degree of doneness.

4. Transfer the lamb to a warm platter and force the gravy through a sieve, or purée in an electric blender.

An Herb and Spice Cook Book

CRAIG CLAIBORNE

THIS SMALLER BOOK of Mr. Claiborne's, which is hot off the presses, is a more personal affair. In a way, it is a love letter to herbs and spices, the fragrant condiments that contribute countless nuances to food. In general, the recipes are grouped under the herb or spice predominant therein and, besides stimulating the imagination of the accomplished cook, they should be a boon to those who are not quite sure about seasoning, encouraging the timid and restraining the too-often heavy hand of the bold.

TAPÉNADE

Traditionally, in Provence, this sauce is made by pounding the ingredients in a large mortar with a pestle. Today an electric blender is more effective and the results are similar, although the handmade version is coarser.

¼ cup capers
3 two-ounce cans flat anchovy fillets
1 seven-ounce can tuna fish
1 clove garlic, or more to taste
18 black olives (preferably Greek or Italian), pitted

Juice of two lemons
½ cup olive oil
3 tablespoons cognac
Freshly ground black pepper to taste

1. Place the capers, anchovies and tuna, with the oil in which they were packed, and the garlic, olives and lemon juice in the container of an electric blender.
2. Blend at medium speed 2 to 5 minutes, stopping the motor to stir

---

down occasionally with a rubber spatula. (It may be stirred with the motor running, but care must be taken not to touch the blades.)

3. Gradually add the olive oil. When all the oil is blended, the sauce should be like medium-thick mayonnaise.

4. Blend in the cognac and pepper. Serve at room temperature over hard-cooked eggs, cold poached fish or cold boiled beef.

Yield: About 2½ cups of sauce.

[NOTE: Another version of this dish, Jim Beard's, may be found in "Recipes from My Files," page 223. — P. H.]

WATERZOOIE CHICKEN

¼ cup (½ stick) butter	½ bay leaf
1 seven- to eight-pound capon, cut into large pieces	4 cloves
4 leeks, washed and trimmed	6 cups chicken broth
8 stalks celery, chopped	1 lemon, thinly sliced
1 carrot, chopped	1 tablespoon chopped parsley
1 small onion, quartered	4 egg yolks
4 sprigs parsley	¼ cup heavy cream
¼ teaspoon nutmeg	¼ teaspoon thyme

1. Heat the butter in a large skillet and brown the capon on all sides.

2. Place the capon with the vegetables and seasonings in a heat-proof casserole. Cover with chicken broth and bring to a boil. Reduce the heat and simmer until tender, about 40 minutes.

3. Remove the capon from the liquid. Remove and discard skin and bones. Cut the meat into large pieces; reserve.

4. Strain the liquid and skim off excess fat. Place over high heat. Add the lemon and chopped parsley.

5. Beat the egg yolks and cream together. Stir into the soup and allow to thicken slightly, but do not boil. Add pieces of chicken and heat briefly.

Yield: 6 servings.

[NOTE: Waterzooie, or Waterzootjie, is sometimes made with fish and sometimes, as in this case, with chicken. Both are equally popular in Belgium and Holland and are the Flemish versions of Bouillabaisse and Poule au Pot respectively. In some recipes, a little white wine is added to the broth after the boiling point has been reached. Steamed or boiled carrots, potatoes, and onions or leeks are the classic accompaniments. Each serving may be sprinkled with bread crumbs if desired. — P. H.]

VEAL RONDELLES WITH EGG-AND-LEMON SAUCE

1 pound ground veal
¾ cup fresh bread crumbs
1 egg
1 tablespoon chopped parsley
½ teaspoon salt
Freshly ground black pepper to taste
½ teaspoon nutmeg, preferably
  freshly grated

⅓ cup heavy cream
Flour for dredging
2 tablespoons butter
2 tablespoons olive oil or peanut oil
2 cups egg-and-lemon sauce
  (recipe follows)

1. Combine the veal, bread crumbs, egg, parsley, salt, pepper, nutmeg and cream in a mixing bowl. Work the mixture lightly with the hands until well blended.

2. Shape the mixture into balls about 1½ inches in diameter. Dredge with flour.

3. Heat the butter and oil in a large skillet and brown the meat balls on all sides over medium heat. Reduce the heat to low and cook, tossing the meat balls in the skillet occasionally, until done, 10 to 15 minutes. Serve with egg-and-lemon sauce.

Yield: Four to six servings.

Avgolémono (Egg-and-Lemon Sauce)
National Sauce of Greece

2 cups chicken broth
2 tablespoons cornstarch

2 egg yolks
3 tablespoons lemon juice, or to taste

1. Bring 1½ cups of the chicken broth to a boil. Combine the cornstarch with the remaining half cup of broth and stir well to blend. Add the hot chicken broth to the cornstarch mixture, stirring constantly. Return to the pan and heat until the mixture is thickened and smooth. Remove from the heat.

2. Combine the egg yolks and lemon juice and beat lightly. Add a little of the hot chicken broth to the yolks, then pour the egg-yolk mixture into the remaining hot broth, stirring rapidly. Place over very low heat and

cook, stirring, to thicken and reheat but do not allow to boil or the eggs will curdle. Serve hot.

Yield: 2 cups of sauce.

[NOTE: Sauce may be served over cooked vegetables. — P. H.]

SICILIAN CASSATA

1 ten-inch spongecake, homemade or purchased	½ ounce bitter chocolate, chopped
1½ pounds ricotta cheese	½ cup chopped toasted almonds
⅓ cup sugar	¼ cup rum
½ cup milk or cream	⅔ cup finely diced candied fruit
2 to 3 tablespoons rose water	Cassata frosting (recipe follows)

1. Cut the spongecake into 2 or 3 layers. Chill.

2. Mix the ricotta, sugar, milk and rose water. Rub through a sieve or whip until smooth.

3. Add the chocolate, almonds and candied fruit and mix well. Chill.

4. Place a spongecake layer on a serving plate and spread with half the ricotta filling for three layers, all if only two layers are used. Top with final cake layer. Sprinkle with rum. Refrigerate until shortly before serving time.

5. Frost the cake, reserving a small amount of the frosting.

6. Beat enough additional confectioners' sugar into remaining frosting to give it stiff peaks when the beater is withdrawn. Color a delicate pink with red food coloring and use in a pastry tube to decorate the cassata as desired.

Yield: Twelve servings.

Cassata Frosting

1 egg white	1 teaspoon almond extract
2 cups or more confectioners' sugar	1 tablespoon lemon juice

Mix all ingredients until smooth. If necessary, add a little water.

Italian Food

ELIZABETH DAVID

W HEN I REVIEWED this book for a magazine several years
ago, I gave it what I felt to be the highest compliment that
one cookbook writer could give another. I said that I wished I had
written it. Aside from the recipes, which are presented with clarity
and precision and which seem to me to have more variety than those
in most Italian cookbooks, there are bits of engaging historical in-
formation, excerpts from classic books on Italian food and, from
beginning to end, there is the joy of Elizabeth David's extraordi-
narily vivid writing. This is a book for the bedside table or the arm
chair, as well as for the kitchen.

SFORMATO OF GREEN PEAS

A sformato, a dish which figures largely in Italian home cooking but never
in restaurants, is a cross between a soufflé and what we should call a pudding. It is a capital way of using green peas, green beans, spinach, fennel,
or any vegetables which are plentiful but no longer in the tender stage when
they may be eaten simply with butter. A sformato takes trouble to prepare,
but requires fewer eggs than a soufflé and is not at all exacting to cook. It
may be served as a separate course with some kind of sauce, or as a back-
ground to meat (scaloppini, for example), or lamb cutlets, or small pieces
of veal grilled on a skewer. For a sformato of fresh green peas you need
about 3 lb. of peas, 3 eggs, ¼ cup broth, a small piece of cooked ham, 1

small onion, 3 oz. butter, ¼ cup of grated Parmesan, 1 tablespoon of flour, 1 cupful of milk.

First sauté the chopped onion very lightly in half the butter; add the shelled peas and cover them with water. Season them with salt and let them simmer until they are completely cooked.

While the peas are cooking prepare a little very thick Béchamel with 1 oz. of butter, 1 tablespoon of flour, and the milk previously heated. Season it well, add to it the ham cut into small strips and the grated cheese. When the peas are cooked, strain them and put them through a sieve, keeping a few apart. Return the purée to the saucepan with a spoonful of butter, and add the Béchamel and the whole peas. Give it a stir or two so that the mixture is well amalgamated.

Leave it to cool, and then stir in the yolks of the eggs, and lastly the beaten whites. Pour the whole mixture into a buttered baking dish, and steam it, with a cover on the pan, for about an hour. Turn the sformato out on to a dish and either pour a sauce over it, or arrange round it whatever meat it is to accompany. Apart from meat, shrimp or scallops cooked in butter go nicely with the green pea sformato, or a mushroom sauce or poached eggs.

This sformato may be made very successfully with frozen green peas.

RICOTTA AL CAFFÈ
(Ricotta with Coffee)

For 4 people, allow 8-10 oz. of ricotta, ¾ cup of sugar, 4 dessertspoonfuls of freshly roasted, very finely ground coffee, and ¼ cup of rum. Put the cheese through a sieve, add the sugar, the coffee, and the rum and stir it until it is smooth and thick. Make the cream at least 2 hours before serving so that the coffee flavor has time to develop. Keep in a cold place.

Serve it with, if possible, fresh cream and thin wafer biscuits.

French Provincial Cooking

ELIZABETH DAVID

THIS MORE RECENT book of Mrs. David's is, once again, a volume to be read as well as used. The French provinces — Normandy, Burgundy, Anjou and the rest — are evoked in all their physical aspects, as well as in their history and their regional dishes. Interspersed with the excellent recipes and sound advice on marketing, cooking utensils and ingredients are fragments of anecdote and personal recollection couched in the author's individual style. I particularly recommend to you the following dissertation on veal.

ESCALOPES DE VEAU CAUCHOISE
(Veal Scallops with Apple)

One of the most difficult cuts of meat to get a butcher to supply in perfection is an escalope of veal. They should be cut on the bias, in clean, even slices from the topside of the leg of veal or from the boned loin or fillet without seam, gristle or skin and weighing a little over 3 ounces each. They should be thin enough not to need the whacking out with a heavy bat with which the majority of butchers remove all life and hope from the clumsily hacked lumps of meat which they sell as escalopes . . . I am quite well aware that the question of cutting veal escalopes is deeply involved with the economics of butchering . . . the situation is that the English (and American) method of cutting a leg of veal crosswise, into joints for roasting, precludes the possibility of cutting proper escalopes because of the seams which run through the meat.

[This being the case, Mrs. David suggests an alternative — a "do-it-yourself" way of procuring your escalopes. — P. H.] Buy a solid piece of that little joint from the leg which is rather the shape of a sausage which corresponds to the roll of silverside . . . in beef, and which is sometimes, although incorrectly, called the fillet. From this little joint it is easy to cut your own slices of meat into whatever thickness you require. Cut very thin and slightly flattened out they constitute the dish which the Italians called *scaloppine* or *frittura piccata*, miniature escalopes which are cooked in a minute or two. Cut about ½ inch thick . . . they become *médaillons*, which after a preliminary cooking in butter are simmered gently for about 25 minutes. In either case the garnish and sauces, the cream, wine, mushrooms and so on given in recipes for escalopes can be adapted to these cuts, so long as the cooking times are adjusted.

[NOTE: For the following recipe, if you cannot get 3½ to 4 oz. escalopes cut correctly, use 2 or 3 *scaloppine* per person depending on weight. — P. H.]

Quantities for 2 people, apart from two fine escalopes, cut slightly on the bias from the wide part of the leg and without seams, but not beaten out too flat, are half a sweet apple, ¼ pint of thick cream, butter, seasonings, Calvados.

Cut the peeled half apple into little cubes; season the meat plentifully with salt, pepper and lemon juice. Melt about 1½ oz. of butter in a thick frying-pan. When it starts to foam, put in the meat, let it take color rapidly on each side; add the apple cubes. Heat a liqueur glass (about 2 tablespoons) of Calvados in a little pan; set light to it. Pour it flaming over the meat, at the same time turning up the heat under the pan. Rotate the pan until the flames die down. Pour in the cream. Lower the heat. Cook gently another 2 minutes or so, stirring the sauce and scraping up the juices all the time. As soon as the cream has thickened, transfer the meat to the serving dish, arrange the apples on top of each escalope and pour the sauce all around.

Cognac, Armagnac, *marc*, or even whisky, which, curiously enough, is the best substitute, can be used instead of Calvados, but then, of course, it is no longer quite the dish of the Pays de Caux.

Although triangles of bread fried in butter would not be out of place as a garnish, vegetables should be kept until afterwards, as always with these creamy dishes, for one doesn't want them floating about the plate and getting mixed up with the sauce. Also, however tempted one may be to cook the whole apple just for the sake of using it up, it would be a mistake to do so. It is just that little hint of a sweet taste and contrasting texture that gives the dish its originality. More would be heavy-handed.

NOISETTES DE PORC AUX PRUNEAUX
(Pork with Prunes)

From Touraine comes . . . a remarkable dish of pork garnished with enormous, rich, juicy prunes which are a speciality of the Tours district.

8 noisettes cut from the boned and skinned chump end of a loin of pork, each weighing about 3 oz.
1 lb. (about 2 dozen) large California prunes
½ bottle white wine, preferably Vouvray

1 tablespoon red currant jelly
½ pint heavy cream
2 oz. butter
Flour
Salt, pepper

Both the utensil for cooking the pork and the dish to serve it in are important. The first should be a shallow and heavy pan to go on top of the stove. The second should be a big oval one, preferably one which can go into the oven for a few minutes without risk.

First, put the prunes to steep overnight in a bowl covered with ½ pint of the wine. Next day, cover them and put them in a very slow oven to cook. They can stay there an hour or more, the longer the better, so long as the wine does not dry up.

Season the pork well with freshly milled pepper and salt and sprinkle each noisette with flour. Melt the butter in the pan, put in the meat, let it gently take color on one side and turn it. Keep the heat low because the butter must not brown. After 10 minutes pour in the remaining wine. Cover the pan. Cook very gently, covered, on top of the stove for approximately 45 minutes to an hour. Test it with a skewer to see if it is tender. When it is nearly ready, pour the juice from the prunes over the meat. Keep the prunes themselves hot in the oven. When the juice has bubbled and reduced a little, transfer the meat to the serving dish and keep it hot.

To the sauce in the pan, add the jelly and stir until it has dissolved. Now pour in some of the cream; if the pan is wide enough it will almost instantly start bubbling and thickening. Stir it, shake the pan and add a little more cream. When the sauce is just beginning to get shiny and really thick, pour it over the meat, arrange the prunes all around and serve it quickly. The amount of cream you use depends on how much juice there was from the prunes and how quickly the sauce has thickened; sometimes it gets too thick too quickly and a little more cream must be added. In any case there should be enough sauce to cover the meat but not, of course, the prunes. These are served as they are, not "boned" as the French cooks say.

On the whole, I think it is better to drink red wine than white with this dish. And, of course, you do not serve any vegetables with it. Even with light first and last course dishes, 8 noisettes should be enough for four people.

[NOTE: I would suggest a clear consommé to start with and a fruit mélange for dessert. — P. H.]

POTAGE CRÈME DE POTIRON AUX CREVETTES
(Cream of Pumpkin and Shrimp Soup)

Peel a 2 lb. slice of pumpkin, throw away the seeds and the cottony center, cut the flesh into small pieces, salt and pepper them, and put them into a thick saucepan with a stick of celery cut in pieces. Cover them with 1½ pints of milk previously boiled, and 1 pint of mild stock or water, and simmer until the pumpkin is quite soft, about 30 minutes. Sieve the mixture; return the purée to a clean pan. Mash or pound in a mortar 4 oz. of peeled prawns or shrimp, adding a few drops of lemon juice. Dilute with a little of the pumpkin purée, add this mixture to the soup, simmer gently for 10 minutes or so, sieve again if the soup is not quite smooth, taste for seasoning and, when reheating, thin with a little more hot milk or stock if necessary. Immediately before serving stir in a good lump of butter. Ample for six.

Pumpkin is a vegetable which tends to go sour very quickly, so this soup should be used up on the day, or day after, it is made.

FOUR RECIPES FROM

Louis Diat's Home Cookbook

LOUIS DIAT WROTE three cookbooks, all of them of the caliber that one would expect from the master chef whose name was, for forty-odd years, practically synonymous with Ritz-Carlton. This one, subtitled *La Cuisine de Ma Mère,* has always been my favorite. In it, Mr. Diat has recaptured, as he set out to do, the essence and spirit of the French home cooking of his youth. His mother, Annette Alajoinine Diat, was famous throughout Auvergne for her culinary skill as was her mother before her. Her children became little gourmets with their first solid food. It was her leek and potato soup, served hot in winter and cold in summer, to which her son, years later, added cream to create his famous Vichyssoise. While important recipes from other regions are included in this book, the majority are for the Bourbonnais dishes that Madame Diat served to her family; dishes that were Louis Diat's first inspiration and which decided his career.

CARBONNADE DE BOEUF FLAMANDE

[Most of the best meat in France goes to the big cities where it fetches higher prices. As a result, the country housewife must, more often than not, meet the challenge of making something delicious out of the less desirable and sometimes tougher cuts. This she does, if she is a *bonne ménagère,* with consummate artistry. It is not simply long cooking that is required to accomplish this; the stewing, boiling or braising must be a slow and gentle process and the seasonings must be selected and incorporated with the utmost care. This Carbonnade is a case in point. — P. H.]

2 lbs. beef (chuck or other lean beef)	3 ·cups stock (may be made from bones)
1 teaspoon salt	1 teaspoon sugar
A little pepper	2 tablespoons butter
2 tablespoons beef or veal fat	3 large onions minced
2 tablespoons flour	1 sprig parsley, 1 stalk celery, a little
1 glass beer	thyme, 1 bay leaf, tied in a faggot
2 tablespoons vinegar	

Have the butcher cut meat into 12 slices and flatten them a little with a mallet. Season the slices with salt and pepper. Put fat in frying pan and when very hot sauté the meat, a few pieces at a time, until brown on both sides. Remove meat from pan, add flour to fat in pan and cook, stirring, until golden brown. Add beer, vinegar, stock and sugar and boil slowly, stirring until smooth. Melt butter in another saucepan, add onions and cook until golden. Put meat and onions in layers in a casserole, add faggot and strain the sauce over. Bring to a boil, cover and put in a hot oven of 425 degrees F. and cook 1½ to 2 hours or until meat is tender. Discard faggot, skim off all the fat from the top and serve from the casserole. If desired, the meat may be removed to a serving platter and the sauce strained over it to remove the onions.

Serve boiled potatoes with this dish. Serves 6.

CREAMED TOMATOES

[One of the reasons why vegetables are usually served as a separate course in fine French restaurants may well be because that is the custom in bourgeois kitchens whence came the solid foundations on which *haute cuisine* was built. In the country, vegetables are important and are eaten, generally, only when they are in season unless, like carrots, onions and potatoes, they can be stored for a time. If you are willing to wait, as the French countryfolk are, for fresh vegetables at their peak of perfection, it makes sense to serve them by themselves so that they may be truly savored and appreciated. — P. H.]

6-8 medium tomatoes	1 teaspoon butter
2 tablespoons butter	½ teaspoon flour
½ cup top milk (or cream)	½ teaspoon sugar

Peel tomatoes, cut in half and gently press out seeds and water. Season with salt. Melt 2 tablespoons butter in frying pan and when quite hot add tomatoes. Sauté on both sides. Add milk (or cream), bring to a boil and cook slowly about 8 to 10 minutes. Remove tomatoes to serving dish. Cook liquid in pan until reduced to about ½ the original quantity, then thicken with *manié* butter, made by creaming together the teaspoon butter with the flour and adding to the liquid in the pan. Correct the seasoning, add sugar and pour over tomato slices. Serves 3 to 4.

POTATO PIE

Potato Pie is one of those typical Bourbonnaise dishes so common in the country from which I came that we had it about once every week or at least every other week. But I do not think it is familiar at all to Americans. It is delicious and rather unusual.

6 medium potatoes	1 teaspoon chopped parsley
1½ teaspoons salt	2 tablespoons butter
A little pepper	1 lb. tart pastry
1 large onion, chopped	1½ cups cream

Peel potatoes and cut in thin slices, season with salt and pepper and mix with onion and parsley. Roll out one half the pastry about ¼ inch thick in either a round or oblong shape and place on a baking sheet. Drain potatoes and arrange about 1½ inches thick on the pastry, leaving an edge of pastry at least an inch wide. Roll out remaining pastry and place on the potatoes. Moisten lower edge to hold top and bottom crusts together and roll the two edges together so that no juice can escape. Prick or cut a few tiny gashes in the top. Brush top with an egg mixed with a little milk. Bake 1 to 1¼ hours in a moderately hot oven of 375 to 400 degrees. Cut a small round opening in the top and test with a knife to make sure potatoes are done. If they are done pour the cream into the hot pie through the opening. Let cool a little and serve either warm or cold. Serves 6.

SALADE MAISON

[Although a green salad is the traditional accompaniment to a French meal, the thrifty cook often makes other kinds, such as this. She serves it either as a main course for a light luncheon or supper or as part of a platter of hors d'oeuvres. — P. H.]

1 cup cooked cauliflower	½ tablespoon vinegar
1 cup cooked string beans	6 tablespoons salad oil
2 tomatoes, peeled, seeded and chopped	½ teaspoon dry mustard
	½ teaspoon salt
1 cup sliced leftover cooked chicken	Pepper
2 hard-boiled eggs	½ teaspoon fines herbes

Put cauliflower, string beans, tomatoes, and chicken in salad bowl. Separate eggs, cut whites in julienne, and add to bowl. Crush the yolks to a smooth paste and combine with seasoning, vinegar and oil, then add this dressing to the ingredients in the bowl. Sprinkle top with fines herbes. Serves 6.

Menus for Entertaining

JULIETTE ELKTON AND ELAINE ROSS

COOKBOOKS FEATURING MENUS have a tendency to be didactic, but that is not the case here. While every possible kind of party is described and the recipes supplied, you are invited, even urged, to vary, simplify or elaborate. A great deal of imagination has gone into the creation, and/or selection of recipes due to the authors' tenet of "give them what they want but surprise them a little, too." The following recipes are guaranteed to produce a stir of excitement and surprise at any party.

SAUCISSON EN CROÛTE
(Sausage in Crust)

The particular sausage we suggest for the Saucisson en Croûte is not mandatory. There are any number of varieties — Hungarian, Polish, Italian, Spanish, German, Scandinavian. Some are milder, some spicier, made of beef, pork, or a combination of meats. If you have access to a shop that specializes in sausages, you will want to experiment with several. We are particularly fond of German *bratwurst*, a light, delicately flavored veal sausage, the size of a large frankfurter. For this recipe, we order it especially in a large size. Some sausages are not precooked; parboil any uncooked sausage, remove the skin, and cool it before you wrap it in the pastry. Serve the Saucisson warm on a hot-plate if it has to wait. To go with it, 2 or 3 types of mustard — Bahamian, English, or a Dijon white wine mustard are all good.

Into a chilled mixing bowl sift together 2 cups flour and 1 teaspoon salt. With a pastry blender cut ¼ lb. plus 3 tablespoons chilled sweet butter into flour until butter is the size of peas. Moisten it with ¼ cup ice water and toss with a fork until mixture holds together, but no more; minimum handling is important. If more water is needed, add a teaspoon at a time. Chill dough 10 minutes. Place between sheets of waxed paper and roll out into rectangle large enough to enclose sausage.

Preheat oven to 375 degrees. Cut a 3 lb. Danish Summer Sausage in half crosswise, and reserve half for other uses. With a sharp knife make several long incisions in casing of sausage and peel off. Brush sausage with ¼ cup Riesling and wrap in crust. Brush edges of crust on top and at both ends with beaten egg, press edges together, and seal and crimp with a fork or flute with fingers. Bake on a greased jelly-roll pan for 30 minutes, or until crust is well browned. Serve warm, cut in 1-inch slices.

2 cups flour	Danish Summer Sausage
1 teaspoon salt	¼ cup Riesling
⅔ cup sweet butter	1 egg
¼ cup ice water	

CAVIAR ROULADE

[These roulades may be made early on the day of the party. Fill them and place them on a buttered cookie sheet; envelop the whole thing loosely in foil, to be reheated later. If in reheating, the roulades must still be kept warm, place the cookie sheets over pots of simmering water. — P. H.]

Preheat oven to 325 degrees. In a saucepan over medium heat, melt 4 tablespoons butter and add ½ cup flour, stirring with a whisk or wooden spoon for about 1 minute. Then gradually, still stirring, pour in 2 cups milk and cook for 4 minutes. Remove from heat and add 1 teaspoon sugar and 4 egg yolks. Beat 4 egg whites until stiff but not dry, and fold in. Grease a 10 x 15 inch jelly-roll tin and line it with waxed paper, then grease and lightly flour the paper. Spread batter on the paper and bake 40 minutes, or until slightly golden. Turn out on another piece of waxed paper and peel off top paper. Spread with a filling made of 2 ounces cream cheese, 2 ounces grey or black caviar and 2 tablespoons sour cream taken from a ½ pint jar. Roll and place on a heated serving platter. With the hot roulade, serve separately a cold sauce made of 2 more ounces caviar stirred into rest of sour cream.

4 tablespoons butter	4 egg whites
½ cup flour	4 ounces grey or black caviar, in all
2 cups milk	2 ounces cream cheese
1 teaspoon sugar	½ pint sour cream
4 egg yolks	

The Fannie Merritt Farmer
Boston Cooking School Cookbook

THIS BOOK SCARCELY needs an introduction. Its record speaks for itself: approximately three million copies have been sold since it first appeared in 1896. That recipes from it should be included in an anthology of this sort goes without saying, but I feel that perhaps I should explain why I chose these particular ones. While Fannie Farmer was the first to teach European cooking to American cooks and housewives, innumerable books have since been published which concentrate on Continental cuisine. The *Boston Cooking School Cookbook,* however, has always been one of the best sources of authentic New England recipes, and so it is from these that I have made my selections.

NEW ENGLAND CLAM CHOWDER

This is the traditional chowder. Old-fashioned cooks discarded the pork scraps, but they add a savory touch to the chowder.

Clean and pick over 1 quart clams using 1 cup cold water. Drain, reserving the liquid. Strain if it is sandy. Chop the hard parts of the clams. Put in a deep pan a 1½-inch cube fat salt pork, diced. Cook slowly until the fat melts and the scraps are crisp and brown. Remove the pork scraps and set them aside so they will be crisp when they are added. Add to the fat 1 onion, chopped fine. Cook slowly until the onion is golden.

Prepare 3 cups cubed potatoes. Put the potatoes and the chopped clams into the pan in layers, dredging each layer with flour and salt and pepper. Add 2½ cups boiling water. Simmer until the potatoes are tender (about 20 minutes). Add the soft part of the clams and cook 2 minutes. Add 4 cups hot milk, 4 tablespoons butter, salt and pepper to taste. Add at the last (to avoid curdling) the reserved clam water thickened with 1 tablespoon butter and 1 tablespoon flour.

Sprinkle some of the pork scraps on each serving. Serves 8 generously.

OLD-FASHIONED FISH CHOWDER

Fish stock made with bones improves the flavor of the chowder. There was a time when New Englanders always put into the chowder common or Boston crackers soaked in milk. Nowadays the crackers are usually omitted.

Order a 4-pound cod or haddock. Have the butcher skin it, remove the fish from the backbone and give you the head, tail and bone. Put the head, tail and bone (broken in pieces) in a deep kettle. Add 2 cups cold water. Simmer slowly 10 minutes. Drain and save the liquid. Put in a small frying pan a 1½ inch cube fat salt pork, diced. Cook slowly 5 minutes. Add 1 onion, sliced thin. Cook until the onion is soft (about 5 minutes). Strain the fat into a deep pan and set the crisp scraps aside. Add to the kettle 4 cups thinly sliced potatoes and 2 cups boiling water. Cook 5 minutes. Add the fish, cut in 2-inch pieces, and the liquid drained from the bones. Cover and simmer 10 minutes. Add the scraps of onion and pork. Add 4 cups scalded milk or cream, 1 tablespoon salt, ⅛ teaspoon pepper, 3 tablespoons butter.

Heat but do not boil. Serves 8 generously.

STUFFED CLAMS UNION LEAGUE

Put in a kettle 4 tablespoons butter and ½ teaspoon finely chopped shallot or onion. Cook 5 minutes. Add 18 small clams (in the shell) and ½ cup dry white wine or water. Cover and cook until the shells open. Remove the clams from the shells and chop. Cook the liquid in the kettle down to ⅓ cup. In a saucepan, melt 2 tablespoons butter. Blend in 2 tablespoons flour.

Stir in the clam liquid, little by little. Add the clams and ¼ cup cream. Season with salt and pepper. Spoon into the shells. Sprinkle with chopped parsley. Put on each bacon, diced, or buttered crumbs mixed with grated cheese.

Bake at 400 degrees until the bacon is crisp or the crumbs are brown.

Serves 3, or 6 as a first course.

BOSTON BAKED BEANS

Boston baked beans are always flavored with molasses and baked to a rich dark brown. The preferred beans to use are small California or New York pea beans, but kidney beans are delicious, too, baked in the same fashion.

Wash, discarding imperfect ones, 2 pounds California or New York pea beans. Cover with 2 quarts water. Bring to the boiling point, boil 2 minutes and soak 1 hour or more. Without draining, cook slowly until the skins burst when you take a few on the tip of a spoon and blow on them. Drain, reserving the cooking water. Cover with boiling water ½ pound fat salt pork. Let stand 2 minutes, drain and cut 1-inch gashes every ½ inch without cutting through the rind. Put the beans in the bean pot. Push the pork down into the beans until all but the rind is covered. Mix 2 teaspoons salt, 1 cup molasses, 1 teaspoon dry mustard, 2 tablespoons sugar, brown or white.

Add 1 cup of the reserved water and bring to boiling point. Pour over the beans and add enough more water to cover the beans. Cover the bean pot. Bake 6 to 8 hours at 250 degrees. Add water as needed to keep the beans moist. Uncover the last hour of baking so that the rind will be brown and crisp.

10 or more servings.

To flavor the beans with onion, rub the inside of the pot with onion and add a few slivers of onion. If you like a pronounced onion flavor, put a peeled onion in the pot with the beans and remove it when you serve them.

OLD-FASHIONED RICE PUDDING

Very soft and creamy. For a firm pudding, use ½ cup of rice. Brown rice gives a delicious flavor. For a richer pudding, stir in 1 or 2 well-beaten eggs 30 minutes before the pudding is done.

Put in a casserole 4 cups milk, ⅔ cup sugar, ¼ cup uncooked rice, ½ teaspoon salt, 1 teaspoon vanilla or a dash of nutmeg or the grated rind of ½ lemon.

Bake, uncovered, 3 hours at 300 degrees. During the first hour stir three times with a fork so that the rice will not settle. After the first hour, stir in ½ cup raisins, dates or figs cut small.

CLUB INDIAN PUDDING

Similar to traditional Indian Pudding but firmer and baked in a shorter time.

Scald in a double boiler 1 quart milk. Stir in slowly 5 tablespoons corn meal. Cook over hot water 20 minutes. Add 2 tablespoons butter, 1 cup molasses, 1 teaspoon salt, 1 teaspoon cinnamon, 2 eggs, well beaten. Spoon into a buttered baking dish. Pour over it 1 cup cold milk. Bake 1 hour at 350 degrees. Serves 8.

To vary the seasoning, use ¾ teaspoon cinnamon and ¼ teaspoon ginger or nutmeg.

The Gourmet Cookbook

VOLUME I

NO ANTHOLOGY of fine recipes would be complete unless the *Gourmet Cookbooks* were represented therein. Over the years since 1941, practically every gastronome worth his salt has written for *Gourmet* magazine, from which, of course, recipes were selected to make up these books. The roster of contributors includes, among others, Louis P. de Gouy, Samuel Chamberlain, Alec Waugh, Louis Diat, Leslie Charteris, Frances Parkinson Keyes, Lucius Beebe, James A. Beard, Stephen Longstreet, Frank Schoonmaker, Kay Boyle, Idwal Jones, Robert P. T. Coffin, George Jean Nathan, Charles Hanson Towne and Vincent Starrett. While there is no way of telling whose recipe is whose, unless you have back issues of the magazine, you can be assured, under the circumstances, that a high level of excellence prevails throughout both books.

HAM AND RAISIN CROQUETTES CREOLE

Rinse ½ cup seedless raisins, drain and dry them, and grind them in the meat chopper. Also grind 3 cups cooked hominy and 2½ cups cooked lean ham. Blend well and add 2 teaspoons prepared mustard. Beat 2 eggs with 2 tablespoons flour and blend thoroughly into the ham-raisin mixture. Season to taste with salt, pepper and nutmeg. Shape into croquettes, dip in egg, then in fine bread crumbs, and chill thoroughly. When ready to use, place a few croquettes at a time in a wire basket and fry them in hot deep fat until delicately browned. Drain on absorbent paper and serve on a bed of spinach with noodles, mashed potatoes, or curried rice. Serves 6.

MARINATED SHORT RIBS

Have your butcher cut 3 pounds of beef short ribs into serving pieces. Wipe the meat with a damp cloth and put it into a deep bowl. Mix together 2 tablespoons hot mustard, 3 teaspoons salt, a generous amount of black pepper, ½ teaspoon chili powder, ½ teaspoon sugar, 1 tablespoon lemon juice, and 6 tablespoons olive oil. Shake well with a crushed clove of garlic. Pour this marinade over the meat and wedge a few thick slices of onion between the pieces of beef. Cover and keep in a cool place for 8 to 24 hours, stirring occasionally. Put the ribs into a roasting pan, reserving the excess sauce and the onion slices. Brown the meat in a hot oven for about 15 minutes. Add the onions and the marinade to the pan. Cover, reduce the heat to moderate, and bake for 1 hour. Remove the cover and bake until the onions are brown and the fat crisp. Serve with baked potatoes and barbecue sauce or gravy made from the drippings. Serves 6.

BRAISED OXTAILS DUNKERQUE

Have 3 oxtails cut in pieces at the joints. Wash quickly and dry. In a braising kettle or a cast-iron pot, place a layer of ⅓ cup each coarsely chopped carrots, onions, and the white parts of a leek, ⅓ cup chopped fat salt pork, 2 small calf's feet, boned, 1 clove garlic, mashed, and a bouquet garni. Cover the kettle and cook over a fast flame for 15 minutes, shaking the kettle frequently. Add the oxtail and cook for 10 minutes longer, stirring almost constantly. Add beef bouillon and dry white wine in equal parts to cover. Season to taste with salt and pepper, cover the kettle and braise in a very slow oven for 4 hours.

Remove the oxtail pieces to a large shallow saucepan. Skim the fat off the liquid in the braising kettle and pour the remaining liquid through a fine sieve into the saucepan. Add ⅓ pound small fresh mushroom caps, 12 small white onions, parboiled and drained, 1 dozen small pork sausages, pricked with a fork and precooked in a pan to remove their excess fat, and 6 small hearts of lettuce, parboiled and held in shape with thread. Cover the saucepan and set it in a moderate oven for 35 to 40 minutes. Correct the seasoning.

Place the oxtails in the center of a heated deep platter and arrange the vegetables and sausages around them. Heat a soup ladle, pour into it 2 tablespoons warmed brandy, set aflame, and sprinkle the oxtail pieces with the flaming spirit. Garnish the dish with finely chopped parsley and serve with small potato balls. Serves 6.

RABBIT SAUTÉED WITH TARRAGON

Skin and clean a rabbit, reserving the liver, cut it into pieces, and dust them very lightly with a little flour seasoned with salt. Melt ¼ pound butter in a large skillet, add the pieces of rabbit, and brown them quickly on all sides, being careful not to let the butter burn. When the pieces are nicely colored, reduce the heat, add ⅔ cup dry white wine, and cover. Simmer very gently for about 45 minutes, or until the rabbit is tender.

Remove the cover and add 2 tablespoons fresh tarragon leaves or 1 teaspoon dried tarragon soaked in ¼ cup white wine for 30 minutes. Increase the heat, turn the pieces of meat to distribute the tarragon, and cook for another 5 minutes. Remove the pieces of rabbit to a heated platter, add ½ tablespoon meat glaze to the sauce in the pan, and pour over the rabbit. Serve immediately. The liver may be sautéed in butter for 5 minutes and added to the dish just before serving. Serves 6.

SWEDISH LAMB, DILL SAUCE

Cook a neck of lamb, weighing about 3 pounds, in 2 quarts salted water with 3 or 4 dill stalks.

When the water boils, cover the saucepan and simmer the lamb very gently for 2 to 2½ hours, or until it is tender but not falling apart. Divide the lamb into 6 serving portions and serve it hot with dill sauce:

In a saucepan over a low flame blend 1 tablespoon butter with 2 tablespoons flour without letting it brown, stirring almost constantly. Gradually add 2 cups hot stock from the boiled lamb and season with a scant 2 tablespoons chopped fresh dill, or the same amount of dill salt, 1½ tablespoons vinegar, ¾ tablespoon sugar, a pinch of white pepper, and salt to taste. Bring the sauce to a gentle boil, stirring frequently from the bottom of the pan, and simmer for 5 minutes. Remove it from the fire and beat in 1 large egg yolk well blended with 2 tablespoons lamb stock. Serves 6.

CAPON SOUVAROFF

In cleaning the capon, the opening should be kept as small as possible, and the skin should not be broken when the pin feathers are removed. Stuff the bird with Poultry Stuffing Souvaroff (see below) and sew the vents. Season with salt and spread with drippings of pork or beef or with lard. Cover the bird with thin slices of fat pork and truss with string.

Lay the bird on its side in a deep roasting pan. Sear for 30 minutes in a hot oven, turning it after 15 minutes to sear the other side. Reduce the heat to moderate and cook for 2½ hours longer, turning the bird every 15 minutes and basting frequently. Transfer to an earthenware casserole. Remove the trussing strings and lay the bird on its back.

Skim off the fat from the juices in the roasting pan and add the juice from the can of truffles, ½ cup brown sauce or rich gravy made with beef extract, 3 ounces Madeira or sherry, and ¼ cup truffles, coarsely chopped. Pour this sauce around the bird in the casserole. Cover the casserole tightly. Make a stiff dough of 2 cups flour and a little water. Shape the dough into a thick roll and seal the casserole cover with it. Set the casserole in a hot oven to bake for 30 minutes. The dough should be well browned.

Serve at once. Remove the dough seal and the casserole cover at the table. This method is also used for pheasant or partridge. Serves 6.

Poultry Stuffing Souvaroff

Combine 1½ cups goose liver cut in large pieces, 6 to 8 fresh or canned truffles, cut in half if very large, and 1 tablespoon *glace de viande*, or meat extract. Moisten with 2 ounces cognac and 3 ounces Madeira. Pâté de foie gras may be used instead of goose liver. [NOTE: This is not a large amount of stuffing, but it is very rich. Stuff only the body cavity. If the capon weighs 5 pounds or over, double the amount of stuffing. You can economize slightly by using a South American brand of paté. — P. H.]

TWO RECIPES FROM

The Gourmet Cookbook

VOLUME II

SOUSED CAMEMBERT

Soak a whole Camembert overnight in enough dry white wine to just cover. Next day scrape off any discolored portion of the crust and mash the cheese with ½ cup soft sweet butter until the mixture is smooth. Chill and re-form the cheese into its original shape. Cover the top and sides with finely chopped toasted almonds and chill again. Remove the Camembert from the refrigerator about 30 minutes before serving and serve with hot toasted crackers as a dessert. Serves 6.

EGGPLANT WITH PROSCIUTTO

Cut 3 medium eggplants in half. Cut the flesh away from the skin, lift it out and cut it into ½ inch slices. Sprinkle the slices with salt and pepper. Cover the bottom of a skillet generously with olive oil and in it sauté 3 onions, finely sliced, until the onions are transparent.

Add the eggplant slices and sauté them quickly for 3 minutes on each side. Return the slices, with the onions, to the eggplant shells and cover with thin slices of prosciutto. Sprinkle generously with grated Parmesan cheese and bake in a moderate (350 degree) oven for 10 minutes.

Serves 6.

Compiled and edited by Gourmet, Inc., 1957. Published by Gourmet Distributing Corp. Reprinted by permission.

The Gold Cook Book

LOUIS P. DE GOUY

LOUIS P. DE GOUY learned his chosen profession from his father, who was Esquire of Cuisine at the court of Franz Josef of Austria and from Escoffier himself, the "chef of kings and the king of chefs." During his long and distinguished career as Master Chef, Mr. De Gouy wrote many cookbooks, but this one is his masterpiece, the culmination of sixty years of experience. It is a monumental work of over 2000 recipes for American and European dishes; a most felicitous combination, as Savarin St. Sure put it, of "sane kitchen instructions, valid philosophical observations and edifying food lore." It belongs in the library of anyone interested in any aspect of gastronomy.

VEAL CUTLET À LA SACHER

This most delicious dish may be made with individual veal cutlets or with one large one cut a generous inch thick, which, in the opinion of gourmets, is the best as well as the original method of this Viennese super-dish.

Have the veal cut from top of the leg; it should be fully an inch in thickness and weigh about 2-2½ pounds. Pound it with a rolling pin with salt and freshly ground black pepper for a few seconds, so as to break down the tissues, but do not flatten too much. Sauté 1 cup of thinly sliced onions, preferably small ones, in 3 tablespoons of butter over a low flame until lightly browned, adding more butter if necessary, because veal, being naturally lean, absorbs plenty of fat. Now, dredge the cutlet with flour. When onions are lightly browned, yet still underdone, bank them to one side of the pan, put cutlet in pan and brown on both sides; pour in 1 cup of heavy, scalded sour cream, and spoon the onions on top of the meat. Cover the pan and cook very, very gently, about 35-40 minutes, or until cutlet is tender, turning it once during the cooking, and again spooning the onions on to the top side of the meat. Serve with sliced carrots fried in plenty of butter until browned, and a side dish of Noodles Amandine.

Serves 6.

NOODLES AMANDINE

Blanch ½ cup of almonds; skin, cut into thin slivers and sauté in butter or margarine until crisp and golden brown. Meanwhile, peel and slice thin ½ pound fresh mushrooms, using both stems and caps, and cook in 1¾ to 2 tablespoons of butter or margarine over a gentle flame for 4 or 5 minutes, stirring frequently; then add 2 tablespoons of grated onion, or finely minced shallots, if available. Combine the almonds and mushroom mixture and gradually stir in 2 generous cups of rich cream sauce, adding a little more cream, if needed. Cook 1 package of noodles or its equivalent of homemade noodles and drain. Toss the noodles in the sauce; turn into a deep, heated platter, and sprinkle with ¾ cup of grated Swiss cheese. Serve at once.

Serves 6.

Season to Taste

PEGGY HARVEY

IT IS WITH considerable humility that I include recipes from one of my own books in this collection. It is not that I am apologizing for them; I can vouch for their quality and, as a matter of fact, lay no claim to their complete originality. It is just that I regret allotting them space which is thereby denied to others. I defer, however, to the wishes of my publishers both as to their inclusion and selection.

BEEF À LA MODE
(Must be prepared long in advance)

Serves 6 to 8.

Long ago when I first decided to tackle this classic French pot roast I found that the recipe was slightly different in each of my important cookbooks. That being the case, I decided to make a chart similar to those I used to make in my high-school history class. Across the top of the page I wrote the names of my mentors — Escoffier, Louis Diat, June Platt, Julian Street, Clémentine, and Louis P. de Gouy. In a box under each name I put the marinade, if any. (Clémentine, for instance, doesn't marinate.) Below this I wrote down what each one said to do next — what liquid to use for the braising and how much of it, when the vegetables were to be added, the seasoning, and so forth. Having pooled the knowledge of these experts I evolved what is now our standard recipe for Beef à la Mode. We sometimes serve snails as a first course. No vegetable is necessary; just hot French bread, a green salad, plenty of good red wine, and an Apricot Mousse or a chiffon pie for dessert.

Shopping List

One 5-pound rolled rump roast of beef, without much fat	Brandy
1 veal knuckle, cracked	Parsley
Salt, black peppercorns	Butter
Monosodium glutamate	Small white onions
Nutmeg	1 can condensed tomato soup
1 quart good domestic red burgundy or claret	Whole cloves
Carrots, onions, celery	Sugar
Thyme, marjoram, bay leaf	Powdered cloves
¼ pound fat salt pork cut in ¼-inch slices	Arrowroot flour or cornstarch

Get a 5-pound rolled rump of beef without much fat on it, 1 veal knuckle, cracked, and ¼ pound fat salt pork cut in ¼-inch slices for larding.

Cut the pork in ¼-inch strips and marinate them for a few minutes in ¼ cup brandy and 1 teaspoon chopped parsley. Insert these in the meat with the grain using an ice pick or larding needle. We find the former satisfactory. Make a hole with it and then use it to push the strip of salt pork into the hole. This must be done the night before the meat is cooked.

When the larding has been accomplished rub the meat with salt, freshly ground black pepper, and a little nutmeg. Put it in a bowl with 1 quart good domestic red burgundy or claret and ¼ cup brandy. Let it stand in a cool place overnight. Turn it occasionally.

A rich broth must be made out of the veal knuckle bone and it is best to make this the day before also. Besides, if you do this, you can leave the broth in the refrigerator overnight and be able to lift the congealed fat off the next day. Put 1 sliced carrot, 1 quartered onion, some celery leaves, and a bouquet garni or pinches of thyme and marjoram and 1 bay leaf in a pot with the knuckle. Add cold water to cover, 1 teaspoon salt, freshly ground black pepper and a pinch of monosodium glutamate. Bring to a boil, skim, and simmer, covered, for 2 or more hours. Strain and chill the broth and save the bits of veal.

Next day drain the beef and dry it well, saving the marinade. Brown the meat carefully on all sides in butter or drippings in an iron pot. Drain the fat from the pot when the meat has browned and add the strained marinade.

Cover and cook over a slow fire for 2½ hours. Turn the meat from time to time.

Remove the fat from the veal broth and add the broth to the meat and marinade. Continue cooking for ½ hour and add 12 or more carrots cut in the shape of olives (thick slices, if you are lazy), 12 small peeled white onions each stuck with a clove and sautéed for 20 minutes in butter and a little sugar for glazing, ½ can condensed tomato soup and 1 teaspoon powdered cloves. Cook 1 hour more, over a slow fire, correct the seasoning, and thicken with 1 scant tablespoon arrowroot flour or cornstarch mixed with ¼ cup cold water. Use more of the thickening agent if necessary. Add the bits of veal, minced.

Slice the meat across the grain, dust with chopped parsley, and serve.

CHICKEN SUZANNE
(May be prepared in advance)

Serves 4.

When I was writing the first edition of this book, a friend, who knew very little about cooking, appointed herself official tester for many of the recipes. The idea was that if she could make it, anyone could. Chicken Suzanne was one of her first triumphs. Her family could not believe that she had cooked it herself. I usually serve green beans or a purée of peas with it, and for dessert, an ice or a compote of fruit.

Shopping List

Two 2 to 2½ lb. broilers, quartered	3 pounds small white onions
1 can clear chicken broth	Butter
1 pint light cream	Long-grain rice
Salt, black peppercorns	Bourbon whisky

Have the butcher quarter 2 small broilers.

Peel 3 pounds small white onions and cook them in ½ pound butter in a double boiler, covered, for 1 hour. Do not let them brown.

Measure 1 can clear chicken broth and add enough water to make 3½ cups liquid. Simmer the chicken in this until tender. The process will take approximately as long as the onions. When the chicken is done, remove it and put it in a casserole, saving the broth. Cover the chickens with the onions and add 1 pint light cream.

Allowing for evaporation you should have 3 cups chicken broth. If not, add water to make up the difference. Put this in the top of a double boiler over direct heat and bring to a boil. Stir in slowly 1 cup washed and dried long-grain rice. Cook for 5 minutes, stirring over medium heat, then cover and place over boiling water. Cook until rice is tender, stirring frequently. This will take about 45 minutes.

When ready to serve, stir the rice into the chicken in the casserole, warm over low heat, and add 4 ounces of bourbon whisky. Taste for seasoning. Add salt, if necessary, and freshly ground black pepper.

Note: Although this dish does not taste "oniony," you may, if you prefer, use half onions and half mushrooms and cook them together in the butter. Try young quartered pheasants this way sometime.

GRILLED LEG OF LAMB DEKKER

Serves 4 to 6.

Albert Dekker, actor, raconteur, and amateur chef, cooked this for us first, and we have been doing it happily ever since. It lends itself equally well to outdoor grill cooking except that, as you will see, the process is reversed. The odd thing is that the meat does not taste particularly like lamb. As proof of this you will find that devotees of mint jelly or mint sauce are apt to pass it up when the lamb is cooked in this manner. The meat, from which the bone has been removed, is of varying thickness and, if the cooking time is, as I recommend, between 45 and 50 minutes, there will be some rare meat, some faintly pink, and quite a lot well done. If there is no one in the group who cares for underdone lamb, the cooking time may be extended for ten or fifteen minutes. Artichokes with Hollandaise Sauce, Acorn Squash, or Eggplant Soufflé are all good accompaniments. Cheese Cake or a Strawberry Soufflé are my choices for dessert. As for how many may be served, allow a little more than the normal half-pound per person, as I have found that even people who usually eat like birds are apt to have a second helping.

Shopping List

One 4 to 5 lb. leg of lamb boned but not rolled	Garlic
	Seasoned salt
Sage	Black peppercorns

Have the butcher remove the bone from a leg of lamb. He should do this by making a long cut on the under, not the fell (fat) side. Do not let him roll it up. Spread it out flat so that it looks like a large irregularly shaped butterfly.

For kitchen cooking, pre-heat the broiler to 450 degrees. Rub the cut side of the lamb with a little sage and place the meat, spread out, fell-side up, on the rack close to the flame. Practically burn it for 30 minutes on this side. Turn it then and rub the cut side with garlic and season with salt and freshly ground black pepper. Broil it for 15 to 30 minutes, depending on the degree of doneness required. Lower the flame of the broiler slightly for this cooking.

On an outdoor grill place the meat fell-side down so that it cooks first. When it has been turned, the fat bastes the meat. Cooking times are comparable.

When the meat is done let it rest, keeping warm, for 15-20 minutes. Place it on a platter with the blackened, fell side up. The meat will have "drawn up," so to speak, and will look more attractive than you would expect. Carve it perpendicularly as you would a steak.

Note: You will find the leftover meat, if any, delightfully moist for serving cold with a salad of green beans for luncheon.

[NOTE: This was the entrée at a Wine and Food Society dinner in Mobile, Alabama in 1961, as I learned from André Simon's *A Gastronomical Quarterly*. Both Mr. Dekker and I were pleased and proud. — P. H.]

PASTETSEO

Serves 6 to 8.

A friend brought me the directions for this, a dish from his favorite Greek restaurant, and asked me to make it for him. The eventual effect, he said, would be a macaroni loaf with a little meat lurking in it and half an inch of custard on top. Since neither my husband nor I were macaroni enthusiasts, we asked permission to change the proportions a bit and used considerably more meat than originally specified. We also worried a little about the amount of onions involved but our fears proved groundless. This is one of those creations in which, as Marcel Boulestin remarked in connection with something else, "raw materials are transformed, flavors are blended, smells altered, miracles performed." It is a wonderful entrée for a buffet supper.

Shopping List

3 large onions	Large macaroni
Powdered cinnamon	Eggs
Salt, black peppercorns	Parmesan cheese
2 lbs. lean ground round steak	Cornstarch
Butter	Milk
1 No. 2 can tomatoes	
Nutmeg	

Dice 3 large onions and put them, with 1 teaspoon powdered cinnamon and 1 teaspoon salt, in a large iron skillet. Add ½ glass water and simmer, uncovered, for ½ hour. Add 2 pounds lean ground round steak and stir until the water has been absorbed. Add ¼ pound butter and let the meat and onions brown over medium heat. Add half a No. 2 can tomatoes, more salt, if necessary, freshly ground black pepper, and ½ teaspoon nutmeg. Cook until all liquid has been absorbed. This seems to take a long time but it does happen eventually — and must. Break up ⅓ lb. large macaroni, boil, and drain thoroughly. Add this to the meat-and-tomato mixture and mix well. Add 3 beaten eggs and ¼ pound freshly grated Parmesan cheese.

Put the mixture into an oblong baking dish or a straight-sided casserole. The receptacle should be just deep enough to hold the meat plus ½ inch of custard.

For the custard, melt ½ tablespoon butter in a saucepan and add 1 teaspoon cornstarch and 1 pint milk. Simmer and stir for a few minutes and add 3 beaten eggs. Cook over medium heat, stirring until creamy. Pour 1 tablespoon melted butter over the meat and macaroni, pour on the custard, sprinkle with a little freshly grated Parmesan cheese and bake in a preheated 325-degree oven for ½ hour.

Note: If you want to make the Pastetseo early, do everything (including the baking) except sprinkling the cheese on the custard. Leave the casserole, uncovered, in a warm place and sprinkle the cheese on top when you put it in a 250-degree oven to heat. I feel that I must warn you that the custard will not look like a perfect, baked custard. Do not worry. It is the taste that counts.

ACORN SQUASH

Serves 4.

Ardell cooked with and for us for five years and this is one of her valuable contributions to the Harvey cuisine. I have never encountered it in any other cookbook.

Shopping List

4 acorn squash split lengthwise	Salt, black peppercorns
Butter	Powdered ginger
Light cream	Brown sugar

Have 4 acorn squash split lengthwise. Remove seeds and scrape cavities. Place the halves, cut-side down, in a shallow baking dish with 1 teaspoon water. Bake in a 325-degree oven for 1 hour or until tender. Remove from oven and scoop out the pulp, saving 4 of the best skins. Beat into the mashed pulp 1 tablespoon butter, 1 tablespoon light cream, ½ teaspoon powdered ginger. Add salt, freshly ground black pepper, and brown sugar to taste.

Stuff the 4 shells heaping full and put them back in the baking dish. They may now wait, keeping warm, until just before serving. At that time put them in a pre-heated broiler 1 inch or so below a medium flame, to brown.

ZUCCHINI FOUQUET

Serves as many as desired.

I first tasted this at Fouquet's in Paris. Even if you feel, as I do, that zucchini is best unpeeled, please try it. It must be peeled for this dish because it should have a cream-colored appearance. In both looks and tastes delicate.

Shopping List

1 large zucchini per person	Butter
Salt	Parmesan cheese

Peel 1 large zucchini, about the size of a medium cucumber, per person. Let them stand 30 minutes or so in cold water, salted. Steam them whole or boil them whole in a very little water if you do not own a steaming gadget. (A colander is a good substitute for a steamer, however.) Do not let the zucchini get too soft — cook only until tender. Meanwhile, grate sufficient Parmesan cheese so that you have 1 generous tablespoon for each person.

Melt enough butter so that you have slightly more than 1 tablespoon per zucchini. Do not let the butter brown.

Drain the zucchini and make a deep lengthwise slit in each one. Fill the slit with the cheese and pour the melted butter over all.

Note: If there is to be any sauce on the meat when you are serving zucchini like this, it is wise to put the zucchini on a separate plate or, as we sometimes do, in a corn boat.

EGGPLANT SOUFFLÉ

Serves 4.

This is one vegetable soufflé which must vary from the general rule because of the wateriness of eggplant. Some recipes call for bread crumbs to take care of this, but I think that fresh cracker crumbs are better. If the taste is too bland, 1 tablespoon of grated onion may be added, more cheese, or 1 tablespoon of tomato catsup. Personally I find the taste subtle rather than bland without these additions. The soufflé is an excellent accompaniment to grilled or roast lamb or baked ham.

Shopping List

1 medium-sized eggplant	Flour
Salt	Soda crackers, unsalted
Butter	or lightly salted
Flour	Parmesan cheese
Milk	Black peppercorns
Light cream	

Pare 1 medium-sized eggplant and cut it into ½-inch dice. Soak in cold salted water for at least 1 hour. (Put a plate over the eggplant pieces to hold them down under the water.) Drain well and cook, in sufficient water to cover, until very tender. Drain thoroughly and mash with a fork.

Melt 2 tablespoons butter and stir in 2 tablespoons flour. Cook and stir, over medium heat, until smooth. Add gradually 1 cup half milk and half light cream, which have been heated together. Cook and stir until thick and smooth. Blend in 1 tablespoon freshly grated Parmesan cheese.

Beat 2 egg yolks with a rotary beater until they are light in color. Combine with the cream sauce in the usual manner.

Crush enough fresh soda crackers (preferably unsalted) to make 1 cup fine crumbs. Add these to the mashed eggplant. Combine with the cream sauce, season to taste with salt and freshly ground black pepper, and cool.

Beat 4 egg whites until stiff and fold them into the soufflé mixture. Pour into an unbuttered 1½ quart soufflé dish and bake in a pre-heated 350-degree oven for 45 minutes. This soufflé will not rise as high as some, but it is lovely and light and equally good.

FIVE RECIPES FROM

Good Taste — Volume I

HARRIET HEALY

HARRIET HEALY is one of the most indefatigable and enthusiastic culinary experts I've ever met. She recently sold and,
to all intents and purposes, retired from active participation in her
successful nine-year-old cooking school, Au Bon Goût, in Palm
Beach. No sooner had this been done than she was off to Paris to
take lessons at L'École des Trois Gourmandes (run by Mesdames
Beck, Bertholle and Child) and to shop for cooking equipment at
Les Halles. Upon her return to Florida the new second kitchen that
she had been having added to her house was ready and she went to
work in it on her new project, a line of frozen foods. As a sort of
busman's holiday she still teaches once a week at the school. And,
of course, there are these two little cook books which she found
time to write between 1956 and 1960. They are collections of
recipes developed at the school. I think you will find these samples
original and practicable, as I do.

BLACK MUSHROOM SOUP (Serves 4)

½ pound mushrooms (preferably
   the ones that are black inside)
2 cans Campbell's consommé
2 tablespoons butter

1½ tablespoons potato starch mixed
   with ¼ cup cold water
Freshly ground pepper to taste
1 tablespoon dry French vermouth

Wipe mushrooms (don't wash). Chop stems and simmer them in 1 can of
consommé until soft. Strain through a sieve, mashing the stems. Throw the

stems away. Now chop mushroom tops quite finely and cook them in a little butter for about 8 minutes. Add the other can of consommé and simmer for 10 to 15 minutes. Add the mushroom stem juice and again strain through a sieve, mashing the mushroom tops. Stir in potato starch and bring to a boil, stirring constantly. Season with ground pepper (no salt) and stir in vermouth. Take a little bit of the fat off the top of the soup by blotting it quickly with a paper napkin. (Sherry can be used instead of vermouth.)

If you wish, you can serve this soup like a Boula by spooning whipped cream on top of the soup in the cups and running them under the broiler for a minute to brown. It will not crack your cups.

POUNDED BEEF

1. Ask your butcher to cut a filet mignon into slices a little over ¼ inch thick. Take these slices, put them between wax paper and pound them with the flat side of a cleaver until meat is paper thin (even thinner than veal scallopini). Make a Bordelaise sauce (heat it preferably at table in a chafing dish). When it is bubbling, place the filets in the sauce for about 1 minute. Turn them and cook for about ½ minute longer. They must be pink inside.

2. Ask your butcher to cut minute steaks as thinly as a slice of roast beef, removing any bone. Pound the meat in the above fashion. Sauté the slices quickly in butter and serve with Bordelaise or Béarnaise sauce or with just a little sauce made in the pan with flour, *glace de viande*, Worcestershire sauce and water. Sprinkle with chopped parsley.

3. You can also cut slices from an uncooked roast of beef and treat them in the same way.

POUNDED LAMB
(An expensive but delicious way to serve a lamb chop)

Have your butcher (or you can do it yourself with a sharp knife) bone a double rib lamb chop or a loin chop, taking off all fat and gristle. Pound the meat between two pieces of wax paper until it is about ½ inch thick.

(Not as paper thin as the filet of beef.) Sauté in butter quickly (must be pink inside) and serve in the following ways:

1. For a special dinner party, sauté slices of bread in butter quickly on both sides. Spread with pâté de foie gras and keep them warm on a platter. Place sautéed pounded chop on top and cover with a sauce made as follows:

Heat a glass of currant jelly to the boiling point and stir in 1 scant tablespoon potato starch mixed with ¼ cup cold water. Bring to a boil, stirring, and add dry sherry to taste. Garnish with watercress.

2. Sauté pounded lamb chops as in the above recipe. Place meat on a warm serving platter and pour over it a sauce made as follows:

To thick Béchamel sauce add a little lamb stock. (Ask butcher for lamb bones and a little meat to make stock.) Cook meat and bones in water to cover with a little celery, bay leaf, peppercorns, salt and a carrot. (Do this the day before so that all fat can be skimmed off.) Then add 3 tablespoons capers and a little of the caper juice and at least ½ cup chopped parsley.

3. Sauté pounded lamb chops as in the above recipe. Place each chop on a piece of sautéed toast the size of the chop and put a large spoonful of Béarnaise on top. (Try to have plenty of fresh tarragon in your sauce). Sprinkle with chopped parsley.

4. Serve sautéed pounded lamb chops with a border of Curry Rice and pass chutney. Sautéed toast may be put under each chop if desired.

POUNDED CHICKEN

1. Buy a three-pound broiler (unless you can buy chicken breasts which have not been frozen). Cut the raw meat off the breast bone and pound it thinly between wax paper. Sauté the chicken meat quickly in butter for about 3 minutes on each side and place it on sautéed toast spread with cooked chopped chicken livers. Make a pan sauce using a little flour, 2 tablespoons *glace de viande* and a little white wine or sherry. Cover chicken breast with the sauce and place a broiled mushroom cap on top. Surround by watercress.

2. Cook pounded chicken as above and place on sautéed toast. Make a rich Béchamel sauce with chopped shallots or onions and add chopped fresh tarragon. Pour the sauce over the chicken breast.

3. Cook pounded chicken as above and place on sautéed toast spread with cooked chopped chicken livers. Make sauce as follows:

To a rich Béchamel sauce add ½ cup fresh grated horseradish. Strain out horseradish after tasting the sauce. Add sherry to taste and pour over the chicken breast.

4. Sauté pounded chicken for about 3 minutes on each side. This can be done ahead of time. When ready to serve, place chicken on a thin slice of sautéed ham. Put a slice of Mozzarella cheese on the chicken and sprinkle generously with grated Parmesan. Put under the broiler, quite far from the flame so that chicken will be thoroughly warmed and the cheese hot and brown.

BLACK RICE

1 medium onion, finely chopped
¾ stick butter
1 cup unwashed long grain rice
2⅔ cups chicken stock
1 teaspoon Beau Monde (Spice Islands)
½ pound mushrooms (preferably the ones that are black inside)

In a frying pan, sauté the onion in the butter until onion is golden brown. Add rice and cook, stirring until rice is golden (not brown). Add chicken stock and Beau Monde seasoning, cover and simmer for 30 minutes.

Meanwhile cut the stems from the mushrooms, chop stems finely and simmer in water to cover for 10 minutes or until mushrooms are tender. Strain, mashing stems against sieve, and reserve the juice. Chop mushroom tops finely and sauté them in a little butter for about 5 minutes. With a fork stir mushroom caps and juice into the rice and cook for 10 minutes longer.

Good Taste — Volume II

Harriet Healy

CRAB CUCUMBER TARRAGON

Serves 6.

Hollow out 3 raw, peeled cucumbers with apple corer. Fill with ½ lb. (or less) cooked crabmeat mixed with 2 sprigs of chopped tarragon leaves or 1 tablespoon dry tarragon. Season with salt, pepper, onion juice and 2 tablespoons lemon juice. Roll filled cucumber in aluminum foil, closing ends tightly by folding under. Bake in 375-degree oven for about 20 to 40 minutes or until tender. Cut foil, slide cucumber on hot baking dish and cover with Béarnaise or Hollandaise sauce.

Cucumber can also be stuffed with canned shad roe mashed with lemon juice and Worcestershire sauce.

CHICKEN AU BON GOÛT (Serves 6)

1 roasting chicken, 5½ to 6 lbs., or 6 chicken breasts	⅛ teaspoon pepper
	1 small onion or shallot
½ lb. ground round (twice ground)	1 egg
3 slices white bread, crust removed	1¾ cup thin cream
2½ teaspoons salt	

First: Place chicken in a 350-degree oven for 6 minutes to make boning easier. Remove all white meat from bone and take out sinews. (There are usually three to a breast.) Remove skin and cut meat into small pieces. Put ½ cup cream and half of chicken in Waring Blender with peeled onion. Blend several times; take long rubber spatula and loosen meat around blades of blender.

Place this in a bowl and repeat with rest of chicken and ½ cup cream. At last put in ground round and pieces of bread which have been soaked in ¾ cup cream. When done, add egg, beating for a few seconds. Place all in bowl and beat again by hand to make even more light and fluffy. Let cool 2 hours or more in refrigerator. Beat again. Mold with wet hands into patties and drop as fast as possible in a hot iron skillet in which you have melted butter. Sear patties on both sides quickly, careful not to over-brown. Turn heat down and cook down slowly for 20 minutes, turning twice. Place a small lemon parsley butter ball or a mushroom on top of each cake.

Leaves of 3 sprigs of tarragon or 1 tablespoon dry tarragon may be used in patty mixture. Then use tarragon butter balls in place of lemon parsley.

This can be made a day ahead and kept in ice box; also any remaining raw or cooked mixture freezes well. Cooked mixture sliced makes delicious sandwiches.

GREEN CAULIFLOWER WITH CROÛTONS

Clean cauliflower and insert sharp knife in core from bottom making an X. Place lemon slices* to cover top, tie in cheesecloth. Boil in salted water for 25 to 40 minutes according to size of cauliflower. While this is cooking, prepare Seabrook** frozen peas as directed on package adding one medium sliced onion. Drain and place peas in blender with 1 tablespoon of butter and ¼ cup thin cream. Blend until a smooth purée, add salt and pepper. Drain cauliflower well, having removed cheesecloth and lemon. Keep purée very hot adding a little more cream if necessary to coat cauliflower. Dot with sautéed croûtons or tiny cherry tomatoes.

[NOTE: To make perfect, evenly browned croûtons that will stay crisp, melt butter in a skillet and turn off the heat. Add diced, day-old bread and mix thoroughly with the butter until each cube is completely covered. Turn the heat on low and brown the croûtons carefully, stirring with a fork. Drain on absorbent paper. Croûtons made this way may be added to garlic oil for a Caesar Salad and may be left in the oil overnight without losing their crispness. — P. H.]

---

* Lemon keeps cauliflower white.
** Seabrook peas are the only frozen peas that can be used in a blender.

House and Garden's Cook Book

F OR SEVERAL YEARS *House and Garden* has had a complete cookbook in each issue of the magazine. Each cookbook is devoted to a specific culinary area and is the work of one person. Many of the most illustrious contemporary food authorities, such as Dione Lucas, James Beard, Charlotte Turgeon, and Helen Evans Brown, have been responsible for these features. In 1958 a sizable and representative selection of these recipes was published in book form. Seven of my personal favorites are reprinted here, and several others, which appeared after the book was published, are to be found in the section entitled "Recipes from My Files."

HOT SHRIMP RAMEKINS

[Credit for this one goes to Charlotte Turgeon. — P. H.]

1½ pounds raw shrimp	¾ teaspoon salt
½ cup dry white wine	Melted butter
1 cup water	Garlic salt
½ bay leaf	Grated Parmesan cheese
Pinch of thyme	Chopped parsley

Put the shrimp in a pan with wine, water, bay leaf, thyme and salt and bring to a slow boil. Cover and simmer 10 minutes. Remove and drain. Shell and devein the shrimp. Place the shrimp in individual ramekins. Pour a generous amount of hot melted butter over each serving. Sprinkle with garlic salt and Parmesan cheese and place in a 425-degree oven until the butter sizzles — about 3-4 minutes. Sprinkle with chopped parsley and serve immediately.

Serves 6.

SHAD ROE EN PAPILLOTE

[This is one of the simplest and most delicious ways to prepare shad roe. It is the brainchild of Mr. Beard. — P. H.]

Shad roe is a great delicacy if properly prepared. There is nothing worse, however, if it is overcooked and dry. Cooking *en papillote* seems to bring out its best qualities. Shad roe is generally sold in pairs. Allow 1 or a whole pair per serving, depending on the size.

Take a piece of foil for each roe and brush it with melted butter on each side. Place the roe in the center, season it with salt and freshly ground pepper, and add liberal dabs of butter. Top with a generous amount of finely chopped parsley and fold the foil up over the roe, closing it tightly. Fold up the ends of the foil. Heat the oven to 400 degrees and bake the roe for 20 minutes.

Variations: Substitute a partially cooked strip of bacon for the butter on top of the roe.

Add a good tablespoon of chopped chives to the roe.

Add a teaspoon or more of duxelles according to taste.

CELERY AMANDINE

[This is by Dione Lucas. I clipped it from the magazine long ago and it became a family institution; lovely with Beef Wellington. — P. H.]

4 cups young celery stalks, diced
Salt and pepper
8 tablespoons butter
2 tablespoons finely chopped fresh
    chives
2 tablespoons grated onion
1 cup blanched shredded almonds
½ teaspoon finely chopped garlic
2 tablespoons dry white wine

Dice the celery stalks, wash and drain and put them into a pan. Season lightly with salt and pepper and add 4 tablespoons of butter. Cover the pan closely and cook very slowly until the celery is tender, shaking the pan frequently to prevent scorching. During cooking, sprinkle the celery with chives and onion. When celery is cooked, arrange it on a small oval serving dish. Melt the rest of the butter in a shallow, heavy pan, add the blanched, shredded almonds and shake them over a medium fire until brown. Then add the chopped garlic, salt, pepper, and the white wine. Cook for 1 minute, pour over the celery and serve at once.

Serves 4.

GREEN POTATOES

[When potatoes are a must on the menu but more color is needed, this creation of Eloise Davison's solves the problem tastefully. — P. H.]

6 medium potatoes	2 tablespoons shortening
1 cup finely chopped raw spinach	Salt, pepper
1 cup chopped parsley	

Wash, peel and slice potatoes. Boil in salted water until almost tender; drain and dry over heat. Combine spinach and parsley and steam 7 to 10 minutes. Drain and add them to the potatoes. Sauté in hot shortening about 5 minutes. Season well with salt and pepper.

Serves 6.

LAMBS' TONGUES POULETTE

[This is another of Jim Beard's — for a so-called variety meat that is too often ignored. — P. H.]

You will need about 2 or 3 tongues per person. Cover the tongues with water and add 1 onion stuck with 2 cloves, 1 bay leaf, 1 teaspoon salt, 1 teaspoon freshly ground black pepper, 1 carrot and 1 stalk celery. Bring to a boil, then lower the heat and simmer until the tongues are tender when tested with a fork. Remove the cooked tongues and, when they are cool enough to handle, skin and trim them carefully. Return them to the broth for several minutes to reheat while you go about preparing the following *Sauce Poulette*.

In a saucepan blend 3 tablespoons butter and 3 tablespoons flour. When they have cooked for a few minutes, add salt and pepper to taste and 1½ cups of the broth in which the tongues cooked. Stir and cook until smooth and thick and add the juice of a lemon. Beat 2 egg yolks lightly and blend with a few spoonfuls of the sauce. Stir this into the sauce thoroughly and reheat but do not allow it to boil. Taste for flavoring. You may find you prefer a little more lemon in the sauce.

CHICKEN JASMINE (India)

[A Helen Evans Brown contribution; excellent for the element of surprise which I consider one of the most important ingredients of a successful dinner party. — P. H.]

3-pound chicken	½ pound butter
½ teaspoon black pepper	1½ pints yogurt
1½ teaspoons powdered ginger	Pinch chili powder (optional)
½ teaspoon salt	

For this recipe use pale, unsalted butter or shortening. Wash and dry the chicken. Prick it all over with a sharp pointed knife and rub the pepper and ginger inside the cavity and on the outside. Truss the chicken. Heat the butter in a very heavy skillet and mix in the salt and yogurt. Put in the trussed chicken and raise the heat high. Cook for 3 minutes, then reduce heat to medium low and cook for 45 minutes. Baste the chicken as it cooks. Cook first on one side then on the other; then on the breast side and finally turn it on its back. By this time the chicken is well done, and has a delicious pearl or jasmine white appearance, except on the parts where it is nicely mottled and reddened. Now sprinkle the chili powder over the chicken, spoon the butter-yogurt mixture over it and cook for a few minutes in a 275-degree oven.

Serves 4.

ROAST DUCK WITH FIGS

[A welcome change from oranges, black cherries or applesauce is this recipe which is unmistakably Dione Lucas's. — P. H.]

2 Long Island ducklings, each 3½ lbs.
Salt, freshly cracked pepper
2 small peeled oranges
2 small peeled onions
1 peeled garlic clove
1 stick butter
2½ cups strong chicken stock
1 cup mixed sliced onions, carrots, celery, leek
4 level tablespoons flour
2 teaspoons tomato paste
2 teaspoons meat glaze
1½ cups mushroom peelings and stalks (or 2 sliced mushrooms)
1 very ripe tomato, skinned and cut up
1 tablespoon red currant jelly
12 green, 12 black figs soaked for 24 hours in 3 cups white Sauterne
½ cup brandy
1 truffle, finely chopped
2 cups each diced carrots, turnips, green beans
6 slices bread, diced and fried in a little chicken fat

Wash the ducks well inside and out and dry thoroughly. Season inside with salt and pepper. Stuff each with 1 orange, 1 onion and ½ clove garlic. Tie up carefully and rub salt and pepper all over the outsides. Place on roasting racks and brush with melted butter. Pour a little stock in the roasting pan and roast at 375 degrees for 20 minutes. Remove, baste well, add a little water to the pan and brush ducks with a little more melted butter. Reduce heat to 350 degrees and continue roasting for a further ½-hour. Remove and cool.

Dissolve ½ stick butter in a small heavy pan. Add sliced vegetables and cook very slowly, without browning, for 3-4 minutes. Add flour and cook slowly until dark nut-brown. Stir in, off the fire, the tomato paste, meat glaze, mushroom peelings and tomato. Pour on remaining stock and currant jelly and stir over the fire until it comes to a boil.

Strain the liquid from the soaked figs and add to the sauce. Stir over fire until it comes to a boil and cook until reduced to the consistency of heavy cream. Remove legs from ducks and cut them in half. Place in bottom of a large heavy casserole. Cut figs in four and place on top of legs. Cut off breasts of ducks in one piece and slice them lengthwise, thinly. Arrange slices overlapping to top of figs. Heat and flame the brandy and pour over the duck. Strain the brown sauce, add the truffle and pour over the duck. Cover casserole with wax paper and the lid and put in 350-degree oven for ½ to ¾ hour. Meanwhile put diced vegetables in a pan and cover with water. Bring to a boil and drain. Melt a little butter in a pan and add the vegetables. Cover with wax paper and the lid and cook for 15 minutes in 350-degree oven.

To serve, pile up vegetables in the center of a flat serving dish. Arrange duck legs on top, then the figs, then the breast of duck. Pour over the sauce and surround with the fried croutons.

Serves 4.

Eight Immortal Flavors

JOHNNY KAN AND CHARLES L. LEONG

WHILE I HAVE HAD but limited experience with Cantonese food, it was not difficult for me to recognize the finest when I was exposed to it. This happened at one of Johnny Kan's three California restaurants, Kan's on Grant Avenue in San Francisco. Jim Beard and I were there on a food assignment. Jim and his "cousin" Johnny have known each other since childhood, and in his foreword to the book Jim says that the first thing he does upon arriving in San Francisco is to go to Johnny's to feast and reminisce. On this occasion we went to borrow the big silver steamer ornamented with gold lobsters for our demonstration and Jim arranged for a banquet three days later. Several days of preparation are necessary for this kind of Chinese dinner and the host thus has time to round up the traditional number (ten) of guests; not hard to do when the banquet is to be at Kan's.

It was an unforgettable evening, but so many wonderful dishes were served that I find that I am only able to remember the highlights: Winter Melon Soup which, miraculously, did not burst the seams of the huge, gray-green melon that contained it; Peking Duck with Thousand Layer Buns, Chicken with Walnuts (the recipe for which appears here), Deep-Fried Chicken Wings and, at the end, an exquisite almond drink, the name of which escapes me.

Now, Johnny Kan, with the able assistance of Charles L. Leong, who plays the historian's role in the collaboration, has written the only cookbook to emanate from San Francisco's Chinatown. For twenty years these two gentlemen of Cantonese descent, one a restaurateur and the other a professional writer and Chinese food researcher, have spread the gospel of the virtues of true California Chinese cooking in a serial newspaper column. The response they received from readers all over the country persuaded them to put all these facts about Cantonese cooking between the covers of a book; a book for the benefit of Chinese-Americans who have forgotten how to cook their family recipes, as well as for that of the many Americans who, according to supermarket statistics, are buying millions of dollars worth of canned and frozen American-packed Oriental products a year for home consumption, but who don't really know the proper way to cook them. Mr. Kan and Mr. Leong feel, and rightly so, that it is an unforgivable sin to misrepresent Chinese cuisine, which, with its recorded history of forty-seven centuries, is one of the world's oldest and finest. So forget Chop Suey, which is not even authentically Chinese. Read this book and start, without benefit of special utensils or ingredients, to cook the simple dishes and graduate, as you will wish to, to the more elaborate specialties. The basic Eight Immortal Flavors are to be found in both. They are, incidentally, Hom (salty), Tom (bland), Teem (sweet), Seen (sour), Foo (bitter), Lot (hot), Heong (fragrant), and Gum (golden).

MUSTARD GREENS SOUP
(Goi Choy Tong)

In a soup pot, place: 5 cups basic or chicken soup stock

Bring to a boil.
Add: 1 lb. washed Chinese mustard greens
                                 cut into 2-inch lengths
                                 ¼ cup raw sliced beef or pork
                                 2 thin slices fresh ginger root
                                 ½ teaspoon monosodium glutamate
                                 Salt to taste

Cook at low heat 10 to 15 minutes, skim off fat. Just before placing on table, break 1 raw egg over soup (optional). Serves 4.

DEEP-FRIED SQUAB
(Sang Jow Bok Opp)

In a large mixing bowl, place:	**2 young dressed uncooked squabs cut into 1½-x-1½-inch pieces**
Add:	**¼ teaspoon monosodium glutamate**
	2 teaspoons soy sauce
	½ teaspoon salt
	¼ teaspoon ground pepper
	½ teaspoon minced garlic
	1 beaten egg
	1 cup water-chestnut flour
	1 teaspoon minced onion

Stir and mix squab with mixture thoroughly.

In a deep fry utensil, place:	**1 quart vegetable oil**
Bring to a violent boil and add:	**Coated squab segments**

Deep fry at high heat for 10 minutes. Remove squab with strainer, drain on absorbent toweling, then transfer to serving platter. Serves 4.

The Chinese are masters in the preparation of squab, especially in crisp, deep-fried dishes such as this. The secret of the light crispness is in the water-chestnut flour batter.

WALNUT CHICKEN
(Hop To Gai Kow)

Have prepared:	**1 cup boned uncooked chicken cut into ¾-x-¾-inch pieces**
	¼ cup canned bamboo shoots, sliced ⅛ inch thick and into ¾-inch squares
	1 cup blanched and deep-fried walnut halves
In a preheated wok or skillet place:	**2 tablespoons vegetable oil**
	¼ teaspoon salt
Bring oil to sizzling point and add:	**Diced chicken**

Toss and turn at high heat 1 minute and add:	1 teaspoon soy sauce ¼ teaspoon monosodium glutamate Sliced bamboo shoots
Toss and cook at high heat 1 minute and add:	¾ cup chicken stock
Cover and cook at high heat 2 to 3 minutes. Uncover. Add:	Walnut halves
Turn and mix thoroughly with other ingredients. Add gradually:	2 tablespoons cornstarch. Make paste with 2 tablespoons water.

Turn all ingredients until sauce thickens, about 2 minutes. Serve with steamed or fried rice. Serves 3 or 4.

SAUTÉED FRESH SCALLOPS WITH VEGETABLES
(Sang Gong Yow Chee Chow Choy)

Have prepared:	½ pound fresh scallops cut into halves ½ cup canned bamboo shoots, sliced about ¼ inch thick and into ½-inch pieces ½ cup celery sliced ¼ inch thick ½ cup sliced dried onion 6-8 Chinese snow peas. Remove tips and strings, wash and drain.
In a preheated wok or skillet place:	2 tablespoons vegetable oil 1 teaspoon salt
Bring oil to sizzling point at high heat. Add:	Scallops and all the prepared vegetables
Toss cook at high heat for 2 minutes. Add:	½ teaspoon sugar 1 teaspoon soy sauce ½ teaspoon monosodium glutamate 1 cup chicken stock

Turn all ingredients until well mixed. Cover and cook at high heat 5 minutes. Uncover.

Add gradually: 1 tablespoon cornstarch. Make paste
                                                  with 1 tablespoon water.

Toss and turn until sauce thickens. Serve immediately, accompanied with hot steamed rice. Serves 4.

FIVE RECIPES FROM

The Perfect Hostess Cook Book

MILDRED O. KNOPF

T HIS BOOK IS the work of a lady who, according to many mutual friends fortunate enough to have enjoyed her hospitality
in Hollywood, has every right to call herself "The Perfect Hostess."
This, however, is not the intent of the title. Rather than blowing her
own horn, Mrs. Knopf shows you how to blow yours. The clearly
defined recipes come from world-famous European and American
restaurants, from the files of noted hostesses, as well as from the
penciled notes of obscure family cooks and the fertile imagination
of Mrs. Knopf, her friends, her "uncompromising gourmet" husband and a daughter who shares her parents' interest in and talent
for fine cooking.

YOUNG PHEASANT WITH RAISIN PURÉE
(Preheat oven to 350°)

Young pheasant	½ cup sherry
Brandy	1 cup chicken broth
½ lemon	1 cup seeded raisins
Salt, pepper	2 tablespoons sugar
Nutmeg	Pheasant liver
4 slices bacon	½ cup chicken broth
2 thin slices ham	Parsley
1 tablespoon melted butter	

Serves 4.

FIRST: Wash 1 young pheasant with a cloth wet with brandy, dipping the cloth several times and not sparing the brandy. Rub the bird, inside and out, with ½ lemon and allow to dry. Season with salt, pepper, and a pinch of nutmeg. Stuff the inside of the bird with 4 slices of bacon and 2 thin slices of ham.

SECOND: Cover the bottom of a roasting-pan with 1 tablespoon melted butter combined with ½ cup of sherry and ½ cup of chicken broth. Place the pheasant in this pan and set in a 350-degree oven. Baste frequently. When it begins to brown, cover.

THIRD: Cook 1 cup seeded raisins in salted water until tender. Add 2 tablespoons sugar and press through a sieve. Set aside. Cook the pheasant liver for 5 minutes in ½ cup chicken broth. Mash and set aside.

FOURTH: Remove the bacon and ham from inside of the bird, put through a meat grinder and place in a pan with the mashed liver and all the remaining broth. Heat well. Serve the bird garnished with parsley and with a side dish containing the gravy. Just before serving, spread the raisin purée thickly on the gravy.

Serve with mashed potatoes.

SWEETBREAD SALAD

2 pairs boiled sweetbreads	**Capers**
¼ firm head lettuce	**Paprika**
¼ cup mayonnaise	**Green olives and sweet pickles, sliced**

Serves 4.

FIRST: Cut 2 pairs boiled sweetbreads into even slices. Shred ¼ head lettuce. Make a bed of the lettuce and place the slices of sweetbreads on top. Cover with ½ cup mayonnaise.

SECOND: Scatter capers on top, sprinkle with paprika, and decorate with slices of green olives and sweet pickles. Serve very cold.

Note: This is the original recipe the French use on their fabulous hors d'oeuvre tray; but, for those who prefer a tart French dressing this may be used instead of the mayonnaise.

POLISH BEETS

12 small, young beets
1 tablespoon cider vinegar
1 tablespoon tarragon vinegar
2 tablespoons sugar
3 tablespoons olive oil

Salt, pepper
1 tablespoon flour
1 tablespoon lemon juice
½ cup sour cream

Serves 4.

FIRST: Boil 12 small, young beets. Skin and slice them.

SECOND: Blend 1 tablespoon cider vinegar, 1 tablespoon tarragon vinegar, 2 tablespoons sugar, 2 tablespoons olive oil, and salt and pepper to taste. Add to beets.

THIRD: Heat 1 tablespoon olive oil in a saucepan and rub in 1 tablespoon flour. When smooth, add 1 tablespoon lemon juice and then the beet mixture. Fold in ½ cup sour cream. Heat well (do not boil) and serve.

PARSNIPS IN PARMESAN

6 boiled, thick parsnips
2 ounces butter
Salt, pepper

Grated Parmesan cheese
Paprika

Serves 6.

FIRST: Cut off the narrow ends from 6 boiled, thick parsnips and slice the tops in half.

SECOND: Render 2 ounces butter in a skillet. Place the pieces of parsnips in the butter and fry lightly until slightly brown on one side. Season with salt and pepper. Turn and fry lightly on the other side.

THIRD: Turn once again and sprinkle with grated Parmesan. Cook until the cheese blends with the butter. Place on a flat serving-dish and pour the butter over the parsnips. Sprinkle lightly with paprika and serve hot.

Note: Artichoke hearts also lend themselves beautifully to this treatment.

PEAS AND SOUR CREAM

3 pounds fresh peas

1 tablespoon melted butter

1 cup sour cream

Chopped mint or chives (optional)

Serves 4.

FIRST: Boil 3 pounds fresh peas in as little lightly salted boiling water as possible. The cooking time cannot be accurately estimated, since it depends entirely on the freshness and the size of the peas. But for very young peas, 10 minutes should suffice.

SECOND: Drain the peas and put them back in the pot with 1 tablespoon butter. Shake the pot over the flame — not on it — until the peas are coated with the melted butter.

THIRD: Add 1 cup of sour cream to the peas and fold in quickly until well distributed. It is not necessary to heat the cream. The peas will be hot, the cream cool. It makes a very novel combination of temperatures and flavors. Sprinkle, if you wish, with chopped mint or chopped chives. In any case, serve immediately.

TWO RECIPES FROM

Cook, My Darling Daughter

MILDRED O. KNOPF

MILDRED KNOPF did not expect to write another cookbook after her successful *Perfect Hostess*. She was perfectly happy, as she puts it, sitting on her laurels. But her daughter's young friends wanted a book written for *them*; not a primer complete with instructions on how to boil water, but a book to teach them how to *love* to cook. So Mrs. Knopf's goal, which she unquestionably attained, was to collect and/or create a group of recipes that would instill in young housewives the excitement that makes creative cooking such a joy.

QUICHE LORRAINE, FRUITS OF THE SEA
(Preheat oven to 375 degrees)

1 unbaked 9-inch pastry shell	Cayenne
½ lb. unsliced Swiss cheese	2 tablespoons melted butter
2 cups light cream	2 tablespoons sherry wine
4 eggs	1 cup freshly picked crab meat
1 tablespoon flour	½ cup tiny shrimp (or)
Salt, pepper	½ cup larger shrimp cut into small
¼ teaspoon nutmeg	pieces

Serves 6 to 8.

FIRST: Cut ½ pound unsliced Swiss cheese into finger-length pieces about ¼ inch thick and cover the bottom and sides of 1 unbaked 9-inch pastry shell.

SECOND: Combine the following ingredients: 2 cups light cream, 4 beaten whole eggs, 1 tablespoon flour, salt, pepper, ¼ teaspoon nutmeg, and cayenne to taste. Stir in 2 tablespoons melted butter and 2 tablespoons sherry wine. Beat everything together until well blended. Strain over cheese in pastry shell.

THIRD: Add 1 cup freshly picked crab meat and ½ cup tiny shrimp or, failing that, ½ cup larger shrimp, cut into small pieces. Put the seafood in carefully, pushing it down carefully with a fork or the back of a spoon so that the custard mixture covers it well.

FOURTH: Bake in a preheated 375-degree oven for approximately 40 minutes or until nicely browned on top. Now, this bit is important: do not try to serve it piping hot, straight out of the oven, unless you wish to burn your mouth! The thing to do is serve it warm, not hot. Standing 20 minutes in the kitchen before serving will just do the trick.

Note: In the classic, original version of Quiche Lorraine, prepare as above, overlapping pieces of crisp, dry bacon alternately with the cheese pieces. Cover with the custard mixture, perhaps adding a little grated onion or chopped chives, and away you go! Of course, no seafood. That was my own idea, inspired by a Parisian friend's imaginative dinner.

SNOW PEAS

[Most recipes for these peas call for bits of pork or beef, which is, of course, authentically Chinese, or — on the rare occasions when they are recognized in an American cookbook — the cooking time is much too long. I like Mrs. Knopf's method, although I have a few suggestions. — P. H.]

2 lbs. Snow Peas	1 teaspoon salt
5 stalks celery, tender	¼ teaspoon pepper
2 tablespoons vegetable oil	Pinch basil or thyme
2 tablespoons butter	

FIRST: Wash and string the peas. Cut 3 tender stalks of celery into small pieces (do not chop).

SECOND: Heat the oil and butter in a skillet and add the salt, pepper and a good pinch of basil or thyme. Add the vegetables. *Do not cover.* Cook over moderate flame for 5 minutes or a little less, turning the vegetables constantly.

[NOTE: As to the use of basil or thyme, tastes differ, but I highly recommend the latter. Also, when the peas go into the pan for their very brief cooking I suggest sprinkling them with a pinch of sugar, a pinch of monosodium glutamate and the juice of ¼ lime. Cook only until the peas are heated, have turned a little darker and brighter green and are hardly wilted. — P. H.]

The Cordon Bleu Cook Book

DIONE LUCAS

WHEN DIONE LUCAS enrolled at L'École du Cordon Bleu in the golden days when the distinguished Henri Pellaprat was co-director, she had no idea that she was taking her first step toward a long and successful career. She was, at the time, a serious music student at the Paris Conservatoire and the cooking lessons were embarked upon for the sole purpose of becoming slightly more adept at her hobby. As her training progressed, however, she realized that she had found her niche; that whatever talents she had were best expressed in the alchemy of the kitchen. By the time she had acquired her coveted diploma she had decided to go into partnership with a fellow student and establish a cooking school and restaurant in London. In order to be able to use the name Cordon Bleu in connection with both of these ventures, additional examinations were undertaken and passed, and the two young women were on their way. For Dione Lucas this meant that after successfully launching the London school and restaurant she repeated the process in New York. Demonstrations in other cities followed, as did cookbooks, magazine articles and television appearances. In the thirty-odd years since she made her decision and switched from the cello to the skillet, Madame Lucas has indeed become one of the most outstanding figures in her chosen field.

BROCCOLI WITH SAUTÉED TOMATOES

4 or 5 tomatoes	1 tablespoon tarragon vinegar
2 tablespoons hot oil	1 tablespoon cream
Chopped fresh marjoram or dried	1 teaspoon tomato paste
marjoram & parsley	2 tablespoons butter
Broccoli	½ teaspoon meat glaze
2 egg yolks	1 tablespoon fresh herbs
Salt	Drop of lemon juice
Cayenne pepper	

Skin tomatoes, cut in very thick slices and cook briskly in hot oil. Sprinkle with chopped marjoram. Arrange on a serving dish, place sprigs of cooked broccoli on top, and pour on the following sauce:

Sauce: Put yolks in a bowl with salt, cayenne pepper and vinegar, add cream and tomato paste. Beat with a whisk over a slow fire in a pan of hot water until the sauce begins to thicken; then add butter bit by bit. Lastly add meat glaze, herbs and lemon juice. Pour over the broccoli and serve.

Serves four.

BREAST OF CHICKEN PARISIENNE

4 double breasts of chicken	1 tablespoon currant jelly
2 tablespoons hot Marsala wine	1 tablespoon grated Parmesan cheese
½ teaspoon tomato paste	4 tablespoons butter
1 tablespoon flour	2 cups mushrooms
Scant ½ cup stock	Cayenne pepper
1 to 1½ cups sour cream	1 tablespoon sherry
Salt and pepper	1 tablespoon finely chopped dill

Remove meat from bone, leaving little wing bone at end. Dust lightly with flour, brown quickly in foaming butter, then pour over wine. Remove chicken and add to the pan tomato paste and flour; stir in the stock. Stir over the fire until the mixture thickens; then add very carefully, with a whisk, the sour cream. Season with salt and pepper, jelly and cheese. Put back the breasts, cover and cook gently for 15 to 20 minutes. Remove, arrange on a serving dish, pour over the sauce, sprinkle with grated cheese, dot with butter and brown under the broiler. Serve with the following:

Mushrooms with Wine and Dill: Slice the mushrooms finely, put into very hot butter and add salt and cayenne pepper. Cook briskly for 3 to 4 minutes; then pour over sherry and finely chopped dill.

Serves eight.

POULET SAUTÉ AU CITRON
(Chicken with Lemon Cream Sauce)

1 4-pound chicken	1 small orange
½ cup butter	2 teaspoons lemon juice
1 tablespoon sherry	Salt and pepper
1 tablespoon white wine	1 cup thin cream
1 large lemon	Little grated cheese

Cut the chicken up carefully, as for casserole. Cook until brown all over in foaming butter. Cover with the lid and continue sautéing over a slow fire until nearly cooked. Remove the chicken and stir into the pan the sherry and white wine. Add the grated rind of the large lemon, the grated rind of the orange, the lemon juice, and season with salt and pepper. Turn up the fire and stir in the cream slowly. Put back the chicken and toss over the fire for a few minutes. Arrange on a serving dish. Pour over the sauce and sprinkle with the grated cheese. Put a few thin slices of lemon and a few small pieces of butter on top. Brown under the broiler.

Serves four.

SWEETBREADS BRAISED WITH PEA PURÉE

4 pairs sweetbreads	2½ cups chicken stock
Butter	1 bay leaf
4 tablespoons hot sherry	3 tablespoons red wine
5 or 6 mushrooms	3 packages frozen peas
Salt and pepper	1 tablespoon fat
1 teaspoon tomato paste	2 tablespoons flour
3 teaspoons potato flour	3 or 4 tablespoons cream

Blanch the sweetbreads by bringing to a boil in cold water; drain, remove all skin and gristle. Brown very quickly in hot butter and pour over the sherry. Remove breads and add to the pan the mushrooms, which have

been finely sliced (add butter if necessary) ; cook briskly for 3 or 4 min·
utes. Season with salt and pepper and stir in the tomato paste and flour.
Blend well off the fire; then pour on chicken stock. Stir over the fire until
the mixture comes to a boil; return breads with bay leaf and wine. Cover
and cook gently for 15 minutes.

Pea Purée: Cook, drain and rub peas through a strainer. Melt the fat
in a pan; remove from the fire and stir in the flour, salt and pepper. Brown
slowly and add puréed peas; cook a few minutes and add cream. Arrange
on a serving dish in loaf form, lay sweetbreads on top, pour sauce over
all and serve.

Serves eight.

A Wine Lover's Cook Book

JEANNE OWEN

NOVEMBER 1962 saw the eighth printing of what Jeanne Owen calls her "modest little book." Modest it may be in size and in the simplicity of its dishes, but it was the first authentic and practical book written for Americans on the use of wines in cooking, and as such has, in the past twenty years, established itself as a classic. Mrs. Owen, who has been Secretary of the Wine and Food Society of New York for twenty-seven years, has been variously described as "the one woman in America who knows wine" and "the *grande dame* of American gastronomy."

CHICKEN CALANDRIA
(purely Mexican)

Our "Guest" cook, Calandria, who had found her way to California from Guadalajara, near the west coast of Mexico, won her way into the hearts of the household with her Mexican dishes. Once a month she arrived carrying a well-worn bag that contained her own knives, mixing spoons, a cap and several clean aprons, for she was nothing if not spotless, this stately slender person whose dignity confirmed her origin.

First came the marketing, and long were the lists of ingredients. The shopping hours were drawn out by a little supplementary conversation at the "Botica" where one bought the *ajonjoli* (sesame seeds to the simple, when translated). Only the pharmacy had them; there were no spice shops in those days.

Peppers, corn, spices, almonds — all had to be ground on the *metate*, and preparations for the feast lasted at least three days.

With abbreviated living, and a short cut to everything — even to all varieties of perfection — we have had to adapt some of our favorites. However, the revised recipe is good and will fit into the small kitchen.

This one can be done with young turkey, or chicken; but unless the party is a big one the chicken will do nicely.

1 four- or five-pound chicken, cut up as for fricassee

½ cup white waterground corn meal

½ cup olive oil

1 cup of almonds, blanched, and green olives

4 tablespoons of sweet chili powder (the dark unprepared powder), or more if desired

6 ounces of Claret

3 white onions, finely chopped

3 cloves of garlic, finely chopped

1 teaspoon sesame seed

½ teaspoon caraway seed

A pinch each of mace and marjoram

In a large iron skillet or Dutch oven heat the olive oil. When hot but not smoking put in the pieces of chicken that have been dredged in the waterground corn meal. (This meal is used, as it has more of the flavor of the home-ground meal.) Sear the pieces of chicken slightly, lower the flame and add the onions and garlic and mix well with chicken. Add the Claret that has been heated, and the spices; then three cups of boiling water. Salt to taste and cover to allow simmering for 1 hour. Do not let it boil actively.

The almonds, olives and chili powder last, and simmer another hour, stirring occasionally.

Mix a little of the corn meal with water and add to thicken to desired consistency; in doing this be sure to keep stirring until the thickening takes place, as the corn meal is apt to go to the bottom of the pot and stick.

Put aside and re-heat when wanted, as this dish is much better re-heated. It can be made the day before using.

The advantage of the "sweet" chili powder is that it makes the seasoning less violent and the flavor is much better.

FROGS' LEGS SAUTÉ WITH SNAILS

This is a native dish of Burgundy and popular with gentlemen who go on "Wine Tours." Something different and worth an experiment.

The preparation of snails is too difficult for the Queen of the Small Kitchen, so we recommend those packed in tins already prepared.

For 4 people:

Two dozen snails, the preserved ones, put in a strainer and washed under running water; drain and chop in fairly large pieces.

Put 2 ounces of butter in a pan, 1 clove of garlic finely chopped, and 2 or 3 shallots chopped. Add the snails, then 4 ounces of white wine. In another skillet sauté in butter two dozen small frogs' legs, that have been dipped in milk and rolled in flour; add salt and freshly ground black pepper. When the frogs' legs are almost done put them into the pan with the snails, raise the flame and finish cooking quickly.

Turn out on a hot platter and sprinkle generously with plenty of chopped parsley for color.

A bottle of white Burgundy has a way with this dish; Meursault or Musigny, well chilled.

POULET VALLÉE D'AUGE

[A specialty of Normandy. — P. H.]

For 4 people:

Two small chickens, each cut into four pices. Sauté the pieces in 4 ounces of fresh butter and when they are about half cooked pour over them 2 or 3 ounces of Calvados (Apple Brandy) and blaze; then add six shallots, chopped, and 1 tablespoon parsley, 1 sprig of fresh small leafed thyme (it can be removed before serving), salt and pepper. Blend well and add three ounces of cider; cover and finish cooking. Just before serving add, slowly, 3 ounces of thick cream, stirring it into the juices of the pan; rectify the seasoning and serve.

TWO RECIPES FROM

Lunching and Dining at Home

JEANNE OWEN

UNHAPPILY, this excellent book is out of print. Happily, quite a few recipes and menus from it are to be found in *A Vintage Food Sampler*, edited by Narcissa G. Chamberlain and also published by Alfred A. Knopf. I take pleasure in presenting two more which were not included in that collection.

FILET OF BEEF WITH OLIVES

Choose 4 filets (or steaks cut from the eye of the round) cut at least 2 inches thick. Marinate in 1 pint of red wine to which has been added a pinch of thyme, 1 bay leaf broken up, 2 whole cloves, 2 thin slices of lemon — including rind — and 1 clove of garlic, to taste. Turn the meat occasionally.

When ready to cook, rub the meat with coarse salt and sear it on both sides — quickly — in butter. Put the meat in a casserole, adding the butter in which it was seared, 1 carrot chopped very fine, 2 tablespoons of chopped parsley, and a little freshly ground pepper.

Bring the marinade (the wine and spices in which the meat was soaked) to a boil, strain and pour over the meat. Cover the casserole and simmer gently on top of the stove for 30 minutes. Add ⅔ cup of pitted olives, green and ripe mixed, and a slice of *glace de viande* (meat jelly) equal to 2 tablespoons. Simmer 20 or 30 minutes longer, or a little less if rarer meat is desired.

Serve with parsley potatoes.

Serves 4.

STUFFED BAKED BROILERS

Broilers weighing no more than 2 pounds are best for this — cut in half, ½ per person.

Prepare stuffing as follows:

Soak 2 slices of whole-wheat bread in milk and squeeze fairly dry. Combine with ¾ cup of finely ground boiled ham. When well blended, add 2 tablespoons of finely chopped celery, 1 tablespoon of chopped parsley, 1 white onion that has been chopped and sautéed in butter — add butter in pan also — a pinch of thyme, ½ bay leaf finely crushed, pepper, and ½ teaspoon of Spice Islands Beau Monde Seasoning Salt.

Hold together with 1 egg beaten with a little of the milk in which the bread has soaked.

Brush two chickens, split in halves, with melted butter and dust lightly with salt and pepper. Place under the preheated broiler, skin-side down, and broil for 3 or 4 minutes. Turn and broil skin-side up the same length of time.

Place in a baking dish, skin-side down, and fill the cavities with stuffing, piling toward center. Dust tops with toasted bread crumbs, top with bits of butter, and bake for 30 minutes in a moderate oven (375 degrees), basting with butter occasionally.

Serves 4.

The Art of Fine Baking
PAULA PECK

NO MATTER HOW GOOD today's cake and pastry mixes are — and they certainly are good — there is really nothing that compares with the aroma, taste and texture of thoroughly home-made bread, cake, cookies or pastry. By the same token, few other culinary successes give the cook quite such a sense of high achievement as does perfect baking. Baking is no longer as time-consuming, difficult or tiring as it used to be, thanks to the electric mixer, the freezer and the blender and thanks also to the revolutionary ideas developed by Paula Peck. Her short cuts involve organization and simplification, short cuts which in no way sacrifice quality. Mrs. Peck's enthusiasm for her favorite field of cooking is infectious and I admonish anyone who enjoys the kitchen but who is timid about baking to arm himself or herself with freezer, mixer, blender and Mrs. Peck's book.

CROISSANTS

After years of experimentation with croissant recipes, I have finally discovered the knack of making perfect, flaky croissants at home. Actually, the proportions given in almost any standard recipe for croissants could be followed, if only the method for making and shaping them were made clear.

2 pkgs. dry yeast or 1 oz. fresh yeast	1½ cups sweet butter
1 tablespoon sugar	1 cup cold milk (approximately)
2 teaspoons salt	2 egg yolks mixed with
4 cups flour	2 teaspoons cream

It is important to use only a small amount of yeast in croissants so that the dough never rises before it is placed in the oven. If dry yeast is used, follow directions on package. If fresh yeast is used, cream it with sugar and salt to make a syrup.

Place 3½ cups flour in a large bowl. Make a well in the center. Add yeast, 2 tablespoons butter cut into pieces, and enough cold milk to make a medium-firm dough — not as firm as a bread dough, but not sticky. Knead dough a few minutes, only until it is smooth, not elastic. If the dough is kneaded too long, the croissants will not be tender and flaky. Place dough in refrigerator to rest for 10 minutes.

While dough is resting, shape butter into a flattened brick, rolling it in some of remaining flour to prevent sticking. Place butter on a sheet of waxed paper. Sprinkle it with flour and cover with another sheet of waxed paper. Then roll out butter into a square ¼ inch thick. Cut square in half. Wrap pieces in waxed paper and place in refrigerator.

Remove dough from refrigerator and roll it out on a cloth well dusted with flour, making a rectangle about 3 times longer than it is wide. Brush off excess flour from surface of dough. Place a piece of butter in center. Fold one end of dough over butter. Place remaining butter on top. Fold second end of dough over butter. Press edges together. Place dough on cloth so that the short ends are parallel to the edge of the table nearest you. Roll out on floured cloth into a long rectangle as before. Brush off excess flour. Fold both ends to meet in the center. Then fold once more, in half, as if you were pressing the pages of a book, making 4 layers.

Press all edges together. Wrap and chill for 1 hour. Place dough on floured cloth, again being sure that the short ends are parallel to the edge of the table nearest you. Roll out dough. Fold ends to meet in the center, then fold once again as before.

Chill dough at least 2 or 3 hours, or until it is very cold.

Cut dough in half. Roll out each half separately into a sheet ⅛ inch thick. Cut into long strips 5 inches wide. Divide strips into triangles. Roll up widest side of triangles toward opposite point fairly tightly, stretching slightly, as you roll, to make them longer. Do not try to shape further now. First chill rolls, preferably in freezer, for ½ hour.

Then, removing only 4 or 5 at a time, make each into a thinner, longer and more compact shape by rolling it firmly against the pastry cloth with open palm of hand. Place on greased baking sheet, curving each into a croissant. Chill again until very cold.

Set oven at 475 degrees.

Brush with egg yolks mixed with cream. Place in preheated oven for 5 minutes. Reduce heat to 400 degrees. Continue baking about 8 minutes longer, or until croissants are golden brown.

Yield: approximately 3 dozen.

Note: These freeze well after baking.

MELTING TEA CAKE

[This recipe was selected not only because I like it but because Mrs. Peck particularly requested its inclusion. — P. H.]

Half sponge, half pound cake, light but buttery, this cake literally melts in your mouth.

½ cup whole, blanched almonds	4 egg yolks
1 teaspoon vanilla	1 cup sugar
1 teaspoon grated lemon rind	1½ cups sifted flour
1 cup butter, melted	2 tablespoons sifted cornstarch
4 eggs	⅛ teaspoon mace

Set oven at 350 degrees. Grease and dust with flour a 9-inch kugelhopf pan or a deep 9-inch tube pan. Arrange blanched almonds around bottom of pan.

Add vanilla and grated lemon rind to butter, melted over low heat and cool to lukewarm but not clarified.

In a large bowl combine eggs, egg yolks and sugar. Beat for a minute. Set bowl over a saucepan of hot water, and place saucepan over low heat for about 10 minutes, or until eggs are slightly warmer than lukewarm. Do not let water boil. Stir eggs occasionally while they are being heated to prevent them from cooking on bottom of bowl. When eggs are warm, beat until they are cool, thick and tripled in bulk. Sprinkle flour, cornstarch, and mace on top. Fold in gently, adding butter at the same time. Continue to fold until there is no trace of butter. Be careful not to overmix.

Pour batter into prepared pan. Bake about 45 minutes, or until cake is golden brown and comes away from sides of pan.

Kyra's Secrets of Russian Cooking

KYRA PETROVSKAYA

THIS IS A COLLECTION of White Russian recipes adapted for American kitchens by a woman who is both a child of the revolution and a grandchild of the aristocracy. She was taught to cook by her grandmother, who had been forced to teach *herself* to cook when she was, abruptly, bereft of the men of her family, her home and her servants. The cuisine of the Russian nobility was largely derivative, but the original French and Italian dishes that were its foundation became, in time, transformed in bizarre and exotic ways. The three recipes I have selected from Miss Petrovskaya's book are as characteristically Russian as a glass of vodka or an astrakhan hat.

VERY QUICK BLINI

These tiny blini make a perfect base for all kinds of cocktail spreads. As their name suggests, they are very easy to prepare and they can be offered to the guests as long as there is a demand for them, which, I dare to predict, will hardly ever end.

1 cup buckwheat flour	1 tablespoon melted butter
1 teaspoon baking powder	1 teaspoon sugar
1 egg slightly beaten	2 tablespoons sour cream
¾ cup lukewarm milk	Dash of salt

Sift together three times flour, baking powder, sugar and salt. Beat egg very slightly, add sour cream and melted butter. Blend well. Add lukewarm milk. Add sifted ingredients and mix thoroughly.

Fry in butter on a pre-heated griddle, making each cake no bigger than 2 inches in diameter.

Put the blini on the platter, top with 1 tablespoon of heavy sour cream for each pancake. Put 1 teaspoon of black or red caviar on the top of sour cream and serve at once.

Double or triple the recipe for larger amount of people. If caviar is not available, top your little blini with any kind of smoked fish or small chunks of baked ham, or with sardines.

Children love the little blini when they are topped with apricot or strawberry jam. I love them just with plain sour cream.

PIROZHKI AND THREE FILLINGS

A true Russian (or anyone who's ever tasted real Russian pirozhki or pirogi) can grow rhapsodic just talking about them. There is nothing more mouth-watering than a platter of hot pirozhki or a large, oblong pirog, which are as traditional holiday dishes in Russia as turkey or baked ham are traditional holiday dishes in America.

Pirogi are large, oblong pastries, made of the same dough as pirozhki and with the same stuffings, only they are huge in size, about 12 by 18 inches. They are more difficult to make and they are more difficult to eat, particularly at a buffet-style party, when most people eat standing up. Besides, the dainty pirozhki are more attractive and I have found they rarely remain on the platter for more than a few minutes.

Raised Dough

1 cake yeast	½ cup butter
1 cup lukewarm milk	2 teaspoons sugar
5 cups sifted flour	1 extra egg yolk
3-4 eggs	1 teaspoon salt

Dissolve yeast in the lukewarm milk. Stir in 1 cup of flour and let it stand for 1 hour in a warm place. Beat the eggs slightly and add salt and sugar. Add melted but cool butter. Combine with the yeast mixture. Add the rest of the flour and knead thoroughly with your hands. Form the dough into a ball and put it in a large bowl, slightly greased. Cover with a clean towel and put in a warm place to rise for the second time. It will take from 3-4 hours to rise, so be patient.

Pinch off a small amount of dough for each pirozhok (the singular of "pirozhki"). Roll into an oval or round shape ¼ inch thick. Put 1 tablespoon of filling in the center of the rolled dough and carefully seal the edges. Let pirozhki stand and rise some more for 12-15 minutes. Brush their tops with the egg yolk, diluted with a little water.

Slightly grease a heavy cookie sheet and sprinkle it with flour. Bake pirozhki in a hot oven (400 degrees) for 12-15 minutes, then reduce the heat and bake them for another 15 minutes, or until ready.

You may also fry these pirozhki in deep fat. Then watch them come up to the top of the pan just like doughnuts.

Cabbage Filling

5-6 cups cabbage, chopped fine	1 tablespoon dill or parsley, minced
2 large onions, chopped fine	1 tablespoon salt
2 hard-boiled eggs, chopped	Salt and pepper to taste
4-5 tablespoons butter	

Chop very fine the inside leaves of a firm, white cabbage. Sprinkle with 1 tablespoon salt and let stand for 10-15 minutes. Squeeze the cabbage dry. Pour boiling water over it and let it drain.

Meanwhile, sauté the onions in butter. Add cabbage and some more butter and continue to sauté very slowly (without letting the cabbage get brown) for another 20-25 minutes.

Add chopped eggs and minced dill or parsley. Add salt and pepper. Use 1½ heaping tablespoons of cabbage filling for each pirozhok.

Beef Filling

1 lb. ground beef	2 tablespoons minced dill or parsley
2 hard-boiled eggs, chopped	1 tablespoon flour
2 medium-sized onions, chopped	Salt and pepper to taste
5 tablespoons butter	

Sauté the onions until slightly brown in 2 tablespoons butter. Add the remaining butter and meat and continue to sauté until the meat turns brown. Add salt and pepper.

Remove the meat from the pan and mix it with dill or parsley. Cool the meat. Sprinkle flour into the pan where the meat was sautéed and brown it slightly, stirring constantly with a fork. Add a little water and bring to a quick boil. Add to the meat and mix thoroughly. Add the chopped eggs and start filling your pirozhki.

Mushroom and Onion Filling

4 cups mushrooms sliced very thin
2 onions
4 tablespoons butter

3 heaping tablespoons sour cream
Salt and pepper to taste

Sauté mushrooms in 2 tablespoons butter, adding a little more butter if necessary. In a separate pan sauté the onions in another 2 tablespoons butter. When both ingredients are tender, combine them, add salt and pepper and blend in the sour cream. Use 1½ tablespoons of filling for each pirozhok.

PASKHA
(Traditional Easter Dessert)

2½ lbs. dry cottage cheese (must be very dry)
5 large eggs
½ lb. melted butter
1 lb. sugar
½ pint sour cream

1 teaspoon vanilla
½ lb. almonds, blanched and shredded
½ cup candied orange or lemon peel or mixture of both
½ cup seedless raisins

The main secret in making really good paskha is to have very dry cottage cheese. Don't even attempt to make paskha unless you are able to get it, the kind that hasn't been creamed. I have tried to make paskha with creamed cottage cheese and each time it was a complete failure. Finally, someone recommended that I try so-called Hoop Cottage Cheese, which is sold packed like any creamed cheese. This cheese is very dry and it makes an excellent paskha. [NOTE: In many localities there is a packaged cottage cheese known as Hunter's Style. It is equally dry. I also recommend the use of a food mill as opposed to a sieve; much less effort is involved. — P. H.]

Crumble the cheese (if you are using the commercial prepacked Hoop cheese) and force it through a coarse sieve twice.

Beat egg yolks with sugar until very light. Add vanilla and sour cream. Slowly add melted butter; continue to beat until all the ingredients are completely mixed. Combine the cottage cheese with the egg yolk mixture. Beat the egg whites with a dash of salt until stiff. Fold carefully into cottage cheese and mix thoroughly. Add almonds, raisins and candied oranges or lemon peel.

Cook on a very slow fire until the bubbles form at the edges of the kettle. Remove from fire and chill in the same kettle.

When cool, pour the mixture into a colander, lined with cheesecloth or a napkin, and let it drip for 2-3 hours.

Without removing the cheesecloth or the napkin, place the mixture in a conical form (a large, unglazed, clay flower pot served me beautifully, for, like the majority of American women, I don't have the traditional Russian paskha form).

Place a small saucepan over the folded ends of the cheesecloth or napkin, put a weight over it and let the excess of moisture come out through the draining hole of the flower pot. To make sure that the moisture drips freely, place the flower pot in such a way that its bottom doesn't touch the drippings below it.

Put the whole contraption in the refrigerator for several hours (I usually leave it there overnight).

Just before serving paskha, remove the weights, unfold the edges of the cheesecloth or napkin, place a large plate or platter over the flower pot and turn it over very carefully. Remove the cheesecloth with the utmost care, for the paskha might break.

Decorate the very top with an artificial flower (it looks naïve, but it is traditional).

Slice horizontally and serve with koolich [Russian cake — P. H.]. Paskha will keep for a long time in the refrigerator, but cover it tightly with waxed paper to prevent drying out.

Serves 6 to 10.

The Picayune Creole Cook Book

WHEN I WAS FIRST MARRIED and starting to cook, I had three "bibles": a notebook made up for me by my mother, full of typographical errors and endearingly vague instructions, an invaluable leaflet from the now extinct Washington Market in downtown New York and a very battered copy of this book — which I borrowed from home and still have, thirty-three years later. It is a fascinating book, full of Louisiana history and lore and as didactic as your great-grandmother. For instance, "There is only one way to cook pompano and that is to broil it and serve it with a Sauce Maître d'Hotel." Suiting the action to the word, that's the only recipe they give, adding, at the end, that it is a "dish that a king might envy." Along the same lines, cucumbers should never be cooked — "the only proper way to eat them is *en salade*," and leeks are used *only* for seasoning. One's feeling, on reading such regulations, is "All right, if that's the way you feel about it, but I'll still make Pompano en Papillote, Cucumbers Poulette and Braised Leeks when you're not looking."

The only trouble with the book is, as you may have gathered, that it is such fun to read that dinner is apt to be late. As you turn the pages looking for that sweetbread recipe, your eye falls on something like the paragraph introducing Calas — and you read; or, on your way to the index, you inadvertently glance at some of the twelve-course "Holiday Menus" and you are lost to the world. The book was first printed in 1901, and is available today in its twelfth edition.

CODDLED OYSTERS

6 or 8 oysters to each person	2 sprigs parsley chopped very fine
6 slices of bread	1 bay leaf minced fine
1 large tablespoon butter	3 cloves
½ teaspoon salt	1 blade of mace
½ teaspoon black pepper	1 pint oyster liquor
Dash of cayenne	

Toast 5 or 6 slices of bread to a nice brown and butter them on both sides. Drain the liquor from the oysters and put in a saucepan. When hot, add a large lump of butter. Have ready a baking dish and place the toast within; lay the oysters on the toast, having seasoned well with salt, black pepper, cayenne pepper, chopped parsley, bay leaf, mace and cloves. Put the liquor of the oysters over the toast until it is well absorbed. Set it in an oven and bake for 5 or 6 minutes with a quick fire. [Serves about 6. — P. H.]

CALAS
"Belle Cala! Tout Chaude!"

Under this cry was sold by the ancient Creole negro women in the French Quarter of New Orleans a delicious rice cake, which was eaten with the morning cup of Café au Lait. The Cala woman was a daily figure in the streets until within the last 2 or 3 years. She went her rounds in quaint bandana tignon, guinea blue dress and white apron, and carried on her head a covered bowl in which were the dainty and hot Calas. Her cry, *"Belle Cala! Tout Chaude!"* would penetrate the morning air and the olden Creole cooks would rush to the doors to get the first, fresh, hot Calas to carry to their masters and mistresses with the morning cup of coffee. The Cala women have almost all passed away. But the custom of making Calas still remains. In many an ancient home the good housewife tells her daughter just how "Tante Zizi" made the Calas in her day, and so are preserved these ancient traditional recipes.

From one of the last of the olden Cala women, one who has walked the streets of the French Quarter for 50 years and more, we have the following stablished Creole recipe:

½ cup rice	½ cake of compressed yeast
3 cups water (boiling)	½ teaspoon grated nutmeg
3 eggs	Powdered white sugar
½ cup sugar	Boiling shortening
3 tablespoons flour	

Put 3 cups of water in a saucepan and let it boil hard. Wash half a cup of rice thoroughly, and drain and put in the boiling water. Let it boil until very soft and mushy. Take it out and set it to cool. When cold, mash well and mix with the yeast, which you will have dissolved in a half cup of hot water. Set the rice to rise overnight. In the morning beat three eggs thoroughly, and add to the rice, mixing and beating well. Add a half cup of sugar and 3 tablespoons of flour, to make the rice adhere. Mix well and beat thoroughly, bringing it to a thick batter. Set to rise for 15 minutes longer. Then add about ½ teaspoon of grated nutmeg and mix well. Have ready a frying pan in which there is sufficient quantity of shortening boiling for the rice cakes to swim in it. Test by dropping in a small piece of bread. If it becomes a golden brown the shortening is ready, but if it burns or browns instantly it is too hot. The golden brown color is the true test. Take a large deep spoon and drop a spoonful at a time of the preparation into the boiling shortening, remembering always that the cake must not touch the bottom of the pan. Let fry to a nice brown. The old Cala women used to take the Calas piping hot, wrap them in a clean towel, and put them into a capacious basket or bowl and rush through the streets with the welcome cry, *"Belle Cala! Tout Chaude!"* ringing on the morning air. But in families the cook simply takes the Calas out of the frying pan and drains off the shortening by laying in a colander or on heated pieces of brown paper. They are then placed in a hot dish, and sprinkled over with powdered white sugar, and eaten hot with Café au Lait.

PURÉE DES POIS VERTS À LA ST. GERMAIN
(Purée of Green Peas à la St. Germain)

1 pint of green peas	Pinch each of salt and white pepper
1 pint chicken broth	1 teaspoon powdered sugar
1 pint sweet cream	1 tablespoon butter
1 herb bouquet	8 chicken quenelles to garnish
2 sprigs mint	

Shell and clean the peas and put them in a saucepan with 1 pint of chicken broth and 1 pint sweet cream. Add an herb bouquet in which you will have tied 2 sprigs of mint. Let the peas cook for 20 minutes, or until very tender, and then remove the herb bouquet and mint; take from the fire, and run the peas through a sieve. Season with salt, pepper and a little powdered sugar; add 1 tablespoon butter; set on the fire 5 minutes longer and serve on a hot dish with Chicken Quenelles to garnish. Make the quenelles from the chicken left over from the broth. This is a very recherché dish. Serve as an entrée. Serves 4-6.

CHOUX DE BRUXELLES À LA CRÈME
(Brussels Sprouts à la Crème)

1 quart Brussels sprouts	½ cup cream or milk
2 tablespoons butter	Pinch of nutmeg
1 teaspoon chopped parsley	Salt and pepper to taste

Prepare and boil the Brussels sprouts. Drain thoroughly, and put in a saucepan, with 2 tablespoons butter, and season with salt and pepper to taste and a pinch of nutmeg. Add a half cup of cream or milk and toss lightly with a fork for 5 or 10 minutes, but do not let them boil. Place on a hot dish, garnish nicely and serve hot. [Serves about 4. — P. H.]

MAÏS FRIT
(Fried Corn)

1 dozen ears young, tender corn	Salt and pepper to taste
1 tablespoon shortening	1 minced onion

Score the corn along each row, and then cut from the cob with a knife. Press out all the pulp and corn juice from the cob. Mix all and season well with salt and pepper. Mince the onion fine, and blend with the shortening, which you will have put into the frying pan. Add the corn when the onions begin to brown slightly, and keep stirring and stirring until the grain is cooked, which will be about 15 or 20 minutes. This is a very nice breakfast dish or dinner course. [Serves 4-6. — P. H.]

CHOU-FLEUR BOUILLI AU BEURRE
(Cauliflower Boiled with Butter)

2 medium-sized cauliflowers
2 tablespoons butter
Tablespoon of salt

Pinch of pepper
1 tablespoon vinegar

After picking and washing cauliflower thoroughly put in a saucepan and cover with cold water. Add the salt and pepper and a tablespoon butter. Let it cook for a half hour and then take the cauliflower from the pan and drain through a colander. Place them on a dish and add a sauce made of 1 tablespoon butter, 1 of vinegar and a dash of salt and pepper, all mixed thoroughly and serve hot. [Serves 6-8. — P. H.]

CARROTS SAUTÉES À LA CRÉOLE

9 nice, tender carrots
1 tomato
1 square inch ham
1 tablespoon butter
6 fine chaurice or sausages
2 shallots

1 onion
½ pint bouillon
Salt and pepper to taste
½ cup white wine
Thyme, parsley, bay leaf
½ clove garlic

Boil the carrots for one hour and a half. Then cut into dice or nice slices. Put the butter in a saucepan, and add the onion, minced very fine, and the shallots, greens and whites. Let these brown for a few minutes, and then add the half square inch of ham and the chaurice whole. Let these simmer for 3 minutes, and add the minced herbs. Then add the tomato and its juice, mincing it well. Let all simmer for 3 minutes more, until the tomato has browned, and add ½ pint of bouillon and ½ cup white wine, if you can afford it. Let all this simmer for 10 minutes and then add the carrots, nicely seasoned. Stir well. Cover and let them simmer for about ½ hour. This is the true dish of Carrots à la Créole. [Serves 5-6. — P. H.]

PILAU FRANÇAIS
(A French Chicken Pilaff)

2 chickens	Yolks of 2 eggs
½ cup rice	Bread crumbs
2 tablespoons butter	

Boil the fowls. When done, take out about a pint of the liquor in which they were boiled, and put the rice, which you have washed well, into the remaining boiling broth. Let it cook well for 20 minutes and then add 2 tablespoons butter to the rice. Butter the bottom of a dish and put upon it ½ of the rice, spreading out nicely. Lay upon it the chicken, which you have disjointed and buttered. Add the remaining chicken broth, pouring over the chickens. Then cover the fowls with the other half of the rice. Make the top perfectly smooth. Spread over it the yolks of 2 eggs which have been well beaten. Sprinkle with bread crumbs and dot with bits of butter here and there. Set in the oven, let it brown and serve hot. [Serves 6-8. — P. H.]

BEIGNETS DE POMMES
(Apple Fritters)

3 fresh apples	Grated peel of ½ lemon
½ cup brandy or rum (if desired)	Powdered sugar

Peel and core the apples, which will be all the nicer if they are a little tart. Take out the seeds and core. Cut them into slices more or less thick or thin according to taste. The thin slices are recommended. Soak them in brandy or good whiskey, or rum, for the space of 2 hours, sprinkling with the grated outer skin of a lemon and sugar, according to judgment. Two tablespoons of sugar should be sufficient for the rind of half a lemon. Make a batter à la Créole (See recipe below), and have ready a deep saucepan of boiling shortening. Drain the apples. Dip the slices, one at a time, into the batter, lift out with a large kitchen spoon, drop into the boiling short-ening and fry to a golden brown. Then lift out with a skimmer, and set on brown paper in the mouth of the oven and drain. Sift powdered white sugar over them and serve hot, piling high in pyramidal shape, and sprinkling again with powdered white sugar. Serve as an entremet or as a dessert. [Serves about 6. — P. H.]

Paté de Beignets à la Créole (Fritter Batter à la Créole)

1 cup flour	¼ teaspoon salt
2 eggs	Cold water
2 tablespoons brandy	1 tablespoon butter, melted

Beat the yolks of the eggs well and add the flour, beating very light. Now add the melted butter, salt, and the brandy, and thin with water to the consistency of a very thick starch. Add the whites of eggs, beaten to a stiff froth, and then dip the fruit into this, immersing well at one dipping. The batter must be thick enough to coat the fruit all around in one immersion, yet it must not be so thick as to be overheavily coated or tough.

The June Platt Cook Book

IT IS A MATTER of common knowledge that there are few truly original recipes. Occasionally one is created by accident, as in the famous case of the fried potatoes which, upon being re-fried because a king was late to dinner, puffed up to become Pommes Soufflés. For the most part, however, cooks and chefs adapt, alter and, in various ways, personalize known procedures. On the rare occasions when recipes are invented from scratch, they are more often found to be the creations of men than of women. June Platt is an outstanding exception. She is as adventurous and imaginative as any chef and has a solid foundation of knowledge and experience on which to build. No matter what their sources, lucidity and style distinguish all her recipes, a fact to which I am sure the following samples will attest.

BRAISED ENDIVE ON A BED OF MUSHROOMS
(Preheat oven to 400 degrees)

18 stalks of endive	1 bouquet of parsley and a bay leaf
Juice of 1 lemon	3 tablespoons flour
1 lb. fresh mushrooms	2 cups hot milk
1½ cups clear chicken broth	2 tablespoons grated imported Parmesan cheese
¾ lb. butter	
1 small onion	2 tablespoons grated imported Swiss Gruyère cheese
1 stalk celery	
1 small carrot	⅓ cup heavy cream
1 tablespoon chopped parsley	Salt, pepper

Serves 6-8

Trim and remove outer leaves of 18 stalks of endive. Wash carefully allowing cold water to run into their centers. Shake and dry well on tea cloth. Butter copiously 2 rectangular dishes, 10″ x 6″ x 2″. Butter both sides of 4 sheets of typewriter paper. Lay the endive side by side in the 2 dishes. Sprinkle with the strained juice of 1 lemon and a little salt and pepper, and dot with 2 tablespoons butter for each dish. Pour ½ cup chicken broth over each dish. Cover with buttered typewriter paper and bake until tender through and beginning to brown lightly, about 1½ hours. Remove from oven, discard paper, and while still hot, pour ¼ cup hot chicken broth into each dish; stir mixture in dishes into brown buttery residue to make a small quantity of clear gravy. Keep warm.

Now make a sauce Béchamel. Wash and peel 1 small carrot and cut in tiny cubes. Peel and chop fine 1 small onion. Remove strings from 1 stalk crisp celery, and cut it in fine cubes like the carrot. Melt 3 tablespoons butter in top of enamel double boiler directly over low flame. Add chopped vegetables and cook slowly over low heat for 10 minutes, stirring frequently. Sprinkle with 3 tablespoons flour, stir, and add gradually 2 cups hot milk. Cook, stirring constantly, until thick, then place over boiling water. Add a bouquet of parsley and 1 bay leaf, and season to taste with salt and pepper. Cover and cook, while you prepare the mushrooms.

Wash and dry 1 pound fresh mushrooms. Cut off and discard tough stems. Chop the caps and tender stems until very fine. Melt 4 tablespoons butter in frying pan, add the mushrooms, and cook over moderate heat until all the juice has evaporated, about 10 minutes. Now remove the parsley and bay leaf from the Béchamel sauce; add the mushrooms. Stir in 2 tablespoons grated Parmesan cheese and 2 tablespoons grated Gruyère cheese. Add more salt if necessary and thin with ⅓ cup heavy cream.

Pour into large buttered 2-quart rectangular baking-dish, 12″ x 7½″ x 2″. On this bed place the braised endive crosswise in two rows. Pour over all the brown gravy from both dishes. Sprinkle with chopped parsley and serve at once. This is especially wonderful and well worth the trouble; it should be served as a separate course.

Note: This dish may be prepared ahead of time, if more convenient, but in this case, do not place the endive on the mushrooms until you are ready to assemble and heat the dish. Place in a pre-heated moderate 400-

degree oven until heated through, about 20 minutes. Sprinkle with parsley just before serving.

Celery may be braised in the same manner, and served plain or on a bed of mushrooms.

PROVINCIAL POTATOES

3 lbs. new potatoes	½ teaspoon flour
⅛ lb. butter	Salt, pepper
3 tablespoons olive oil	1 tablespoon chopped parsley
Grated rind of ½ lemon	1 tablespoon chopped chives
¼ teaspoon nutmeg	Juice of 1 lemon

Serves 6-8

Wash and boil in their skins 3 pounds new potatoes. Put ⅛ pound butter in a saucepan. Cut it up and pour over it 3 tablespoons of olive oil, and grate into this the rind of ½ lemon. Add 1 tablespoon chopped parsley, 1 tablespoon chopped chives, ¼ teaspoon freshly grated nutmeg, ½ teaspoon flour, and some salt and pepper. When the potatoes are cooked, peel, cut into quarters or eighths, and put them into the butter mixture. Heat, but don't let the butter boil. When ready to serve, add the juice of 1 lemon.

PURÉE OF FROZEN LIMA BEANS

4 pkgs. large frozen lima beans	4-6 tablespoons butter
¼ cup heavy cream	Chopped parsley

Serves 6-8

Cook lima beans, following directions on wrapper. Place large sturdy sieve over a saucepan and rub the beans and their juice through the sieve, using a heavy wooden spoon or potato-masher. An electric blender may also be used, but do a small portion of the beans at a time. It may be necessary to moisten them with little cream as you go along. If the blender has been used, it may still be necessary to rub the resultant purée through a sieve. Transfer the purée to top of enameled double boiler in which you have placed 2 tablespoons butter. Keep warm over hot water, pouring a little cream over the top to prevent the purée from drying out. When ready to serve, beat well with spoon, adding a little more cream if necessary, to the consistency of mashed potatoes.

Place in a hot vegetable dish, make a depression in the center with the back of a serving-spoon, and place a fresh lump of butter in the depression. Sprinkle with chopped parsley and serve.

BOILED WHITE MARROW BEANS GARNISHED WITH TRUFFLES

2 cups dried white marrow beans	2 truffles (1 can containing 2)
6 tablespoons butter	Salt, coarsely ground pepper
½ cup heavy cream	½ cup white wine

Serves 6-8

Look over carefully 2 cups dried white marrow beans, discarding imperfect ones. Wash with care, cover with cold water, and soak overnight. Drain, put them into 2 quarts lukewarm water, and bring gently to boiling point. Skim carefully. Simmer very gently until tender but not falling apart, 2½ to 3 hours, adding hot water as necessary to keep the beans just covered with water.

When almost done, open a small can of truffles which contains at least two, peel if necessary, and chop moderately fine. Cover with white wine and heat gently. When the beans are done, drain (but save the water for soup). Place 6 tablespoons butter in bean pan, cover with the drained beans and pour over them ½ cup heavy cream. Season lightly to taste with salt and coarsely ground pepper. Shake over low flame until butter has melted and cream is hot. Place beans and juice in hot vegetable dish. Drain the truffles and sprinkle over the beans. Serve at once.

SPANISH CARROTS

3 bunches carrots	2 4-ounce cans pimientos
1 clove garlic	2-3 tablespoons chili sauce
6 tablespoons butter	Salt, pepper

Serves 6-8

Peel 3 bunches carrots, wash and cook in enough salted water to cover until tender, about 45 minutes. Drain and chop fairly fine. Drain and chop

2 cans pimientos. Melt 6 tablespoons butter, add 1 clove garlic, add chopped carrots and pimientos, and season to taste with salt and coarsely ground pepper. Last of all, stir in 2-3 tablespoons chili sauce and serve.

COLACHE

4 small summer squash or 4 Italian squash (zucchini)

4 tablespoons butter and bacon fat mixed (or 2 tablespoons olive oil, instead of bacon fat)

1 large onion

2 green peppers, seeded and quartered

4 peeled tomatoes

Salt, freshly ground black pepper

Cayenne

3 ears fresh corn, or 1 package frozen corn

Serves 6-8

This dish is a kind of vegetable stew which was made by the Spanish in early days in California. Cut into ½-inch squares 4 small summer squash (round, scalloped, light green) or 4 long green Italian squash (known as zucchini). Melt 4 tablespoons butter and bacon fat mixed — or use 2 tablespoons olive oil instead of the bacon fat — and fry the squash in it until partly browned. If too much juice is formed, pour off some of it and put it back in the colache later on.

Next add 1 large onion, sliced thin, and 2 green peppers. Fry a bit, then add 4 peeled tomatoes, or an equal amount of canned ones. Season well with salt, freshly ground black pepper, and cayenne to taste. Add corn cut from 3 ears fresh corn, or 1 package frozen corn, and cook ½ hour. Be sure to season the colache well, for it should be quite hot and peppery. This goes well with chicken dishes.

COLD CHICKEN CURRY

2 young 4-5 lb. roasting chickens cut as for fricassee

2 large Bermuda onions

10 tablespoons butter

1 jigger brandy

Salt, pepper

2 tablespoons curry powder

2 cups heavy cream

Tarragon

2 quartered lemons

Serves 6-8

Singe, wash and dry thoroughly 2 young roasting chickens cut up as for fricassee. Peel 2 large Bermuda onions, quarter, and slice thin. Melt 8 tablespoons butter in large frying pan and brown chicken lightly on both sides, transferring the pieces as they brown to an iron cocotte containing 2 tablespoons butter. The cocotte should be on a very low flame, or better still, on an asbestos mat over a low flame. When all the chicken has been transferred heat 1 jigger brandy, pour over the chicken, and set ablaze, being careful not to burn yourself. When it has burned itself out, cover the chicken with the sliced onions and sprinkle with salt and pepper.

Add ½ cup water to the frying pan and stir over low flame to melt the brown residue in pan, making a small amount of clear gravy. Pour this over the chicken, cover tightly, and simmer gently until the chicken is cooked through and about to fall off the bones, about 1¼ hours. By this time the onions should have collapsed and the chicken should be swimming in plenty of strong broth. Now sprinkle the chicken with 2 tablespoons good curry powder and baste well. Remove from fire and cool until the chicken may be handled, at which time be prepared for the messy job of removing the meat from the bones.

Discard skin, gristle, and bones. Cut breasts in two lengthwise and lay these symmetrically over the bottom of an oblong glass baking-dish, 6″ x 10″ x 2″. Then add the rest of the meat, distributing it evenly over the breasts. Now add 2 cups heavy cream to the onions and buttery juice remaining in the cocotte; stir well, place on low flame, and heat to boiling point. Taste and add more salt if necessary. Do not allow the cream to boil. When it is heated through strain out the onions, using a colander placed over a large pan. Press gently with wooden spoon to extract all the cream. Pour the resulting cream sauce over the chicken in the dish. There should be plenty to cover the chicken completely and fill the dish. When cold, cover with aluminum foil and place in refrigerator for several hours or overnight until jelled and set through like custard.

When ready to serve, run a knife carefully around the edge. Dip the dish into shallow pan of hot water for a few seconds to loosen the bottom, then turn out carefully onto a large oval platter. Garnish prettily with quartered lemons and crisp parsley. Serve accompanied by a bowl of crisp romaine broken in small pieces and dressed with a good French dressing, seasoned if possible with finely chopped fresh herbs, preferably parsley and tarragon.

SALMON COULIBIAC

Pastry:

1 cup all-purpose flour

1 3-oz. package cream cheese

¼ lb. sweet butter

1 egg yolk

Filling:

2 cups (1½ lbs.) boiled fresh salmon

2 hard-boiled eggs

½ cup finely cut fresh dill

Juice of 1 lemon

¼ lb. fresh mushrooms

6 small shallots

2 cups flaky cooked long-grain rice

12 tablespoons butter

½ teaspoon cracked pepper

¼ teaspoon cayenne

2 teaspoons curry powder

Serves 8

The night before, mix the pastry. Sift 1 cup all-purpose flour into a bowl. Work into this with finger tips ¼ lb. sweet butter. Add 3 ounces cream cheese, and using a large, silver fork, work the cheese into the flour and butter until you can gather it all together in a ball. Wrap in wax paper, press into rectangle, and refrigerate overnight. When ready to make the coulibiac, remove pastry from refrigerator and allow to remain at room temperature while you prepare the filling.

Remove tough stems from ¼ lb. fresh mushrooms. Wash and dry caps and chop fine. Peel and chop fine 6 small shallots. Cook them gently in 2 tablespoons butter in small frying-pan for about 1 minute, then add mushrooms and simmer 5 minutes. Season lightly with salt; cool. Prepare ½ cup finely cut fresh dill. Cook ½ cup flaky long-grain rice, following directions on box, which will give you about 2 cups. Boil 2 eggs gently for 12 minutes. Plunge into cold water, remove shells, and chop fine. Have ready 2 cups boiled salmon.

Now preheat the oven to a very hot 500 degrees. Butter a cookie sheet lightly. Cut pastry in half and roll out separately into 2 rectangular sheets approximately 13″ x 9″, making 1 slightly larger than the other. Place smaller one over center of cookie sheet. Then spread about ¾ of the rice over pastry keeping within 1 inch of the edge. Place 2 cups boiled salmon in bowl and squeeze over it the juice of 1 lemon, season with ½ teaspoon cracked pepper, ¼ teaspoon cayenne, and a little salt. Spread salmon over the rice. Sprinkle with ¼ cup cut dill; then cover with chopped eggs, salt lightly, and dot with 4 tablespoons butter. Cover with mushrooms, another ¼ cup cut dill and the remainder of the rice. Moisten edges of pastry on cookie sheet with water; then roll larger piece of pastry up on rolling-pin, and unroll over the whole. Press edges of top-and-bottom pastry together and roll up, making neat rolled edge. Mark edge with prongs of fork; cut 3 deep vents in top to allow steam to escape. Paint with beaten yolk of 1 egg. Place in pre-heated very hot oven and reduce heat immediately to slow 250 degrees. Bake for 25 minutes or until a golden brown and sizzling hot. Have ready 6 tablespoons melted butter, into which you have stirred 2 teaspoons curry powder. Pour this down into the 3 vents of pastry. Transfer with aid of spatula to hot platter and serve at once. Cut with sharp knife in 8 squares, and serve with pie knife.

LE STEAK AU POIVRE

3 lbs. ¾-inch-thick top sirloin steak	¼ lb. sweet butter
1 tablespoon chopped parsley	¼ cup brandy
1 tablespoon cracked pepper	Salt
½ cup white wine	

Serves 6-8

Cut steak into 12 pieces of equal size, discarding fat and gristle. Cover breadboard with heavy waxed paper. Lay steak out on paper and sprinkle with 1 tablespoon coarsely cracked pepper. Cover with more waxed paper and pound with wooden mallet until ⅜ inch thick. Heat a large, heavy iron frying-pan until very hot, add ⅛ lb. butter, and spread it over the entire surface of pan. Add steak and sear quickly on both sides; reduce heat and cook as desired until rare, medium, or well done, 1-4 minutes.

Place steak on large, sturdy hot platter and sprinkle with salt. Add 1 cup dry white wine to brown residue in pan and cook rapidly, stirring with wooden spoon, until reduced to syrupy consistency. Remove from fire and stir in ⅛ pound butter. Now pour ¼ cup heated brandy over steak, light it, and allow it to burn itself out, ladling the brandy over it with a spoon. Pour gravy from pan over all, sprinkle with parsley, and serve at once.

Contemporary French Cooking

WAVERLEY ROOT AND RICHARD DE ROCHEMONT

BOTH OF THE AUTHORS of this book were journalists first and serious food experts later. Under the circumstances they brought some aspects of the journalist's craft, notably objectivity, to the study of food. For this reason they limit themselves, in this book, to contemporary French cooking adapted, as it is, to the facts of life today: the rise of prices, the lack of servants, less space for both cooking and dining, the increase of mechanical conveniences in the kitchen and a new, slightly more austere, attitude toward food. (The present-day Frenchman eats less and less richly than did his grandfather and is a more circumspect drinker also.)

While Mr. Root and Mr. de Rochemont have no wish to subvert classic French cuisine, nor do they do so here, they acknowledge the changes that have been made due to the pace and clamor of the times, report on them and on how it is that the French still eat superbly no matter what income bracket they are in. The aim of this book is to help you enjoy some of the finest dishes of the great French tradition with a modest expenditure of time, money and effort. Many of the recipes, particularly those in the section entitled "Heat and Serve à la Française," come, with slight simplifications, from the kitchens of Air France.

ESCALOPES DE VEAU VALLÉE D'AUGE
(Veal Cutlets Vallée d'Auge)

The Auge Valley in Normandy is particularly noted for the quality of its food. It is, among other things, dairy country, within whose borders are made two of the most famous cheeses of France — Camembert and Pont-l'Évêque. Normandy is also apple cider and apple brandy country. This accounts for the Calvados.

5 thin slices veal, preferably from the leg	¼ cup Calvados (apple brandy) — you can use apple jack or cognac if you can't get Calvados
¼ lb. butter	
1½ lbs. button mushrooms	4 tablespoons heavy cream
½ cup white wine	

Melt three tablespoons of the butter in a casserole, and when it foams, put in the veal cutlets, seasoned to taste with salt and freshly ground pepper. Cook over a low flame to prevent them from taking on color, turning the slices when they are half done. The cooking time will depend on the thickness of the slices, but 10 minutes on each side should be about right.

When they are well done, remove them from the casserole and lay them, overlapping, on a heated serving platter, covering this with another hot plate. Keep warm.

In the same casserole melt another 1¼ tablespoons butter. Put in the mushrooms, which have been peeled, washed and cut into thin slices. Season to taste with salt and pepper. Cook over a high flame until the liquid has evaporated, then pour in the Calvados quickly. Do not light it. The white wine goes in next. Continue cooking until half the mixture has boiled off. Now lower the flame to medium, stir in the cream and continue stirring until the sauce has thickened. Take off the fire and stir in bit by bit 2 tablespoons of butter cut into small pieces. Remove the mushrooms and put them with the veal cutlets on the serving platter. Strain the sauce through a fine sieve, add seasoning if necessary, pour over the veal and mushrooms and serve.

Serves 5.

VEAL KIDNEYS WITH MUSTARD SAUCE

This dish must be prepared quickly, just before the moment of serving, because it can stand neither being kept warm before serving nor reheating. It must pass immediately from stove to stomach. Another warning: most kidney dishes can, if necessary, be made with other than veal kidneys — pork, for instance or lamb — but don't try it with this one.

4 veal kidneys	Salt and pepper
4 tablespoons Dijon prepared mustard	2 tablespoons heavy cream (optional)
Juice of 1 lemon	Chopped tarragon (optional)
3 tablespoons butter	

Remove membrane from kidneys and cut away most of their fat. In a flameproof dish, melt enough butter to brown them, and when butter is very hot, cook the kidneys over a high flame just long enough to brown slightly. Move the dish to the edge of the flame to keep contents warm without boiling, take the kidneys out and put them on a warmed plate. Slice them on the plate. They should at this stage be hardly cooked and should ooze blood as you cut them up.

Keeping the dish still at the edge of the flame, stir in the mustard and the lemon juice, blending it all well into the butter. Now put the cut-up kidneys back into the dish, along with the blood, salt and pepper to taste, and put the dish back on a low flame, stirring constantly until it barely reaches a boil. Prevent it from actually boiling — either by lowering the flame still further or drawing the dish to the edge of the burner — and continue to stir until the kidneys are done, that is to say, until only a little pink shows in the center. Serve from the cooking dish onto very hot plates.

An optional additional touch, which gives a richer taste, is to stir in at the last moment, after you have removed the cooking dish from the fire, 2 tablespoons of heavy cream plus a little chopped tarragon.

This is enough for 4.

MINUTE SQUAB

[I have only one quarrel with this excellent dish: the tenderest squab will be frustratingly difficult to dismember after a mere 25-30 minutes of cooking. The first time I tried it, following the recipe exactly, as I always do to begin with, I was fortunately alone. The bird and the sauce were so good that I couldn't bear to leave a bite. As a result, my blouse, the table mat and my library book were thoroughly splattered and I needed a bath rather than a finger bowl. Obviously this won't do if you are serving guests. The squab or squabs must cook longer before the onion is added. A little more butter is needed, if you do this, and a lid may be put on the pan for the period between the initial browning and the finishing. Even at the sacrifice of slightly underdone squab, which many people seem to prefer, I feel that this period should take about 40 minutes and the entire procedure close to an hour, the name of the recipe notwithstanding. If you cannot bear the idea of cooking the squab this long — and incidentally, the same problem obtains with underdone wild duck and may be similarly solved — have the birds cut into bite-sized pieces, Chinese-style, before cooking or cut them yourself, after cooking, using game shears. Your guests will still have a little difficulty but not quite as much. — P. H.]

1 squab to serve 2

1 tablespoon chopped onion per squab

1 tablespoon cognac per squab

1 tablespoon dissolved meat extract (or *glace de viande*)

½ tablespoon chopped parsley per squab

Butter

Salt and pepper

Cut the squabs in half, lengthwise. Flatten slightly and remove the small bones. Season to taste and sauté in hot butter in a deep pan. Meanwhile sauté the onion in butter separately until it is almost melted. When the birds are almost done (say 20 minutes), add the onion and finish the cooking (another 5 minutes) together.

Take out the squabs and keep warm. Rinse the cooking juices from the sides and bottom of the pan with the cognac, add the meat extract, take off the stove and stir in the parsley. Pour over the birds and serve.

STRING BEANS WITH EGG

2 pounds string beans	1½ tablespoons butter
8 eggs	Salt and pepper

Cook the string beans by boiling but remove them from the water before they are quite cooked. Drain. Beat the eggs lightly (not until they become frothy). Melt the butter, mix well with the beans, salt and pepper to taste, and mix in the beaten egg. Now put the whole into a buttered oven dish and cook in a hot oven for 10 minutes.

Serves 4 amply as a separate dish.

FIVE RECIPES FROM

Table Topics

JULIAN STREET

JULIAN STREET was, and always will be, a name to be con-
jured with in the world of food and wine. This is interesting in
view of the fact that his writing on those subjects constituted but
a minor part of his work. He considered himself a writer of short
stories and travel books and his concern with food and wine was a
hobby to which he turned in times of stress. Be that as it may, his
books on restaurants, at home and abroad, are classic; his small
volume entitled simply *Wines*, which is still in print and is as valid
today as when it was published in 1933, earned him the ribbon of
the Legion of Honor; he helped to found, and was the first member
of, the New York branch of the Wine and Food Society and was,
for many years, a director of Bellows and Company, the wine mer-
chants. As a result of that last connection, we have this charming
book.

When ill health forced him out of city life, he retired to the
country and from 1943 until his death in 1947 turned out a
monthly pamphlet for Bellows. This was entitled *Table Topics* and
was published "in the not disinterested hope" that it might help to
"sustain the civilized tradition of good eating and good bottles
through [that] period of anxiety and difficult living." Based on his
files, his diaries, cellar-books and correspondence, the pamphlets
contained both wit and wisdom and were a joy to all who read

them. In 1959, a selection of the best material from them was published in book form. The selecting and editing were done by Mr. Street's widow, A. I. M. S. Street, and a difficult job it must have been, since it is not easy to skim cream from cream. The recipes, except when otherwise noted, are Mrs. Street's contribution.

ALMOND SOUP

The American friend whose guests we were during our visit to Portugal owns and inhabits for many months in the year a charming ancient house that is also a national monument — a country palace built for the noble Albuquerque family. Among its treasures is a rare collection, in the walls of house and garden, of Portuguese *azulejos*, the glazed tiles the Moors left as mementos in this country; but perhaps its greatest benefaction is its spaciousness and serenity. We were entirely content to sit on the loggia and rest in its beauty. In one such time the question of feeding the guests at the Quinta arose; talk of recipes followed, and among those given us at that time by Mrs. Scoville is the following:

1 tablespoon butter	1½ quarts chicken stock
1 tablespoon cornstarch	1 cup cream
2 tablespoons flour	2 ounces almonds

Cream butter, flour, and cornstarch well. Add the hot stock, stirring constantly. Let boil 5 minutes. Add cream and finely chopped almonds. Serve very hot.

Serves 6.

BURGHUL WITH CHICKEN AND SPICES

Burghul (spelled a number of different ways: boulgour, bulghur, burgol, known as kasha or buckwheat kasha in many lands and bought as cracked wheat in Italian markets) is a food our government has made tentative moves to popularize; but, as so often happens, they seem to be holding the wrong end of the stick, considering it not as a splendid food but as part of the problem of disposing of the wheat that is in surplus all over the country.

Actually, burghul is delicious and nutritious. Its use parallels that of rice, but it has more texture than rice, and its nutty flavor is more exciting to the palate. It is another of the foods that tie us to antiquity: as *arisah* it is mentioned in the Bible, and it continues into the present as a basic food item in Russia, Armenia, and neighboring lands of the Middle East.

[NOTE: See recipe for Steamed Chicken below. — P. H.]

Cut the chicken from the bone and keep hot, or heat later, by simmering in a small quantity of its own broth.

Make a pilaf: melt a lump of butter, simmer in it for 2-3 minutes 1 tablespoon chopped onion; add and mix well together:

½ teaspoon cumin seeds	1 teaspoon coriander, crushed
⅛ teaspoon cardamom, crushed	1 teaspoon grated orange peel
6 peppercorns, crushed	

Add ¾ cup burghul, turn the heat up, stir hard for a few minutes until the grain lightens in shade. Transfer to a baking-casserole; add 1½ cups highly flavored chicken stock on the boil.

Bake at 400 degrees for 25-30 minutes, uncovered until the grain has absorbed the liquid; covered up to the last 5 minutes, then run a long-tined fork through to release the steam; finish baking. Heat 3 tablespoons of good olive oil in a skillet, thinly slice into it 1 medium-sized onion and ¼ kernel of garlic, minced, and cook very slowly until tender, not browned.

Add 1 tablespoon chopped parsley, ¼ cup pine nuts, ¼ cup washed raisins. Mix well and keep hot.

When the burghul is done, spoon it into the skillet, blend together, add salt and pepper as needed.

Serve individually, or on a hot baking-platter, the pieces of chicken lifted from their liquid and laid across the top. Add a salad of endive, a 4th- or 5th-cru claret, fruit — and feast!

Serves 4-5.

Steamed Chicken
(Basic recipe)

For some reason, probably chemical, the broth which results from cooking a chicken slowly in its own steam is richer and more flavorsome than any got by other methods of cookery and the chicken itself emerges tender and juicy.

For 4-6 persons, buy 2 well-found broilers, 2½ to 3 lbs. each, cut into 4 pieces. Wash and dry.

Dust well with flour which has been combined with salt, freshly ground black pepper, ½ teaspoon chervil, ¼ teaspoon marjoram. Melt 2 table-spoons butter in a skillet and brown the chicken well, adding more butter as necessary. Remove the chicken to a casserole, pour over 1½ ounces of cognac and flame.

Melt 1 tablespoon butter in the original skillet and add 2 small white onions, thinly sliced, and cook for 2-3 minutes.

Dissolve 2 chicken bouillon cubes in ¼ cup warm white wine or water; add to onions in skillet, scrape well to catch all the rich chicken juices in pan, pour over chicken in casserole, seal with wax paper and cover tightly. Place casserole on asbestos pad over high heat until it comes to the boil, turn heat down to simmer, where the chicken cooks until done. Depending on the freshness of the birds, this takes upward of 40 minutes.

[NOTE: As Mrs. Street points out, this basic recipe lends itself to many variations. If more broth is needed, as in this case, cook the chicken the day before, reserving necks, backs, wing tips and giblets. When the steaming has been accomplished, remove the meat from the bones in large pieces and reserve to be reheated later. Combine the bones and the uncooked sections, cover with cold water, bring to a boil and simmer, covered, for several hours until a flavorful broth has been obtained. Strain and boil down broth until 2 cups remain. Strengthen to taste with 1 or more chicken bouillon cubes. — P. H.]

SMOKED TONGUE WITH MADEIRA SAUCE

Soak the tongue 24 hours, changing the water frequently. Simmer, well covered with water, until a fork penetrates fairly easily. This process takes from 2 to 3 hours. Cool tongue, skin and trim. Place the tongue on a trivet in an earthenware or similar pot.

Pour over it 4 cups of unsalted beef stock, or 2 cans of undiluted consommé, and add 2 small onions chopped, 2 chopped carrots, a few sprigs of parsley, a small handful of celery tops, 1 small bay leaf or ½ large, a pinch of thyme, 6 peppercorns, crushed.

Seal the lid onto the pot and simmer 1 to 1½ hours, or until the tongue is very tender when pierced by a fork.

Strain the liquid off into a saucepan and reduce by boiling rapidly for several minutes. Taste; if the salt flavor is too strong, finely slice into the broth a peeled potato, boil up, taste and remove the slices when sufficient salt has been absorbed. Add ½ cup well-washed seedless raisins and Madeira to taste — 3 or 4 ounces. Thicken with arrowroot and serve poured over the slices of tongue. (A 3-lb. tongue will serve 6.)

FRUIT COMPOTE MADEIRA

Combine large balls of watermelon and canteloupe, canned red plums, spiced crabapples, and pitted black cherries.

Boil down the juices of the canned fruit. Combine the juices, add Madeira in the proportion of 3 or 4 parts juice to 1 of Madeira.

Marinate the fruit in this mixture for 5 hours, in the icebox. Just before serving, sprinkle the top with fresh blueberries, and over all place paper-thin slices of lemon, covered with finely chopped mint.

FRENCH CREAM—SAVOY PLAZA

Only a few times in a cooking lifetime does one come across a basic recipe which is so good that, once having found it, one never lets it go. Such is a French Cream, part of a recipe given us by a chef of the Savoy Plaza, which seemed in its entirety too complicated for our household, but in so far as it brought us this culinary treasure we shall never cease to be grateful.

A fruit tart, as was mentioned by one of our correspondents, is a most delicious finish to a dinner. To achieve a good one, two things are essential: a tender crust and a smooth cream.

1 pint milk	3 tablespoons cornstarch
4 egg yolks, beaten	Pinch salt
⅔ cup sugar	1 teaspoon vanilla
2 tablespoons sweet butter	

Heat all but a small portion of milk, stir in the egg yolks, sugar, and salt. Beat the cornstarch into the remaining milk and add slowly; add the butter in small pieces, stirring constantly. Beware overcooking. The cream does not come to a boil, but is done when smooth, shiny and thick. Remove from the fire, add the flavoring. The cream is quite thick when finished. If a thinner cream is wanted, reduce the cornstarch ingredient. A double boiler is not essential — use a heavy pot and a round wire whisk.

Basic Pie Crust

1 teaspoon baking-powder	1 cup shortening
2 cups flour	1 egg, beaten
¼ teaspoon salt	5 tablespoons ice water

Sift baking-powder, flour, and salt; add shortening with a pastry-cutter, chop into flour mixture, add egg and water, gradually mix, chopping, not stirring. Gather into a ball, roll into wax paper, put into the icebox until firm enough to roll out.

If the crust is to be used for a fruit pie or tart, add to the flour mixture 6 blanched and grated bitter almonds and 2 teaspoons of sugar.

To complete the tart, cherry or apricot:

Precook the tart shells, baking at 450 degrees for 12-15 minutes — watch them. Draw off the juice from the fruit, flavor and boil down as for a compote. Cool; add Grand Marnier or fruit liqueur to taste. Half fill the shells with cream, cover with fruit, spoon over the juice.

A novel use for French cream, and another surprising dessert:

Pack, not too tightly, a pint mason jar with firm dried prunes, fill the jar with gin, and put in a fairly cool place, not icebox. Turn it frequently and leave it for two weeks — better longer. The prunes absorb the spirit, swell out and emerge tender and full of zing.

We serve this by passing three bowls on a tray; the fruit; the sauce drained from the fruit, and the cream, allowing the guests to combine the three as they will.

The Italian Cookbook

MARIA LUISA TAGLIENTI

FEW PEOPLE, if any, dispute the fact that the art of fine cooking originated in Italy and was introduced to France by Catherine de' Medici who, when she went to Paris as a bride, took with her Italian chefs, Italian cooking utensils — and the fork. Among the delicacies that her well-trained staff prepared for her and the French court were desserts which were destined to become known the world over as "French" pastries.

One must travel extensively in Italy in order to appreciate the great variety of the Italian cuisine. Each region has its own specialties and cooking methods; in Northern Italy butter is used more often than oil; in southern Italy, one encounters more tomatoes and garlic, and in the district around Bologna, more milk and cream are used. This is a collection of recipes from *all* Italian sources. They come from famous restaurants, from ancient cookbooks and from Miss Taglienti's illustrious family and friends. Although all the classic Italian dishes are included, Miss Taglienti has selected from the thousands of regional specialties those which she felt would appeal most to Americans. I find this a most valuable book.

FONDUTA ALLA PIEMONTESE

Fonduta is a delicious Piedmontese soup. The original recipe calls for Fontina, a cheese from Piedmont exported to this country, but when Fontina is not available, (real) Swiss or Muenster cheese may be substituted.

1 lb. Fontina cheese, diced
5 egg yolks
Milk
4 tablespoons butter
⅛ teaspoon white pepper

2 canned white truffles, size of a walnut, minced fine or sliced paper
thin
4 slices of toast, diced

Place cheese in bowl, add enough milk to cover and let stand overnight. Then place cheese and milk in double boiler. Water in bottom of double boiler should be hot but not boiling. Beat with egg beater or stir vigorously with wooden spoon until cheese is dissolved. Then stir in egg yolks and pepper and cook for another minute or two, stirring constantly. Fonduta should have the consistency of thick cream. Correct seasoning and serve with diced toast, sprinkle with truffles.

Serves 6.

[NOTE: Black truffles may be used if you cannot find the white. Also, if you are a truffle devotee, as I am, it's better to slice them than to mince them. — P. H.]

CARCIOFI ALLA GIUDIA
(Artichokes Jewish Style)

In Italy this is the most famous and most generally liked way of preparing artichokes. Its secret lies in their tenderness and in the correct cooking time. Each leaf should look golden and be as crisp as a potato chip.

12 artichokes
4 cups olive oil
Juice of 2 lemons

1 teaspoon salt
½ teaspoon pepper

Peel stalks and cut off tips of artichokes. Remove all tough outer leaves. Spread remaining ones open by pressing down and holding by stem. Remove spiny choke from center with a small sharp knife. Wash artichoke in water to which lemon juice has been added. Drain. Sprinkle inside leaves with salt and pepper. Place oil in deep skillet or saucepan. Fry artichokes, a few at a time, over medium flame, for 8-10 minutes, turning occasionally. Remove to absorbent paper. Let artichokes stand for at least ½ hour (even as long as 3 hours) before continuing preparation. Then reheat oil in skillet and, when hot, hold each artichoke by the stem and dip it in. The artichoke will open, its leaves will curl and become a dark, golden brown color. Re-move to absorbent paper, sprinkle with salt and serve hot.

Serves 4-6.

[NOTE: The artichokes should be as small as possible — about 2 inches high, if you can find such. The oil for each frying should be hot but not smoking. To test it, throw a moistened piece of bread crust into it. If the oil crackles, it is hot. You do not have to use pure olive oil for this preparation. Half olive and half vegetable oil, or all peanut oil will be fine. — P. H.]

SFORMATO DI PATATE MARIA LUISA
(Potatoes Maria Luisa)

[I gather that this dish is the author's own invention since it bears her name. She suggests serving it as an accompaniment to roast lamb, which is a very good idea. — P. H.]

4 lbs. potatoes	3 tablespoons butter
3 eggs, beaten	6 slices prosciutto
½ cup grated Parmesan or Romano cheese	¼ lb. provolone or mozzarella cheese diced
½ teaspoon pepper	¼ cup breadcrumbs
½ teaspoon salt	

Wash potatoes and boil unpeeled in salted water until tender. Peel and mash while hot, taking care that they do not become cold. Put in mixing bowl with eggs, grated cheese, salt, pepper, diced cheese and 2 tablespoons butter. Mix well. Sprinkle greased 8″ x 3″ or 9″ x 2″ baking dish with ½ of breadcrumbs. Pour in half the potato mixture. Level off top with spoon and cover with layer of prosciutto. Cover with remaining potato mixture. Even top with spoon, sprinkle with remaining breadcrumbs, dot with butter and bake in a (pre-heated) 300-degree oven for 35 minutes. Cool for 15 minutes. Turn out on serving dish. Cut in wedges and serve. If desired, it can be served hot immediately, using a spoon for serving. It is also delicious cold.

Serves 6-8.

(*Note:* If the Italian ham, prosciutto, is not available, thin slices of American cooked ham or salami may be substituted.)

FEGATO DI VITELLO ALL' ITALIANO
(Calves' Liver, Italian Style)

1 lb. calves' liver, sliced thin, dipped in flour
½ cup butter
2 slices prosciutto, chopped fine
½ small onion minced
½ teaspoon sage

3 tablespoons parsley, chopped
1 tablespoon flour or cornstarch
½ cup chicken or beef broth
¼ cup dry Marsala wine
Salt, pepper

Fry liver in hot butter until golden on both sides. Remove liver to hot platter. To the butter in skillet, add prosciutto, onion, sage and parsley. Sauté for 3 or 4 minutes or until onion is tender but not brown. Stir in flour, and add broth, Marsala wine, salt and pepper. Simmer for 10 to 12 minutes. Add liver and simmer just long enough to warm up the liver. Serve immediately with lemon wedges.

Serves 4.

ZABAGLIONE GELATO
(Iced Zabaglione)

8 egg yolks
½ cup and 1 tablespoon granulated sugar
Sliced peel of ½ lemon
1 cup dry Marsala wine (preferably imported)

1 teaspoon unflavored gelatin
3 tablespoons Cognac
1 pint heavy cream whipped stiff with ½ teaspoon vanilla and 1 tablespoon sugar

Beat egg yolks, lemon peel and sugar for 3 minutes with electric beater at beating-eggs speed, or 9 minutes with hand beater. Remove lemon peel. Fold in Marsala wine. Place egg mixture in top of double boiler. (The water in the double boiler should be boiling slowly.) Cook for about 6 minutes continuing to beat with beater. Zabaglione is cooked when it stands in soft peaks. Remove from fire. Soften gelatin in 1 tablespoon cold water and dissolve in 2 tablespoons boiling water and add to zabaglione, stirring slowly. When zabaglione is at room temperature blend in Cognac and heavy cream. Place in individual glasses or in a crystal or silver bowl and place in refrigerator for 4 to 5 hours. Serve with cookies or French pastry.

Serves 8.

Thoughts for Food

W HEN, IN 1938, a group of Chicago women produced what I
believe to be one of the first menu cookbooks, they hit upon a
title that was not only inspired as a name for any cookbook, but
which was, in this case, beautifully apt. When anyone is thinking
about food, chances are that he or she is planning a meal and is
searching for suitable dishes and accompaniments. While other
books often had a list of menus tucked away somewhere, this one
was *all* menus — each recipe appearing as part of a well-planned
luncheon or dinner. Owning the book, as I have for many years, has
been like having a trusted and dependable friend in the kitchen;
a friend to whom I could turn for advice when I couldn't, for the
life of me, think what to have with something or even, on occasion,
what to have period. This recipe is an old favorite of mine.

CHICKEN ROLLS

2 cups cold finely diced chicken	1 tablespoon grated onion
2 tablespoons butter	Few grains ginger
2 tablespoons flour	½ teaspoon lemon juice
1 cup hot milk and cream or chicken	Salt, pepper
broth	Pie dough
2 egg yolks	2 tablespoons cream
1 tablespoon minced parsley	1 egg yolk

Melt butter, add flour, and then add the liquid. Cook until thick, then
blend with egg yolks. Add to the chicken with seasonings. Cook over hot
water for 10 minutes. Cool. Roll rich pie paste ⅛ inch thick, cut into 5-inch

squares; spread with chicken mixture and roll. Pinch ends together and place in a greased pan. Brush with additional egg yolk diluted with 2 table-spoons cream, and bake for 30 minutes in hot oven (400 degrees F.). Serve with mushroom sauce.

Serves 4.

TWO RECIPES FROM

Thoughts for Buffets

IT WOULD APPEAR that, in spite of the increasing scarcity of
domestic help these days, entertaining at home is becoming
more and more popular. Hostesses take pride in acquiring a reputation for the originality as well as the excellence of their fare and
many are discovering that the success of a party is even more to be
relished if they have accomplished most or all of the preparation
themselves. *Thoughts for Buffets,* compiled by the same group who
were responsible for *Thoughts for Food,* is geared to today's living
and was one of the first books of its type to include, with each
menu, an advance schedule of preparation. One is also frequently
given one's choice between a short-cut recipe (taking advantage of
frozen foods and ready-mixes) and the more painstaking, classic
procedure. That the recipes are not lacking in imagination is evi-
dent, I believe, in these two examples.

BONED LEG OF LAMB

1 9-pound leg of lamb, boned

Have butcher bone the lamb and shape so that it lies flat.

Marinade:

> 1 clove garlic, crushed
> 1 cup French dressing
> ⅔ cup chopped onions
> 2 teaspoons barbecue spice

> 1 teaspoon salt
> ¼ teaspoon oregano
> 1 bay leaf, crushed

Marinate the lamb overnight in the combined crushed garlic, French dressing, onions and seasonings; drain. When ready to cook, place on wire rack; barbecue 45 minutes to 1 hour, basting with marinade. To cook in oven, place the lamb, fat side up, in a shallow pan; brush with marinade. Place under flame in broiler 4 inches from heat and broil for 10 minutes until golden brown. Turn, baste, and broil 10 more minutes. Bake, fat side up, for 20 minutes per pound of meat in a 350-degree oven. Serves 8.

CRÊPE MERINGUE VIENNESE

Casserole ingredients:

Thin pancakes, cut in ½-inch strips
¼ cup butter (approx.)

1 cup of damson plum or apricot jam
½ cup powdered sugar

Thin pancakes for strips:

3 eggs, beaten
1 cup sifted all-purpose flour
1 cup milk

⅛ teaspoon salt
3 tablespoons powdered sugar
2 teaspoons grated lemon rind

Combine 6 pancake ingredients in order listed. Melt 1 teaspoon butter in 7-inch skillet. Pour 2 tablespoons batter into pan and tilt pan back and forth so that batter covers bottom completely. When lightly browned, turn and brown lightly on the other side. Use 1 teaspoon butter for each pancake. Stack pancakes on breadboard until all batter is used. Then cut pancakes into ½-inch strips and separate. Place a layer in bottom of well-buttered 2-quart casserole. Spread with jam, dust lightly with powdered sugar and dot with butter. Repeat layers until all strips are used. When ready to serve, top with meringue; place in a 325-degree oven for 15 minutes or until meringue is lightly brown. Serve slightly warm.

Meringue:

½ cup egg whites, room temperature

6 tablespoons sugar

Beat egg whites until they stand in peaks. Gradually add sugar, continuing to beat very well.
Serves 8.

The Alice B. Toklas Cook Book

THROUGH MANY rich years of companionship Gertrude Stein talked and wrote while Alice B. Toklas talked and cooked. An extraordinary succession of friends and servants shared their *ménages,* both in this country and in Europe, and many famous people enjoyed the food and the talk at the Toklas-Stein table. From some of these Miss Toklas garnered recipes and from others, anecdotes. Her book is a unique and fascinating mixture of reminiscence and repasts — with recipes for the latter.

STUFFED CUCUMBERS

Cut unpeeled cucumbers in half lengthwise. Boil for 2 minutes. Remove from heat. Put under cold-water tap, drain and dry thoroughly. When cold, with a sharp knife hollow out within ¼ inch of the skin and fill with previously cooked, chilled and diced string beans and green peas. Chill thoroughly and cover with a green mayonnaise. Sprinkle with minutely cut chives.

[NOTE: I suggest using frozen "Petite Peas" for this dish; the beans may be fresh or frozen — preferably fresh. — P. H.]

CAULIFLOWER SALAD WITH SHRIMP

[This excellent and original salad is quite a conversation piece when served at a buffet. It is a delicious accompaniment to cold salmon. — P. H.]

Boil a large whole cauliflower in salted water until the flowerets are tender but no more than that. Drain and press head down in a bowl while still hot so that when cold and removed from the bowl it will keep its shape. Place cauliflower flat side down on a round serving dish. Place 1 lb. shelled (and cooked) giant shrimp between the flowerets, tails pendant. Serve apart:

Sauce Mousseline

Make a sauce Hollandaise by placing in the top of a double boiler the yolks of 3 eggs, ¼ teaspoon salt, a pinch of pepper and the same of nutmeg. Put over very hot but not boiling water. Stir constantly with a wooden spoon, particularly around the sides and at the bottom. Add in very small pieces ¼ lb. butter. Allow each piece to melt before adding the next one. When the butter has melted and the mixture has thickened remove from the heat and add, very slowly, 1 tablespoon lemon juice.

When the sauce is tepid add ½ cup whipped cream. Stir gently and serve.

Serves 6-8.

[NOTE: Since our shrimp are not very pink and their tails curl up rather than being pendant, I suggest using the little Danish shrimp that come in glass jars; even though their tails aren't pendant either, they will add color. Also, if you happen to have some truffles on hand, as I did, scatter a few thin slices over the cauliflower. Last, but not least, if your Hollandaise is quite thick, don't whip the cream too stiff. The sauce must be able to flow over the servings of cauliflower. — P. H.]

MADAME LOUBET'S ASPARAGUS TIPS

[This dish is definitely not for weight-watchers, but then few of the good ones are. It was, according to Miss Toklas, the high point of a luncheon that she and Gertrude Stein enjoyed at the restaurant Sévigné in the tiny town of Grignan in the Drôme, a department of France famous for fine cooking. The restaurant, which dates from the seventeenth century, still exists, according to the Guide Michelin, but no stars are awarded it. Perhaps the inspectors were there on an off day. To do the recipe justice, you must use the very first small green asparagus of the season. — P. H.]

Wash asparagus quickly — do not allow to remain in water — and discard white stems. Tie into neat bundles, plunge into boiling salt water.

Allow about 8 minutes for the cooking. It should not be overcooked; much depends upon its freshness. Put aside. Over a very low flame put in a saucepan 4 tablespoons butter (for 1 lb. asparagus). When butter is melted, add asparagus tips still tied up in bundles. Add 4 tablespoons heavy cream. Do not stir but gently dip saucepan in all directions until the asparagus is coated with butter and cream. Then remove from flame. Place asparagus on preheated round dish with the points facing to the edge of the dish. Gently cut the strings with kitchen scissors. In the center, place ½ cup whipped cream with ½ teaspoon salt mixed in it. Serve before the cream has time to melt. This is a gastronomic feast. And a thing of beauty.

PEACHES GLACÉES

Put 6 fine peaches in hot water only long enough to peel. Prepare a syrup of 1 cup sugar and ¾ cup water. Poach the peaches covered in the syrup over low flame for 4 minutes. Remove peaches and drain. When the syrup is quite thick, after about 3 minutes further cooking, pour over the peaches. See that it adheres. When cold, place peaches on serving dish in the refrigerator for at least 2 hours. Prepare a purée of 1 lb. fresh strawberries, ¼ cup icing sugar, add 2 tablespoons best brandy and 1 cup whipped cream. Put in refrigerator for at least 2 hours. Before serving, pour the purée over the peaches.

[NOTE: The easiest way to make the purée is to slice the berries and put them through a food mill. Do not make the mistake of sweetening the purée more than indicated; the peaches, in their syrup, are quite sweet, and a certain tartness in the purée keeps the dish from being cloying. — P. H.]

CROÛTE À LA BELLE AURORE, HOT SABAYON SAUCE

Cut stale cake into 12 slices ⅓ inch thick. Sprinkle generously with rum. Cover half of them with very thick applesauce to which has been added 1 tablespoon heavy cream to each cup applesauce and 3 tablespoons tiny, dried, mixed glacé fruits. Place the other slices of cake on the prepared ones, pressing so that they hold together. Dip in beaten egg, cover with sifted cracker crumbs and fry in butter over medium heat. Serve with:

Hot Sabayon Sauce

For 6 servings, stir in saucepan over lowest heat 3 yolks of eggs with 8 tablespoons sugar until thoroughly mixed. Add very slowly 2 cups Marsala, beat with a whisk until it thickens. Serve in preheated bowl or sauce boat.

[NOTE: The amount of applesauce depends, of course, on the size of the slices of cake. I used "bought" pound cake and trimmed off the crusts. This required 2 scant cups of applesauce. The glacé fruits are available in jars. Two eggs are necessary, and about 1½ cups crumbs. I always add a little vegetable oil when frying in butter to keep the latter from burning. For the sauce, use either a double boiler or a heavy aluminum or cast-iron saucepan. — P. H.]

Tante Marie's French Kitchen

TRANSLATED AND ADAPTED BY CHARLOTTE TURGEON

ALTHOUGH CHARLOTTE TURGEON has made her mark in practically every area of the culinary field, having written cookbooks, edited them and reviewed them for the New York *Times*, she is probably best known for *Tante Marie*. This small book has been used by generations of French families, and the fact that few changes have been made in the many French editions serves as proof that the fundamental secrets of French cooking are timelessness, simplicity and economy. A few, but only a very few, liberties of addition and omission have been taken by Mrs. Turgeon in her translation and adaptation; these have to do, for the most part, with measurements and occasional modernization of methods. First published in 1949, *Tante Marie's French Kitchen*, known in France as *La Véritable Cuisine de Famille par Tante Marie*, is a veritable classic.

POT-AU-FEU

The famous French *pot-au-feu* provides the basis of a whole week of good meals. Many kitchens start their weekly routine by making this soup. If the dish is to be prepared for the sake of the soup only, any of the cheapest cuts of beef may be used. However, if a slightly better cut is used, the meat can be served hot or cold or in a casserole dish.

3 pounds beef (chuck, shoulder, neck or bottom round, rolled and tied tightly)	2 carrots ½ parsnip 1 turnip

6 quarts cold water	bouquet garni
2 tablespoons salt	3 cloves
1 teaspoon black pepper	1 onion
3 leeks	

Place the meat in a large pot. Add water, salt, and pepper. Bring to a boil over a moderate fire. A white scum will form on the water. Keep skimming this off until it has all disappeared. Slice the leeks lengthwise and tie them together with string so that they may easily be removed. Add the leeks, carrots, parsnips, turnip, bouquet garni, and the onion stuck with the cloves. Let this simmer for at least 4 hours. Pour the broth through a strainer and skim off as much fat as possible before serving. If the color is too pale, add a little kitchen bouquet.

To serve: Place several rounds of stale or toasted bread in the bottom of the soup tureen or individual soup plates. Pour the bouillon over the bread. If bottom round has been used, place on a platter, surround with the vegetables and serve with gravy made of 2 cups of the bouillon thickened with cornstarch or potato starch. The rest of the bouillon should be kept in a cool place for future use.

CHOUX ROUGES AUX POMMES
(Red Cabbage with Apples)

1 medium-sized red cabbage	3 cloves
5 large crabapples	2 tablespoons currant jelly
2 tablespoons butter	1 teaspoon cornstarch
Salt and pepper	1 tablespoon cider vinegar

After removing the outer leaves, wash the cabbage and cover with water. Peel and core the apples. Add the apples, butter, salt, pepper, and cloves to the cabbage. Cover and simmer 2½ hours. Bind the sauce with the currant jelly, mixed with cornstarch and vinegar. Serve very hot. This is a Flemish dish.

SEVEN RECIPES AND A MENU

WITH TIMETABLE FROM

Time to Entertain

CHARLOTTE TURGEON

TIME IS OF THE ESSENCE in this, Mrs. Turgeon's fourth book, which was first published in 1954. After much trial and error, this busy housewife, mother and career woman worked out a system whereby she could be all those things and cook and entertain too. That system is presented here. In spite of the fact that menus are provided, sufficient room is left for the exercise of personal taste, and one can follow Mrs. Turgeon's schedules without feeling unduly regimented and find that, as a result, there has been time for everything including relaxation. To prove this to those of you who are not acquainted with the book, I give one whole menu and schedule. The alternate suggestions are listed, but recipes are given for the original menu only.

DINNER PARTY FOR FOUR

Buy graceful new candles and polish up your silver for this one. It's extra delicious and worth all the loving care the hostess can give it. I think it deserves two wines, but if you decide to serve only one, I recommend the red. And I would suggest to your guests that they leave at least a swallow to accompany the final morsel of bread, cheese, and sweet butter so dear to any Frenchman — and anyone else who has perfected the art of good eating. The veal recipe is adapted from a dish I first ate in Vendôme,

France. The chef was unwilling to part with his secret so I used my diag-
nostic powers and can assure you this is a good translation of the original
French. If you prefer, serve fruit instead of the maple cream, but in any
case, don't rush this meal. The memory of it will linger long with you and
your guests. If you are going to make your own rolls, consult the recipe before planning your time in the kitchen. And if buying French bread, two
loaves, please. More will be eaten with the cheese course than you think.

MUSSEL CANAPÉS

VEAL CUTLETS VENDÔME

RISSOLÉ POTATOES

TOSSED AVOCADO SALAD

ROQUEFORT OR BLUE CHEESE

SWEET BUTTER

CRUSTY WATER ROLLS OR FRENCH BREAD

MAPLE NUT COFFEE CREAM

COFFEE

Wines

White Burgundy (Pouilly Fuissé or Chablis, for instance)

or

California White Pinot

Beaujolais

or

California Cabernet

Alternates

CRAB BISQUE

CHICKEN SANS SOUCI

CAULIFLOWER TIMBALE, HOLLANDAISE SAUCE

TOSSED SALAD

Your Shopping List

1 can (3¼ ounces) smoked mussels	1 large avocado
1 lemon	Roquefort or blue cheese
8 veal cutlets	French bread
¼ lb. mushrooms	1 pint coffee ice cream
½ pint sour cream	½ pint heavy cream
1 head escarole	Chopped walnuts
1 bunch watercress	

Beforehand Preparation:

MUSSEL CANAPÉS

3 tablespoons butter	Salt and black pepper
1 clove garlic, chopped or pressed	4 thick slices white bread
1 can smoked mussels	Lemon slices
1 tablespoon chopped parsley	Parsley sprigs

Melt the butter in a small saucepan and simmer the garlic over moderate heat while chopping the mussels and parsley finely. Add these to the butter and stir gently for 1 minute. Season with a little salt and plenty of freshly ground black pepper. Remove from the heat and cool. Trim the bread and toast it very lightly. Spread with the mussel mixture. Place on a baking sheet, cover and keep in a cool place.

VEAL CUTLETS VENDÔME

8 individual veal cutlets	1 tablespoon chopped onion
Salt and black pepper	3 tablespoons butter
½ lb. mushrooms	2 tablespoons brandy
2 tablespoons butter	1 cup sour cream, scalded

Ask the butcher to cut the cutlets from the top of a leg of veal. They should be cut against the grain and should be free from both fat and gristle. Sprinkle them generously with salt and black pepper and place them on a breadboard. Cover with wax paper and roll them firmly with a rolling pin.

Trim, wash, and chop the mushrooms, using both caps and stems. Cook in a small saucepan with the 2 tablespoons of butter for 10 minutes. They will be dry when they are cooked.

Sauté the chopped onion in the 3 tablespoons of butter, using a large skillet. When the onions are yellow, remove from the skillet with a slotted spoon. Turn the heat up high and sear the veal cutlets on both sides until nicely browned. Place them on an ovenproof platter. Scald the cream while this is going on. Add the brandy to the butter in the skillet and light it with a match. Stir while the flames subside. Stir in the cream. Do not let the sauce boil after the cream has been added. Season with salt and pepper.

Cover the cutlets with the mushrooms and pour the sauce over all. Keep in a cool place.

RISSOLÉ POTATOES

Scoop out 2 cups of potato balls from large white potatoes. Parboil them 5 minutes in boiling salted water. Drain and dry. Canned potato balls can be used very well but they must be thoroughly dried before frying.

TOSSED AVOCADO SALAD

1 head escarole	French dressing
1 bunch watercress	Cut lemon
1 large avocado	

Wash and trim the escarole and watercress, breaking the large escarole leaves into small pieces. Peel the avocado and rub the outside with the cut side of the lemon. Wrap in wax paper. Place everything in the refrigerator crisper to chill. Make the dressing, adding garlic and anchovies.

THE CHEESE

Cheese should be served at room temperature. Ideally, it should never be chilled but stored in a cool place. However, several hours of room temperature restores much of its flavor subdued by refrigeration. Prepare a small platter with balls or pats of sweet butter and several knives, leaving room for the cheese. Keep this in the refrigerator because the coolness of the butter contrasts nicely with the cheese. The cheese may be served as a separate course accompanied by red wine or with the salad.

If you serve it with the salad, forget the wine, for only those in love drink wine with vinegar.

MAPLE NUT COFFEE CREAM

1 egg yolk	⅓ cup chopped walnuts
½ cup maple syrup	1 pint coffee ice cream
½ cup heavy cream, whipped	4 walnut halves

Beat the egg yolk in the top of a small double boiler. Add the maple syrup and cook over hot water until the mixture thickens, stirring constantly. Turn the mixture into a freezer tray and place in the freezing compartment, but do not change the temperature, because too quick freezing will crystallize the mixture. When thoroughly cold combine with the whipped cream and nuts and chill for at least 3 hours, stirring once or twice.

The dessert is served in the following manner: Place a tablespoon of the maple mixture in the bottom of each dessert glass. Fill with coffee ice cream. Top with the maple mixture and a walnut half.

1 Hour Before Dinner
Uncork the red wine to let it "breathe." If it is an old wine it should be decanted an hour or more before serving.

20 Minutes Before the Guests Arrive
1. Preheat the oven to 300 degrees.
2. Prepare a tray with 4 dessert glasses and plates.
3. Heat 1 inch of vegetable shortening in a covered frying pan until it smokes. Add the potatoes and brown lightly on all sides. Reduce the heat as far as possible and continue cooking from 30 to 45 minutes. An occasional shake if you pass through the kitchen is a good idea.
4. Arrange the escarole and watercress attractively in a salad bowl. Cut off the top of the avocado to remove the seed, and to form a cup. Fill the cup with the French dressing. Place the avocado in the center of the salad. Keep in the refrigerator if possible. When it is time to toss the salad, cut up the avocado with salad spoon and fork. This will release the dressing.
5. Place the veal cutlets on the middle rack in the oven, leaving room on the upper rack for the canapés. They will need 30 to 40 minutes of slow cooking but a little more will not harm them.
6. Warm 4 small canapé plates and 4 dinner plates.

10 Minutes Before Serving
1. Place the canapés in the oven. They need 5 to 6 minutes to heat.
2. Fill the water glasses, light the candles.
3. Place the cheese platter, bread, and the salad on a side table in the dining room.
4. Drain the potatoes and place them in an oven-proof vegetable dish.

Sprinkle liberally with salt and keep in the oven during the first course.

5. Start the coffee.

6. Place the canapés on individual plates and garnish with a slice of lemon and a sprig of parsley.

Call your guests.

BAKED STUFFED CHICKEN LOBSTERS

This has a better flavor if made a day in advance.

8 boiled chicken lobsters	3 tablespoons flour
½ lb. mushrooms	½ pint light cream
2 tablespoons butter	4 tablespoons Madeira
1 teaspoon lemon juice	2 teaspoons chopped parsley
¼ cup water	Salt and pepper
1 can mussels	1 cup fine bread crumbs
3 tablespoons butter	2 tablespoons butter

Remove the large and the small claws from the lobsters, keeping the body and tail intact. Reserve the small claws and break the large claws to remove the meat. Carefully take out the meat of the tail and remove the black intestinal strip. Cut the lobster into bite-size pieces. Clean out the body cavities but save the green tomalley (liver). Place the shells in a large roasting pan.

Wash and trim the mushrooms and slice them quite thin. Place them in a saucepan with 2 tablespoons butter, lemon juice and water, bring the liquid to a boil, and simmer over moderate heat for 5 minutes. Drain the mushrooms and reserve the broth.

Drain the mussels and reserve the liquid. Chop them coarsely Heat the 3 tablespoons butter and stir in the flour. Add the mushroom broth and mussel juice. Stir until smooth. Add the cream and Madeira and stir until the sauce boils. Simmer 5 minutes. Add the mussels, mushrooms, parsley, and the lobster meat to the sauce. Mix well and season with salt and pepper. Fill the body and tail cavities with the mixture.

Sauté the bread crumbs in the remaining butter. Add the tomalley and toss with a fork over low heat until well mixed. Spread the mixture over the lobsters. Keep in the refrigerator. [When ready to cook, bake 30 minutes in a 350-degree oven. — P. H.] Serves 8.

SWEET TURNIP CHIPS

8 medium-sized white turnips	1 tablespoon sugar
4 tablespoons butter	½ teaspoon salt
2 cups chicken broth (homemade or canned)	⅛ teaspoon white pepper

Beforehand Preparation.

Pare the turnips and cut them into ⅛ inch slices with a very sharp knife. Place the turnips in a saucepan with the rest of the ingredients. The liquid should just cover the turnips. Cook the turnips over a high heat until almost all the liquid has disappeared. They should be tender but not mushy. Place the turnips in a shallow ovenproof vegetable dish.

Before the Guests Arrive.

Sprinkle the turnips with a little sugar and bake 30 minutes with roast turkey. Serves 8.

Paris Bistro Cookery

ALEXANDER WATT

THIS SLIM VOLUME is both a guidebook and a cookbook. Mr. Watt, who has made a life study, so to speak, of Paris bistros, has selected fifty of them and describes their specialties, their cellars and their peculiarities, i.e., when they are open, how many they accommodate, when they are apt to be crowded and what *types* frequent them. As a guidebook, certain allowances may have to be made for it, since changes do take place as the years go by. Since 1958 some of the little restaurants may have disappeared or lost character, but I know, from my own experience, that many still exist as described. As a cookbook, there need be no qualifications. Mr. Watt has extracted a couple of authentic recipes from each bistro chef and this, as anyone knows who has tried to do so, is no mean trick.

MOULES, FAÇON LUCIEN
(Mussels Lucien)

[To devotees of Moules Marinières, this recipe may seem like gilding the lily but, if one is lucky enough to live in a locality in which these marvelous shellfish are available, it is notably worth trying for a change. It is a specialty of Chez Lucien, a bistro near the Eiffel Tower. — P. H.]

4 pints mussels	1 tablespoon fresh cream
1 onion, finely chopped	Juice of 1 lemon
1 shallot, finely chopped	1 dessertspoon finely chopped pars-
6 parsley stalks, finely chopped	ley, chives, chervil, tarragon

3 tomatoes, peeled, seeded and finely chopped	Pinch pepper
½ cup dry white wine	Sauce Hollandaise

Scrape and brush the mussels well in several waters. Place them in a stewpan. Add the onion, shallot, parsley and wine. Cover the pan tightly and put it on a fast flame. After 2 minutes, shake the pan vigorously. Do this three times more during the cooking of the mussels, which should take only 5 or 6 minutes in all. The mussels should then be cooked and their shells wide open. Remove the mussels and keep hot. Leave the juices in the pan and prepare the

Sauce Hollandaise

3 egg yolks	Salt
1 teaspoon water	1 teaspoon lemon juice
1 cup butter	

Place the egg yolks and water in the top of a double boiler over hot but not boiling water. Whisk until creamy. Add the butter, bit by bit, whisking gently all the time. Season with a pinch of salt, add the lemon juice and strain through cheesecloth. Keep warm.

Pass the juice in the pan in which the mussels cooked through a fine sieve. Return to the rinsed pan, heat and pour in the cream. Bring to a boil, gently whisk, and allow to reduce by half. Heat the tomatoes in a small pan — to evaporate the water — and add to the stewpan. Remove from the fire and pour in the Hollandaise. Reheat but be careful the sauce does not approach the boiling point; otherwise it will turn. Add the lemon juice and pepper but no salt.

Remove the upper shell from each of the mussels and place the mussels on the bottom of 4 hot plates. Pour the sauce over the mussels and sprinkle with herbs. Serve at once.

[NOTE: As Mr. Watt points out in his introduction, most of these bistros' recipes are timed according to the use of copper pans. If you do not possess these he suggests heavy aluminum, and I suggest the coated ironware such as Le Creuset. The point is that the utensil must heat gradually and retain a steady, even, overall temperature. The cream, incidentally, must be heavy or whipping cream — especially if, as in this recipe, the sauce must be reduced. The use of a lighter cream may cause the sauce to turn. If you have your own method of making Hollandaise Sauce, you could use it here, but the amounts of butter, eggs and lemon juice should be as indi-cated. — P. H.]

RIS DE VEAU EN CROÛTE
(Sweetbreads in Crust)

[This recipe comes from Chez Pauline, which specializes in regional dishes from Burgundy. I fed it, several years ago, to a friend who is a Chevalier du Tastevin. He was enchanted, went away with the recipe, and it was served, with tremendous success, at the next dinner of the Chicago chapter. — P. H.]

6 sweetbreads	¼ cup dry white wine
Larding pork	½ cup water
1 large truffle	1 teaspoon tomato purée
1 onion, sliced	8 tablespoons butter
1 carrot, sliced	*beurre manié*
1 egg yolk	bouquet garni
4 tablespoons fresh cream	Salt, pepper
2 tablespoons port wine	Puff pastry

Prepare sufficient puff paste to wrap around each sweetbread.

Soak the sweetbreads in cold water, then blanch them in boiling, salted water for 7 minutes. Remove the membrane and tubes. Chop up the tubes and reserve. Lard the sweetbreads with strips of pork and small strips of truffle.

Place the carrot, onion and tubes in a heavy stewpan with 7 tablespoons butter. Cook for a few minutes, then salt and pepper the sweetbreads and add to the pan on top of the vegetables. Cover with a piece of buttered greaseproof paper and cook in a medium oven for 35 minutes. Remove the sweetbreads and keep hot.

Add the bouquet garni (bay leaf, thyme and parsley tied in cheesecloth), the white wine, water and tomato purée to the pan and cook, covered, for another 30 minutes. Remove from the oven. Pour in the port wine and cream, stirring well. Add a little *beurre manié* [NOTE: soft butter and an equal amount of flour mixed to a paste; use about a dessert spoonful], re-move the bouquet garni and pass the sauce through a sieve. Reheat the sauce but do not let it boil.

Wrap each sweetbread in pastry, brush with the yolk of egg and cook in a medium oven for 20 minutes or so, until the pastry is golden, crisp and cooked. Place on a hot serving dish and serve the sauce separately.

[NOTE: When the sweetbreads come from the braising pan, I put them briefly in a skillet with a little butter and sauté them so that they take on a little color. I think it makes them look more appetizing if the crust falls away from a forkful, and it certainly doesn't hurt the taste. I take a further liberty, if I am not in the mood for making puff paste, of rolling out frozen (thawed) patty shells, two to a sweetbread. Put a sweetbread on an oval of pastry, moisten the edges with cold water, cover with another oval, seal edges, scallop them and paint with egg yolk. It works extremely well. — P. H.]

II

Recipes from My Files

THESE RECIPES have come to me from many sources; some are gifts, others have been begged, borrowed or stolen. By "stolen" I don't mean that I have rifled a chef's master file in the dead of night or ripped a page out of a friend's notebook at high noon, nor have I knowingly taken a recipe from a published book without acknowledgment. But when, as in the case of Strawberries Liberté or Crêpes Fabien, I give a recipe without having received exact instructions or express permission of the chef, I consider it a mild form of theft. As for the few orphans whose parentage I am unable to trace, having omitted to make notes at the time — these *may* have been stolen and, if so, I apologize.

ARTICHOKES WITH A PURÉE OF OYSTERS
FROM THE FORUM OF THE TWELVE CAESARS

Everything at this fine New York restaurant is just a little larger than life with the exception of the kitchen. This is surprisingly compact but so well designed that Chef Freddie Rutracht can see to it that his cheerful and efficient staff of sous-chef, sauciers, grill cooks and so forth can cope with a capacity crowd of 180 people with alacrity as well as perfection. Preparation of the foods in general is deliberately unusual, but flavor is never sacrificed to the bizarre. This sauce, served in the de-choked center of a large, hot artichoke, is a case in point, a conversation piece which is marvelous to taste.

1 teaspoon chopped shallot	1 doz. oysters with juice
1 clove minced garlic	1 cup heavy cream
2 teaspoons minced onion	2 tablespoons arrowroot or corn-
1 oz. butter	starch
1 teaspoon curry powder	Lemon juice
1 oz. dry sherry	Salt, white pepper, Aćcent

Lightly sauté the shallot, garlic and onion in the butter until soft but not brown. Add the curry powder and the sherry and simmer until slightly reduced.

Put the oysters and their juice through the finest blade of the meat grinder or give them 30 seconds in an electric blender. Add to the simmering sauce and bring again to a boil. Simmer for only a minute or two and add the cream. Simmer for another minute or two. Mix the arrowroot or cornstarch with 2 tablespoons cold water and add, stirring, bit by bit. Since arrowroot or cornstarch thickens liquid instantly, you can tell when you have added enough. Thin to the desired "dunking" consistency with lemon juice, or, if you prefer, a little light cream, or both. Season to taste with salt, white pepper and Accent.

Serves 6.

BARQUETTES DE CONCOMBRES NEUFCHÂTEL: A POSTILION RECIPE

Madame Liane Kuony was born in Brussels of a Dutch mother and a French father, both of whom were gourmets. She studied culinary art and interior design in Belgium, France and Switzerland. About fourteen years ago, after extensive traveling in Europe and this country, she and her husband bought a lovely, hundred-year-old house near Fond du Lac, Wisconsin, and started a little French restaurant known as the Postilion. They preferred the Anglicized spelling for the sake of pronunciation. Here, in the intimate atmosphere reminiscent of European inns, they served wonderful French food for six months of the year. During the winter, Madame devoted herself to her many other pursuits and to bringing up her family. At present she is conducting a school of Classic Cooking at the Postilion and the restaurant is only open on special occasions for private dinners. This recipe for Barquettes de Concombres Neufchâtel was one of the *plats de réception* served at a recent dinner given there by the Confréries des Chevaliers du Tastevin, a dinner, incidentally, about which the Chicago Chevaliers are still talking.

For six:

12 4″ pickling gherkins (rough-skinned cucumbers) plus 2 more gherkins for chopping up	½ teaspoon dill (preferably fresh)
1 pint rich chicken stock	2 tablespoons grated Neufchâtel or imported Gruyère cheese
2 tablespoons butter	1 egg yolk
2 tablespoons flour	½ cup heavy cream

Scoop out shallowly 12 gherkins which have been peeled. Remove the seeds from the "meat" you take out, and reserve the latter. Whittle the gherkins down to the shape of Indian canoes and cut slices from the undersides so that the canoes will not tip over. Cut the reserved meat and that of the 2 extra gherkins into miniscule dice. You should have 1 heaping cup of diced gherkins for the 12 barquettes.

Put the barquettes in a saucepan that is large enough to just hold them without overlapping if they are closely placed on the bottom. Poach the barquettes in the chicken stock until they gently resist the pressure of a fork and until the edges are transparent. Remove and drain. Keep warm between 2 linen towels which have been rinsed in hot water and wrung very dry.

Take just enough of the poaching stock to cover the diced gherkins and cook these just long enough to take away any taste of rawness while still retaining their crispness. It is essential that you use a small amount of the stock for this so that you can observe what happens. In the meantime, boil down the remaining poaching liquid to a little less than a cup. Melt the butter and stir in the flour. When the roux is smooth, add the reduced stock, stirring until slightly thickened. Then add the diced gherkins and their stock, the dill and cheese and just cook long enough for the cheese to begin to thread.

Turn off the fire and add the egg yolk, beaten slightly, and added to the cream. Adjust for seasoning.

Take the barquettes and make sure that the cavities are thoroughly dry before filling them. Put under the grill until just palely gilded.

Serve two barquettes per person.

CONSOMMÉ STRACCIATELLA MILANESE

When I lived in Chicago my favorite restaurant there was the Imperial House, and this recipe was given me by my friend, Max Guggieri, the *padrone*. Having first tried the soup as is, add a pinch of nutmeg to the cheese sometime and see how you like it.

2 eggs	2 tablespoons freshly grated Parmesan cheese
Pinch salt	
2 tablespoons semolina or Cream of Wheat	4 cups beef or chicken consommé

Into a mixing bowl break 2 eggs. Add a pinch of salt, the semolina or Cream of Wheat and the cheese. Whip all ingredients thoroughly. Add 1 cup cold consommé. Meanwhile, heat the other 3 cups of consommé. When this comes to a boil, slowly pour in the egg mixture, and simmer for 5 minutes, stirring constantly. In this way you obtain little light flakes floating in clear consommé. Serve in consommé cups and pass grated Parmesan cheese.

Serves 4-5.

JIM BEARD'S COUNTRY PÂTÉ

Jim serves this typical French *pâté de campagne* sliced thin with hot buttered toast.

1 lb. each ground beef, pork and chicken or pork liver	¼ teaspoon each nutmeg and ginger
3 cloves garlic, finely chopped	Pinch powdered cloves
1 teaspoon thyme	3 eggs
1 teaspoon freshly ground black pepper	½ cup finely chopped parsley
1 medium onion chopped fine	¼ cup Cognac
	Salt pork or bacon strips

Combine all ingredients except salt pork or bacon and mix thoroughly. Pack into a well-buttered 1 quart baking dish or mold. Cover with pork or bacon strips. Bake at 350 degrees in a pan of hot water for 1½ hours. Remove from oven and place a weight on the pâté while it cools. Chill and unmold on a bed of greens.

CRÊPES WITH SMOKED SALMON FABIEN

Fabien, on the Rue Duret, is one of the nicest restaurants in Paris. It is not listed in the Guide Michelin, but if it were, it would deserve a star or two rather than a set of crossed cutlery. Perhaps it is just as well that it is not listed; enough people who know good food find their way to this modestly elegant little place so that it is always busy enough but is never uncomfortably crowded. If there is an empty table or two, it is there that the season's specialties are displayed: the *écrevisses,* the big, white asparagus or the *fraises de bois.* This is a fabulous first course with which to begin a light meal.

Make 2 of the lightest buckwheat pancakes possible for each serving. These should be ¼ inch thick and about the size of an American griddle cake. (In fact, you can use a mix.) Keep them warm.

Have enough thinly sliced smoked salmon to cover, generously, 1 pancake per person. Have enough clarified butter heating to afford at least 2 tablespoons per serving.

Also have ready a bowl of half whipped cream and half sour cream or, preferably, one of Crème Fraîche, the recipe for which is to be found among the recipes from *Mastering the Art of French Cooking.* (See index.)

To serve, make sandwiches, so to speak, of the pancakes and salmon. Pour 2 tablespoons hot butter over each and cover with cream, about ½ to ¾ cup per serving.

CURRY CREAM

My acquisition of this recipe is an example of the odd ways in which these things happen. A friend of mine in Chicago gave a dinner party to which a mutual friend was invited. Next day the mutual friend called to say that our friend, his hostess, had served a wonderful, pale yellow, creamy sort of thing for a first course. It had tasted delicately of curry and he thought I should find out about it. I called Francie at once and she promptly and happily gave me the recipe which follows.

You can make it in a ring mold, put chutney in the center and serve it as a first course, as she did, or you can put it in a shallow bowl, unmold it on a plate and surround it with sesame seed wafers as the main attraction at a cocktail party. This amount will serve

8 as a first course. I usually make it in double quantity for a cocktail party, since experience has taught me that people lap it up.

1 envelope unflavored gelatin	Yolks of 6 hard-boiled eggs
2½ cups hot, clear chicken broth	Curry powder to taste

Soften the gelatin in ½ cup cold water. Dissolve it in the chicken broth. Put broth, egg yolks and 1 teaspoon curry powder in an electric blender. Blend for 30 seconds. Taste and add more curry powder if desired. Place in an oiled mold and chill overnight or for at least 4-5 hours.

CRÈME DE TORTUE
(Cream of Turtle Soup)

This lovely soup is the creation of René Valdenaire, presently executive chef of the Mid-America Club in Chicago. When he wrote out the recipe for me he appended this special note: "This Crème de Tortue can be *only as good* as the turtle soup that goes into it." Now you and I are going to use canned soup, so the thing to do is to get the very best brand. As I remember, there were not bits of turtle meat in René's brew but I like to add it, cut in julienne strips.

2½ pints green turtle soup	⅓ pint heavy cream
6 egg yolks	3 ounces butter

Beat the egg yolks with the cream. Add to very hot turtle soup, whipping until it is thick and foamy. Do not let it boil or it will curdle. Take from fire and add 3 ounces soft butter.

Serves 8.

EMPANADAS SALTENAS

This recipe is the gift of Señora de Caballero Tamayo of Bolivia, talented wife of that country's Ambassador to the United Nations.

It is for a favorite Bolivian dish that varies from family to family and which, in this case, has been handed down from one generation to the next but has never before been made public. It is generally served as a main course, but Señora de Caballero Tamayo has also found it a happy solution when something substantial is indicated during the prolonged cocktail hour that often precedes large dinners.

Prepare the filling the day or night before:

1½ lbs. top round steak cut in ½″ cubes	1 teaspoon salt
	½ teaspoon ground cumin
1 lb. potatoes cut in ½″ cubes	2 tablespoons chopped parsley
1 cup peas	1 teaspoon oregano
2 cups finely chopped onions	1 teaspoon prepared mustard
1 tablespoon *aji* (hot ground red pepper; see Note)	1 tablespoon Worcestershire Sauce
	4 cups beef consommé (hot)
½ cup sugar	2 envelopes unflavored gelatin

Parboil potatoes and peas separately. Brown the onion and cook until tender. Dissolve the red pepper in ½ cup water. Add cumin and pour into the onions. Add sugar and salt.

In a big bowl mix the drained potatoes and peas, the meat (raw), the onion mixture, the parsley, oregano, mustard, Worcestershire Sauce and the consommé in which the gelatin has been dissolved. Mix well and chill.

For the pastry:

8 cups flour	1 tablespoon *achiote* or *oruco* seeds (see Note)
1 lb. vegetable shortening	
½ cup sugar	
1½ cups water mixed with 1 teaspoon salt	

The *achiote* or *oruco* seeds are used to color the dough, which should be a deep yellow. Fry them in 1 tablespoon of shortening and strain, reserving the colored oil. Keep it hot.

Mix the flour with the sugar. Heat the shortening and pour over the flour and sugar, adding the oil from frying the seeds. Mix thoroughly with the flour and then add the water and salt, which has been warmed. Knead until the dough is smooth. Work while everything is still warm. Cut into pieces and roll into approximately 2-inch balls. With a rolling pin, flatten the balls until you have a stack of round, very thin pastries.

Before filling the pastries have ready:

4 hard-cooked eggs, sliced	1 6-ounce can black ripe olives,
4 oz. seedless raisins, soaked in water and drained	pitted

Put a tablespoon of the filling crosswise on each pastry round, adding 1 thin slice of egg, 3 raisins and 1 olive. Moisten the edges of the pastry with water, bring the edges together and seal them, rolling them with your thumb so that the closing looks like twisted rope. The finished pastry should resemble a slightly deflated football laced from one end to the other across the top.

Bake in a preheated 400-degree oven until golden brown and serve immediately. Fifty empanadas.

[NOTE: the *aji* and the *achiote* or *oruco* seeds may be obtained from a Puerto Rican grocery store. Cayenne pepper could be substituted for the pepper and you *could* use vegetable coloring for the dough. — P. H.]

ICED TOMATO AND DILL SOUP ELSTON

Friends in California sent me the recipe for this cold soup, and I find it a welcome change from Vichyssoise, Jellied Madrilène and other run-of-the-mill summer soups. The only catch is fresh dill, without which it cannot be accomplished. So, if you do not boast an herb garden or if your grocer does not occasionally post a small sign saying "Fresh Dill," as mine does, you are out of luck.

2 lbs. ripe tomatoes	3 cups water
¼ cup tomato paste	½ cup finely chopped fresh dill
2 medium onions	1½ cups heavy cream
4 tablespoons vegetable oil	Salt, pepper
6 tablespoons rice flour	

Skin 2 tomatoes and set aside. Cut the rest into fine slices. Chop the onions finely and sauté in the oil 5-6 minutes. Add the tomato slices, salt and pepper. Cook very slowly until quite soft. Add the tomato paste and remove from fire. Mix the flour with the water and stir into the first mixture. (Arrowroot flour or cornstarch may be used instead of rice flour.) Stir over medium heat, until boiling. Rub through a fine sieve, add nearly all the dill and chill.

Garnish with the skinned tomatoes, quartered, pipped and shredded. Serve in individual bowls, surrounded with crushed ice. On top of each serving put 1 tablespoon of whipped cream previously mixed with the remaining dill. Serves 6-8.

REMEJEK: A JAVANESE COCKTAIL TIDBIT

Madame Dinar Siagian, born in North Sumatra and raised in Djakarta, is now living in New York where her husband is in the diplomatic service. She is a superb cook and hostess and has a remarkable talent for entertaining all ranks and nationalities in the rather cramped confines of a small apartment. It goes without saying that charm, tact and linguistic ability help to make this possible. She very graciously gave me this recipe for delicious, crisp little hors d'oeuvres. They are popular all over Indonesia, where they are sometimes made with soy beans instead of fresh peanuts.

1 cup coconut milk (see below)	2 tablespoons all-purpose flour
½ cup rice flour (or arrowroot flour or cornstarch)	½ teaspoon garlic powder
	½ teaspoon powdered coriander
½ cup fresh peanuts, shelled, skinned and opened into halves	Salt to taste
	Peanut or vegetable oil for frying

To make the coconut milk put 1 can flaked coconut or 1 package grated coconut (unsweetened) into a saucepan with 1⅓ cups water or milk. Bring to a boil and simmer until the liquid foams, about 2 minutes. Strain. Or . . .

Put the flaked or grated coconut with liquid into an electric blender first and blend for 15 seconds. Then proceed as above. This gives a slightly stronger coconut taste. Or . . .

Do as Madame Siagian does and put the chopped meat of a large coconut in the blender with sufficient water to cover. Blend for 30 seconds and strain into a bowl, pressing the coconut with the back of a wooden spoon.

Mix the coconut milk thoroughly with all other ingredients, adding them one at a time and mixing after each addition. Drop by tablespoonfuls into deep, hot oil and fry until brown, turning several times. Drain on absorbent paper.

This makes about 12 Remejek.

SHAD ROE RING

Personally, I deplore ring molds. I have no idea why; perhaps I was frightened by one as a child. At any rate I do not own one; and when I make a recipe such as this, I use either a shallow bowl or individual molds and serve the sauce on the side. In whatever shape it is molded, this is a superior first course — a gift from a friend in Kentucky.

1 7¾ oz. can shad roe	1 teaspoon salt
½ cup cold water	1 tablespoon lemon juice
1½ tablespoons gelatin, or 2 if the weather is hot	1 cup mayonnaise
	½ cup sour cream
1 10½ oz. can clear chicken consommé	1 small cucumber
	Watercress
¾ cup water or vegetable stock	

Drain the roe, remove the skin and separate the eggs with a fork. Pour ½ cup cold water in a bowl and sprinkle with gelatin. Let stand. Combine the consommé, water or vegetable stock and salt in a saucepan. Bring to a boil. Pour into the soaked gelatin and stir until the gelatin is dissolved. Cool. Add the lemon juice and ½ cup mayonnaise, beating as you do so. Add roe, mix lightly and let stand in the refrigerator if the kitchen is hot, otherwise in a cool place. Stir occasionally until the mixture has thickened sufficiently to keep the roe from settling to the bottom. Turn into a 1 quart ring mold, rinsed in cold water (or into a bowl or individual molds) and chill for 5-6 hours. Unmold and garnish with watercress. For the sauce, mix ½ cup mayonnaise with ½ cup sour cream and add the cucumber, peeled, seeded and diced.

Serves 6.

Note: Fresh shad roe may, of course, be used. Poach a pair in simmering water (salted) in a shallow pan for 15 minutes. Drain and proceed as above.

SHRIMP JAY DE LAVAL

As I have said before, recipes come to a cookbook writer in curious ways. A friend in Acapulco, who had always seemed utterly disinterested in both food and cooking, sent this one to me with the laconic inscription, "Recipe from a famous chef, Jay de Laval." I was never able to find out from my friend who Mr. de Laval was, where he had been a chef or how it happened that she had acquired the recipe. Eventually I lost touch with her but the recipe was tried and found definitely commendable, and here it is as I received it. My alterations or suggestions are in parentheses:

Peel, devein and sauté in (½ cup) butter until pink (4-5 minutes) 3 lbs. shrimp. Set aside.

Put in a saucepan 5 cloves crushed garlic (or less, according to your taste), 2 tablespoons sweet butter, 1 teaspoon chopped tarragon, 1 teaspoon chopped parsley and cook — but not until brown (5 minutes over low heat). Add ½ cup white vinegar and reduce (over low heat) until thick. Add 1 pint dry white wine and reduce until it does not smell strong (about 10-15 minutes over low heat). Add 1 quart heavy cream and boil 5 minutes. (I think 1½ pints of cream are sufficient.) Strain.

If sauce is not the consistency of thick cream, thicken with a little cornstarch mixed with sherry. (A scant tablespoon cornstarch mixed with ¼ cup cold, dry sherry or water.)

Put shrimp in an au gratin dish, pour sauce over, sprinkle with chopped chives and put under the broiler until heated through and slightly browned.

(Serves 8 as a first course.)

STRAWBERRIES LIBERTÉ

The Club Alabam, in Chicago, is one of the oldest night clubs in the country. It started, of course, as a speakeasy and is one of the few such places to survive Repeal. Neither the decor (hand-painted murals and a ceiling arrangement of colored lights and artificial flowers) nor the type of entertainment (red-hot mamas belting out the blues) has changed since the place opened, but in 1958 there was a startling change in the kitchen.

The club hired a young Polish chef–and–maître d'hôtel and ventured, with surprising success, into the world of *haute cuisine*. Word got around, and the carriage trade flocked to sample the specialties they'd heard about. Wearing a ruffled white shirt with his dinner jacket, the young man performed at a wheeled cart beside your table. His staff of attendant waiters was superbly trained. With the precision of skilled O.R. nurses, they slipped sharp knives into the master's hand. Ingredients and partially readied dishes were whisked from the kitchen at exactly the correct moment. Spotlighted by two goosenecked lamps, Mr. C., with incredible speed and expertise, sliced mushrooms paper thin without deigning to give them a glance, made a sauce for a Chateaubriand that involved putting pieces of rare beef through a duck press, skewered and broiled a fine, chunky Shish Kebab or flamed a very unusual chicken. These strawberries were his preprandial specialty and they are surprisingly good:

Select the biggest, firmest ripe strawberries available. Cut a small slice from the tip so that the berry may stand upright.

With a demitasse spoon or a narrow, sharp knife or both, hollow out the stem end of each berry and fill the cavities with fresh caviar. Stand each berry on a slice of lime and sprinkle with vodka.

The very smallest glass jar of caviar will take care of 6 large strawberries.

JIM BEARD'S TAPÉNADE

Whether puréed or chopped, Tapénade does not look as attractive as it tastes. When Mr. Beard serves it at a party in his colorful Greenwich Village kitchen (the classroom for his cooking school) he does not attempt to prettify it. However, for a large cocktail party at a food convention when I assisted him he added mayonnaise, which made the mixture more appealing to the eyes of the uninitiated and tasted good besides. It was served as a dip for raw vegetables and bread sticks.

1 lb. black olives, Italian or Greek ones, finely chopped	12 oz. capers, drained and finely chopped
12 oz. anchovy fillets, finely chopped	1 cup parsley, chopped and blended with
7 oz. tuna fish, crumbled	2 quarts homemade mayonnaise
½ cup Cognac	

Mix all ingredients thoroughly. Serve at room temperature. A slightly different version of Tapénade may be found in the group of recipes from Craig Claiborne's *An Herb and Spice Cook Book*, page 77.

A RECIPE AND AN IDEA FROM THE FERTILE IMAGINATION OF HELEN McCULLY

When I first told my friend Helen McCully that I wanted to include something of hers in this collection, she sent along two original recipes and a revolutionary idea for me to try. One of the recipes and "the idea" have an important culinary maneuver in common: switching the main ingredient of a dish from one kind of food to another. This is the sort of thing that is more often attempted by male than by female cooks, but when someone on the distaff side boasts an adventuresome spirit combined with experience (Miss McCully was food editor of *McCall's* for thirteen years) she can, and does, do it. In the recipe, Miss McCully transforms

Vitello Tonnato into Pollo Tonnato by substituting chicken for veal; in "the idea," she suggests using tuna fish instead of chicken livers in your favorite recipe for pâté. In case you do not have a favorite pâté recipe, I have taken the liberty of giving you mine with Helen's idea incorporated therein.

The second recipe is the lady's by-guess-or-by-God attempt to reproduce an apple confection she encountered in France — and an eminently successful attempt it is. The apples look as enchanting as they taste, and the dish is a great improvement on applesauce even if the latter has been made with loving care. You will come across this recipe a little later on among the desserts. (See Helen McCully's Apple Slices in index.)

Pollo Tonnato

1 5-6 lb. fowl	Pinch thyme
1 large onion, sliced	3 or 4 peppercorns
1 can anchovy fillets (8-10)	Chicken broth (clear)
2 large glasses white wine	Sauce: 1 pint mayonnaise
2 cloves garlic, sliced	lemon juice
1 carrot, cut up	capers
4 stalks celery with tops	

Place fowl in a large, heavy kettle with all ingredients and enough chicken broth to almost cover. Bring to a boil slowly, then reduce heat and simmer, covered until the bird is tender. Allow to cool in the broth. It is preferable to do this a day ahead of time. No salt is added, incidentally. The anchovies will have taken care of that. When the fowl is cool, remove from stock, put stock back on high heat and cook down until you have about 1 pint of liquor. Strain and chill this.

Strip meat from the bones in fairly large pieces, discarding skin and all connecting tissue. Chill.

To make the sauce, add the juice of 1 lemon to the mayonnaise and then enough of the chilled stock to make a smooth sauce that is the consistency of a thin cream sauce. Arrange the chicken on a platter or on individual plates and sprinkle with drained capers. Spoon the sauce over it. Garnish with parsley and sliced tomatoes if desired. Serve extra sauce on the side.

Serves 10-12 as a first course, 8 as an entrée.

Tuna Fish Pâté

1 7¾ oz. can tuna fish in oil	Pinch of cayenne pepper
2 tablespoons grated onion	¼ teaspoon dry mustard
½ cup unsalted butter, softened	⅛ teaspoon powdered cloves

Put the tuna fish through the finest blade of the meat grinder three times, add remaining ingredients and blend well *or* put all ingredients in an electric blender. Pack into a crock or jar and refrigerate for at least 12 hours. This makes about 1 cup of pâté.

MY GAZPACHO ANDALUZ

There are countless recipes for this Spanish soup-salad. This, according to incontrovertible evidence, is how it is made at the Ritz Hotel in Madrid.

1 clove garlic	Salt, cumin, cayenne pepper
½ teaspoon olive oil	Dash Worcestershire Sauce
1 small cucumber, seeded and chopped	1 hard roll soaked in 2 cups water
4 tomatoes, quartered	1 teaspoon wine vinegar
1 small green pepper, seeded and chopped	1 pint light cream

Garnish: seeded and chopped tomatoes, cucumbers, green peppers; toasted and buttered croutons.

Put the first five items through the finest blade of the meat grinder. Repeat 4 or 5 times. Add seasoning to taste. Add the bread and water and beat, with a rotary beater, until smooth. Add the vinegar and cream. Chill. Serve in small pottery bowls topped with the garnish.

Serves 4.

STUFFED PEPPERS FELESIA

A friend of mine who spoke very little Spanish had a Mexican cook who spoke even less English. Fortunately, the whole family liked

Mexican food, so Felesia was given free rein in the kitchen. She did not object to being watched as she cooked, and my friend was able to learn how to make a great many dishes by keeping her eyes open and a pencil and paper handy. This one may be served as an hors d'oeuvre, a luncheon entrée or as a salad accompanying cold meat or fowl. The proportions are difficult to specify since the size of peppers and avocados varies. One small avocado will suffice for one medium-sized pepper, however.

Choose the long, thin variety of peppers which may be red or green. Hold them over a low flame, turning them until they blister. Put them in a paper bag in a moderate oven to steam for 10 minutes. Take them out and when they are cool enough to handle, skin them, cut off one end and remove the pulp through the opening. Chill the peppers until ready to use.

Mash the avocados and season them to taste with minced onion. Stuff the peppers, whole, with the avocado mixture, cover them with sour cream and garnish with slices of Spanish onion which have been marinated in a true French dressing (3 parts olive oil, 1 part vinegar, salt and pepper) for 2 hours.

TRANCHE OF SMOKED STURGEON WITH CAVIAR "FOUR SEASONS"

This was first prepared by Albert Stockli, of the Four Seasons Restaurant in New York, for a Chevaliers du Tastevin dinner given at that restaurant in New York in December 1962. It is a marriage made in heaven, a miraculous though expensive combination. If you cannot find a fish man who has the kind of sturgeon that he can slice transparently thin in fairly large pieces, however, don't attempt to make it. Break open the piggy bank and go have it at the Four Seasons.

Spread each slice of sturgeon with fresh caviar and cover with another slice of sturgeon. (You should be able to see the caviar through the fish.) Scatter a few scraps of peeled and seeded cucumber, sliced as thinly as possible, over the top of each portion and sprinkle with the sieved yolk of a hard-cooked egg. Flank with thinly sliced dark Polish rye bread spread with unsalted butter.

Lemon wedges may accompany the dish, but I do not find the extra flavor necessary.

Serve ice cold and drink vodka or aquavit! And live!

MA HAWLEY'S CODFISH BALLS

With the exception of two unforgettable experiences, one of which involved this recipe, I have always been rabidly anti-codfish. This may be heresy to many people, but there it is; be it fresh or salted, in Norway or in France, it normally leaves me cold. I can even walk away from the much-touted Brandade de Morue.

Once upon a time, however, I had codfish balls — My husband (who was equally anti-cod) and I were spending the weekend in New England at the home of a college classmate of mine whose mother was — and still is — a great cook. On Sunday morning we came down to breakfast in Ma Hawley's big, sunny kitchen and found that lady frying things. "You're in for a treat," she announced happily. "You're going to have my famous codfish balls." With sinking hearts, not daring to look at each other, we sat down and made appropriate noises. Presently we were each given a plateful of spikey, golden-brown objects. They looked pretty, but pretty is as pretty does, so they say. Reluctantly we bit one for politeness' sake and went right on biting through two helpings.

We often talked of that breakfast but I never tried to duplicate it, taking it for granted that I'd not be able to. Recently, while compiling this book, I wrote my friend and asked for the recipe. She sent it and I tried it, albeit with averted eyes, so to speak. To my vast surprise, I came up with Ma Hawley's codfish balls, spikey, golden brown and indescribably good. Here is the recipe, in my friend's inimitable style:

Get a *wooden box* of dried salt cod fillets. [NOTE: This is important; no other codfish will do. The fillets are put out by Salt Water Farms, Damariscotta, Maine, and by the Davis Fish Co., Gloucester, Massachusetts. — P. H.]

Peel and cut into ¾ inch cubes enough potatoes to make 2 cups. Soak fish in cold water for 2 hours. Cut enough fish in chunks like the potatoes to make 1 cup. Boil *together* until potatoes are tender. Drain *thoroughly*. Whip up very well and add 1 well-beaten egg, a little pepper (no salt, needless to say). If you want to be neat, form into croquette shapes but we think it is better simply taken up by large kitchen spoonfuls and dropped, unshaped, into hot, deep fat. I can't tell you the temperature of the fat because Ma says "hot enough." [NOTE: 375 degrees — P. H.]

Fry until brown. You do not roll them or dip them in anything at all before frying.

Make them fresh not long before cooking or they are lousy. If you increase the recipe by more than 50%, add another whole egg.

When the mixture is dropped into the fat by spoonfuls, there are little tiny points of crispness all over them — that is why we prefer the rough surface to a smooth croquette.

BACALAO A LA PAMPLONA

A small group of congenial souls sped the last unmourned hours of 1963 in Mary Hemingway's unfinished doll's house on the top of one of New York's apartment buildings. We crouched around a low cocktail table in front of a little Franklin fireplace (the dining table had not yet arrived) and happily spooned up this aromatic soup-stew, dunking crusty bread in the last of the broth and drinking a venerable white Rioja. When we had finished the salad, cheese, fruitcake and coffee, which followed, we were each given twelve big blue grapes which the Spanish call wine in capsules. According to European tradition, one eats a grape on each stroke of the clock at midnight on New Year's Eve. Champagne was poured into handblown Murano goblets that Mary had designed for the lost Hemingway Finca in Cuba, and we hopefully toasted 1964. This is how Mary made the Bacalao and how I had my second pleasant experience with codfish.

Put 1 lb. package of frozen salt codfish in a strainer and allow hot water to run over it from the tap until no saltiness is left. Feel it carefully as it thaws and remove any bones.

Slice 3 small onions or 1 large one and 1 or more cloves of garlic. Slice the contents of a small jar of pimientos into thin strips. Wash 6 cherry tomatoes. Chop finely 2 stalks celery. Seed 1 green pepper and slice it into thin strips.

Heat about 4 tablespoons olive oil in a cast iron or earthenware pot, add the vegetables and cook, very slowly, covered. When the vegetables are soft, add the codfish, season to taste with oregano and marjoram and simmer, covered, for 40 minutes. Five minutes before the end of the cooking add 1 lb. each of fresh frozen lobster and shrimp.

Serves 4-6.

TWO SPANISH RECIPES BY PAULA LAURENCE

Once upon a time I was doing a magazine article and needed some Spanish recipes for a Twelfth Night Supper party. I called my friend, Paula Laurence, the actress, who is half Spanish and a fine cook. She came through in great style and tossed in a couple of dividends which I liked. This recipe is one and the following Pescados a la Espanola is the other.

Langostinos Salteados a la Catalana
(Lobsters Sautéed à la Catalana)

2 lobsters, 1½ lbs. each	½ cup white wine
4 tablespoons vegetable or olive oil	3 tablespoons tomato sauce
1 medium onion	Salt, pepper
Garlic to taste	3 or 4 sprigs parsley

Remove meat from shells and claws of boiled lobster. Brown in the hot oil in a deep frying pan or chafing dish. Add the onion, finely chopped, the garlic, chopped or put through a press, and 3 or 4 sprigs of cut parsley. Season well with salt and pepper and add the wine and tomato sauce. (The latter may be your own or canned.) Heat through and serve.

Serves 2.

Pescados a la Espanola

4 small trout or 2 lbs. of any filleted white fish, such as sole	½ cup white wine
	Oil
4-5 mushrooms	1 tablespoon chopped parsley
1 tablespoon chopped chives	Salt, pepper
4-5 shallots or scallions	Ground cumin
1 or 2 tablespoons honey	½ cup melted butter

Oil a casserole large enough so that the fish may lie side by side in it. Make a bed of the shallots and chives. Place fish upon this and cover with sliced mushrooms and the parsley. Season with salt, pepper and a sprinkling of cumin. Pour the wine over the fish and dribble with honey and melted butter. Cover with aluminum foil and bake in a moderate oven until fish flakes easily. Serve with a little more melted butter.

Serves 4.

MARY HEMINGWAY'S CURRY

It is Mary Hemingway's contention, with which not everyone agrees, that a respectable curry should, with the first bite, cause tiny beads of perspiration to burst out just beneath your eyes. This cannot be accomplished with commercial curry powder, no matter how much you use. From Indian friends in London during the last war she learned, before rationing became severe, how to make authentic curry. This meant starting from scratch by grinding her own spices with mortar and pestle. It is a well-known fact, of course, that there is the same superiority of aroma in freshly ground spices as there is in that of freshly ground coffee, which accounts for the special flavor of the curries one gets in India or in fine Indian restaurants here or in Europe. However, if you are lazy or pressed for time but still would like to try a hot curry, you can approximate true curry powder by using a good brand of powdered spices and mixing your own. These are the amounts for the basic recipe which is designed to serve 4-6 people.

1 tablespoon each powdered:

cinnamon	cardamom
nutmeg	coriander
mace	ginger
turmeric	cumin

1 teaspoon each:
    red pepper (Chili Pequins — squashed)
    Ceylon cloves (powdered)

For a shrimp curry, Mary suggests a trifle more cardamom because of its lemony flavor; for chicken curry, use a little more nutmeg and cinnamon; for lamb curry, use plenty of turmeric, less cardamom and lots of ginger.

To make the curry, toast the powder in a large iron skillet, stirring with a wooden spoon. There should be ½ inch of powder in the pan. Have the heat low and toast for about 4-5 minutes, until the powder is steaming and "the house is fragrant with the aroma." Blend in ½ teaspoon sugar. Moisten with 1 stick (¼ lb.) unsalted butter and 1 cup of liquid, which may be water or fish, chicken, lamb or beef stock, depending on what you are currying. Add 3 cups of fish, poultry or meat cut in any desired size pieces. Simmer over a very low fire so that the curry can penetrate the other ingredient. Serve with rice and chutney. Bombay duck, which goes wonderfully with fish but not so well with lamb or beef, should be toasted until dry in the oven and then crumbled and either sprinkled on the curry or served on the side. This recipe makes a rather dry curry. More liquid may be added if desired.

CHICKEN HÉLÈNE

It is always gratifying when a dinner guest asks for the recipe for a dish that you have cooked, and it is particularly so when the dish in question is your own invention. This was the case with the following recipe, and I wouldn't be at all surprised if my asking for it was not largely responsible for a pleasant acquaintanceship turning into a firm friendship. That's the way things happen.

Skin, bone and trim six half breasts of chicken. Brown carefully on both sides in hot butter. Pour over 2 tablespoons flaming sherry. Remove chicken, add 1 tablespoon butter to the pan and in it sauté ¾ lb. mushrooms which have been washed, dried and stemmed. Remove the mushrooms and stir in 2 tablespoons flour. Add 1½ cups chicken broth and ¼ cup dry white wine. Stir until boiling. Put the chicken in a casserole with the mushrooms and pour the sauce over all. Cover with wax paper and a lid and cook in a 325-degree oven until chicken is tender. Spread with about 6 tablespoons Hollandaise Sauce and brown for a minute or two under the broiler.
Serves 6.

CHICKEN IN CHAMPAGNE SAUCE
CAFÉ CHAUVERON

When the proprietor of a restaurant is constantly on hand to supervise his kitchen and his dining room and when he may be observed popping in and out of his establishment as early as 9 A.M. to scan the busy street for an anticipated truckload of meat or vegetables, you can be reasonably certain that this is a place where one dines well. Roger Chauveron is such a proprietor. After many years as a successful restaurateur in New York, he went home to France and tried to retire. As so often happens, when a man is dedicated to his chosen profession, he was unable to do so. He came back, fortunately for us, and soon the quietly elegant Café Chauveron took its rightful place among the handful of truly excellent restaurants in Manhattan. If the prices seem high you must remember that one does not shop for rhinestones at Cartier's. This is a Cartier sort of place; one goes there for diamonds and diamonds are what one gets. What's more, Roger Chauveron is on the alert to see that the jewels are flawless and brilliantly set. It was difficult for me to decide what recipe to ask for as an example of M. Chauveron's artistry. Should it be the Quenelles de Brochet, Sauce Nantua? The Moules à la Crème? The snails which are served with the exact amount of garlic that the individual desires? Finally I decided on the Chicken in Champagne Sauce, and I beg you not to substitute any other liquors for the ones stipulated, in particular the white port. The blend of these 3 flavors is the secret of the sauce.

2 3 lb. chickens, cut up	½ lb. butter
⅓ cup white port wine	2 oz. brandy
4 oz. dry champagne or dry white wine	3 cups light cream
	1 cup thick cream sauce

Sauté chicken in butter. When it is lightly browned, season with salt and pepper and cover. Cook slowly for 25 minutes.

Remove the pieces of chicken and pour off the cooked butter. Bring to a boil the brandy, port wine and champagne; simmer for 5 minutes. This will make a sauce. Then add the thick cream sauce and the fresh light cream. Cook over a hot fire for 6 minutes, stirring constantly. Do not boil any more.

Put the chicken back in sauce, simmer for 5 minutes. It is now ready to be served.

Boiled rice or wild rice can be served with the chicken.

Serves 4.

POULET HENRI IV

When M. Max Blouet was presiding over the Ambassador Hotels in Chicago, he proffered this recipe to the Wine and Food Society, and a member of the latter forwarded it to me. It is presented in the special, undetailed language in which one knowledgeable food man describes a dish to another. The parentheses, therefore, are mine — in order to clarify matters to the less initiated.

Take a young hen for stewing (a 4-5 lb. fowl). Remove heart, liver and giblet (gizzard). Chop these and mix with 1 lb. raw ham, 4 oz. salt pork, 3 stalks parsley (chopped), tarragon (1 teaspoon dried or 1 tablespoon fresh), chopped shallots (or green onions — 2 or more — chopped), and a small clove of garlic. Put dressing into a platter with 2 raw eggs, add about 4 oz. breadcrumbs (about ¾ cup) soaked in (chicken) bouillon and mix thoroughly. Spice hotly with herbs (thyme, marjoram, rosemary, crumbled bay leaf), salt and pepper. Stuff the hen with the mixture, sew front and rear, and wrap tightly in cheesecloth. Put in (3 quarts) water with Pot-au-Feu garnish (2-3 carrots, 1 turnip, 1 small parsnip, 2 leeks, 2 stalks celery, 1 medium onion, pinch thyme, 1 bay leaf and 1 teaspoon salt) to simmer 3-4 hours or until chicken is tender. Skim several times.

Cold Serving: Carve hen by removing legs and breasts. Open carcass. Remove dressing as a whole and slice it about ½″ thick a slice. Serve with homemade mayonnaise flavored with tarragon.

Serves 4.

[NOTE: This is a wonderful cold dish but it is also excellent hot. Carve it or not and serve with a sauce made by melting 1 tablespoon butter and stirring in 1 tablespoon flour. When blended, add, slowly, 2 cups hot, strained broth from the chicken. Cook, stirring, until thick and smooth and add enough light cream to thin the sauce to the desired consistency. Season to taste, heat and serve in a sauce boat. The vegetables may be arranged around the chicken or not, as you prefer. Do not, however, forget the rest of the broth. Strain it and serve it either as a prelude to the chicken or at another meal. — P. H.]

TWO RECIPES FROM AVERY ISLAND

Every now and then a pleasant and unexpected fringe benefit is dropped into the lap of a cookbook author. One of the most interesting ever dropped into mine was a trip to Avery Island, Louisiana, where Tabasco Sauce is made. Tabasco is only one of many projects developed by the McIlhenny clan on this piece of land which is not really an island but high ground surrounded by swamps. There is a salt mine, there is sugar cane, there are rice fields, there are oil wells and there is Bird City, a sanctuary known to every egret and heron for miles around. Tabasco, however, is the reason why I and a group of my betters were invited there. We traced the evolution of the famous sauce from seedling pepper plants in a greenhouse to the familiar bottle in the packaging plant. When that had been accomplished we were taken sightseeing and, at what seemed like every possible opportunity, we were royally fed. We had fresh artichoke bottoms covered with sautéed truffles as an accompaniment to quail, steamed Jerusalem artichokes with wild duck (an excellent combination), salad made of a lovely green called roquette, sweet potato pie and a crawfish feast served at the firehouse in the town of Breaux, among other things. One of the recipes that I managed to get was for some especially good fried chicken which was served cold, as part of a picnic lunch on a boat trip down the bayou. Here is the recipe, and don't cut down on the Tabasco, which, in spite of the amount used, imparts only the subtlest flavor to the chicken.

Cajun Fried Chicken

Soak 2 disjointed frying chickens overnight in refrigerator in a mixture of 1 quart milk, 2 well-beaten eggs, 1 teaspoon Tabasco and salt to taste.

Next day roll each piece of chicken in a mixture of half flour and half breadcrumbs — about ½ cup of each.

Heat 1½ inches of Crisco in a skillet that is just large enough to hold the pieces of chicken. When the fat bubbles, add the chicken and brown quickly on all sides. Cover the skillet, lower the heat and cook for 15 minutes. Remove the lid, turn the pieces of chicken and cook 15 minutes longer or until chicken is tender. Serve hot or cold.

Quail Roasted in Cabbage Leaves

[You may question the length of time given for cooking these quail. It is longer than usual, but the birds, which were slightly larger than most, were meltingly tender and not one bit dried out. — P. H.]

Put a piece of salt pork the size of your little finger inside of each bird. Then wrap each in a thin slice of salt pork and then in a scalded cabbage leaf. Fasten with toothpicks. Place the birds close together in a baking pan with a little water. Cover pan with foil. Bake in a 500-degree oven for 30 minutes. Remove foil, leaf and salt pork wrapping. Reduce heat to 400 degrees. Cook, basting, for 15 minutes. When brown, replace foil and keep warm. Cook boiled and ground giblets in butter and add to the pan drippings. Serve the birds on toast with the giblet sauce poured over them.

A BIRD IN THE PAN:

Five Recipes for American Game Birds by Clara Spiegel

When I was associate editor of *Bon Appétit* magazine I occasionally commissioned friends who, while they were not cooking authorities, were accomplished amateurs in their particular fields.

Clara Spiegel, novelist and sportswoman, lives in Ketchum, Idaho, a part of the year and has very definite ideas about how to prepare the birds she shoots. For one thing, she does not approve of disguising them in sauces, no matter how good the latter may be. Game, she feels, should taste like the game it is. Here are five of her tried and true recipes complete with suggestions for accompaniments both liquid and solid.

Mourning Doves

(Figure at least three for each woman and four for each man.)

Ingredients: For 10 doves, 1 stick butter, salt, pepper.

Preparation: If possible, doves should be feathered in the field while they are still warm. It takes about half the time and removes otherwise stubborn pinfeathers. Cut off and throw away the head, feet and wings below the joint and slit up the back. Cut out and clean in cold running water, being careful to remove all lung tissue and glands. Soak in cold salted water for about an hour to draw the blood. The birds will keep unfrozen in water in the refrigerator for several days or will freeze well in water-filled containers for several weeks. Before cooking, wash again in cold running water to remove any extra pieces of skin, fat or clots of blood. Drain on absorbent paper.

Make a paste of soft butter with salt and pepper to taste. Place the doves breast up and not touching each other on a broiling rack with a drip pan and smear the breasts with the butter paste to a thickness of about $\frac{1}{4}''$. Melt the remaining paste in a small saucepan to use as a baste. Put the doves under the broiler at a hand's breadth below the heat and turn on the broiler. After about 5 minutes, baste the birds with the melted paste. At the end of another 5 minutes, pour off the pan drippings into the saucepan, mix them with the remaining baste and from now on baste with this. Repeat this twice more at 5 minute intervals. Turn the birds, baste and brown the backs for 1 minute. Serve at once, using the pan gravy and any leftover baste for the birds and accompanying wild rice.

On the subject of accompaniments to, and preludes for this dish, if you have amenable guests, serve either a light dry sherry or half dry and half sweet vermouth over rocks rather than hard liquor for cocktails. Both of these drinks are pleasant to the taste and will not spoil the delicate flavor of the dove meat. Wild rice prepared your favorite way and a crisp green salad with an oil and vinegar dressing are indicated, as well as French bread. A good dry claret, the finer the better, is perfect to serve with these birds, and a very light dessert such as an ice or, if available, bunches of sweet chilled green and purple grapes.

Partridge of Any Variety or Young Sage Hen

Ingredients: Salt, pepper, flour, bacon grease and/or butter, chicken-rice soup, mushroom caps, marjoram.

Preparation: Clean and skin the birds and cut them up by fileting out the breasts and cutting off the legs. The breasts and legs are all you use.

Season the flour well with salt and pepper. Put it in a paper bag, add the meat and shake well but lightly and quickly so that very little flour clings. Remove the pieces to a platter. In an iron skillet melt enough bacon grease or butter or a combination of the two to form a liquid about an eighth of an inch deep. When this is very hot, brown the birds in it quickly. Cut down the heat to low and, per bird, add ½ can of chicken-rice soup, 1 small tin of mushroom caps and a stingy pinch of marjoram. Simmer covered for about an hour, adding ½ cup of water twice during this time. Check, and if the bottom of the pan is scabbed up, add more water.

When done, serve with the pan gravy in a sauce boat to go on the mashed potatoes which this ranch dish demands. And unless you have an aversion to it, drink beer or ale, although a Rhine wine is also very good. For vegetables try baby beets and/or green beans. Finish off with an apple or peach pie.

Pheasant or Chukkar Partridge
(of any age, but the younger the better)

Ingredients: Salt, paprika, garlic, flour, light cream.

Preparation: Skin out the bird and clean thoroughly. Cut up as you would a frying chicken. A pheasant has membranes dividing each breast into 2 sections. Separate these along the membrane so that there are 4 pieces of breast from each bird.

On a platter season the flour with salt and enough paprika to make the flour a deep pink in color. While preheating an oven to 350 degrees, melt butter in an iron skillet over a low flame, using a half of a stick of butter more or less for each bird, depending on their size. Dry the pieces of pheasant and dredge them very lightly in the flour, so that they are just dusted with it. Then turn up the heat beneath the skillet a bit and brown the meat carefully until golden. When this is done, transfer the birds and the contents of the skillet to a roasting pan. Put a cut clove of garlic in with them, pour a ½ pint of light cream per bird over them, cover and put in the oven for about 2 hours. Baste every thirty minutes with the pan drippings. If more liquid is needed add another ½ pint cream or more. When done, serve with the pan contents as gravy. It will look curdled, which is fine. Don't strain but serve as is. Excellent cold the next day.

Almost anything is good to drink before this, although I lean towards the lighter cocktails. The dish is rich and filling, so a good green salad with a lemon and oil dressing is best and that's usually all I serve except some biscuits or small slices of toast drenched in butter and then thickly covered with poppy seeds. Either a dry white Burgundy or a red Bordeaux seems to complement the meat. For dessert canned pears soaked in Cointreau or cherries in kirsch or any macédoine of fruit is good.

Wild Duck

There is no way of cooking a "trash" duck to make it palatable. So, in both the following recipes it is assumed that the duck itself is good to begin with. Most men will eat a whole duck, so will most women.

Ingredients: The quantities depend on the number of ducks. Butter, salt, onions, apples, water.

Preparation: Whether you are of the hang or don't hang school, do everything you can to find someone else to pick the ducks. In most communities where ducks are hunted there are experienced, well-equipped pickers who will do the job for very little money and will also remove the head, feet and wings. However, when you get your birds back from these Samaritans, clean them thoroughly as in the recipe for doves, go over them for pinfeathers and soak them as you do the doves. They will keep for several days or will freeze.

Preheat the oven to 450 degrees and meanwhile rub the duck cavities well with salt, leaving the grains inside. Cut up the apples and peeled onions and stuff the birds full with these. The manner of cutting is unimportant as the stuffing is discarded before serving. Place the ducks breast up in a roasting pan, cover and cook for 10 minutes.

In a saucepan melt ½ stick of butter for every 2 or 3 birds and add an equal amount of water. Baste the ducks with the above mixture every 10 minutes. If you like them very rare 25 minutes' cooking is enough. If you like them only faintly pink, as I do, 40 minutes should do it. For the last 5 minutes remove the cover and allow the birds to brown. Remove the stuffing and serve.

Filet of Duck Breasts

Ingredients: Butter or imported olive oil, salt, oregano.

Preparation: Cut the breasts carefully away from the carcass in order to have 2 complete pieces of meat from each duck. Soak in cold salted water for an hour. Pat dry. Pound with a pounder or the edge of a saucer.

In an iron skillet melt 1 tablespoon butter or heat 1 tablespoon olive oil per bird. Bring to a high heat. Add very little oregano and a bit of salt. Put the birds in and brown quickly on one side, turn and brown on the other side. Serve at once with pan gravy or Shotgun Sauce.

Shotgun Sauce

This sauce is a purely Western invention. Furthermore, it is delicious and, I suspect, the discovery of a bachelor friend of mine who is an excellent cook as well as a superb field shot.

Ingredients: Butter, currant jelly, Worcestershire Sauce.

In an iron skillet place 1 part butter to 2 parts currant jelly and add a dash of Worcestershire Sauce. Heat, stir up and when hot, serve. Duck is a rich meat but surprisingly enough it can support heavy side dishes. Spiced apples or applesauce are delicious with it and so is wild rice.

ESCARGOTS DE BOURGOGNE
CHEZ MARGUERITE

Two young men who have never been to France own and operate a small, truly French restaurant in San Francisco. The young men, Herbert M. Emery and J. Ross Williams, Jr., are responsible for the warmth of your reception and the charm of the bistro's decor while Chef Eugene Maissa, who has been with them since the beginning, maintains the high standards of the Gallic cuisine. At a "finishing stove" in full view of the 40 diners (when the place is filled to capacity), M. Maissa puts the last touches on his specialties, which include these snails, Belgian Hare Bruxelloise, Tripe à la Créole, and others.

For 1 dozen snails:

Combine ¼ lb. salted butter, 2 teaspoons Worcestershire Sauce, salt and white pepper to taste, 1 crushed clove of garlic, 3 crushed shallots, or chopped green onions, and 1 tablespoon finely chopped parsley. Add the juice of ¼ lemon, 2 drops Tabasco Sauce, and 1 tablespoon fine cracker crumbs.

Sauté the drained, canned snails in regular butter until tender. Cool. Spoon a small amount of the seasoned butter into each shell, insert a snail, fill the shell with more seasoned butter and top with additional fine cracker crumbs. Bake in a 350-degree oven for 10 minutes until the butter bubbles and begins to turn brown.

Serve immediately with lemon wedges and plenty of hot French bread.

[NOTE: If you don't have your own snail plates, half fill a shallow baking dish with rock salt and stud it with the filled snail shells. Serve in soup plates. — P. H.]

CANARD À L'ORANGE CHEZ MARGUERITE

If you are well known at Chez Marguerite or if you come with a friend's recommendation or if Mr. Emery or Mr. Williams likes your looks you are apt to be invited to sample the menu before you order your dinner. You take one of the four or five stools at the tiny bar and let your hosts know which of the specialties interest you. With your cocktail you are served tiny plates on each of which is a small sample of your choices. You take it from there — but it's not easy. As a matter of fact, it's almost harder to make up your mind after sampling than it was just looking at the menu. Here is Chef Maissa's recipe for duck with orange:

2 3- to 3½-lb. ducklings or 1 5- pound duckling	2 cups chicken consommé
2 tablespoons brown sugar	½ cup sherry
2 tablespoons red wine vinegar	3 drops Tabasco
1 cup fresh orange juice	3 drops orange bitters or orange liqueur
2 tablespoons currant jelly	2½ teaspoons cornstarch
Orange peel from 3 oranges	Mandarin orange sections

Place ducklings in low-sided roasting pan on rack; do not cover; do not add water. Roast in 325-degree preheated oven 1½ hours for small size; 2 to 2½ hours for large size until tender. Peel oranges very thinly, avoiding as much white as possible. Cut into fine juliennes. Place in saucepan; cover with boiling water and let stand a few minutes; drain. Set aside. Melt brown sugar in saucepan until it turns to caramel. Add wine vinegar, stirring constantly, cooking until thick. Add orange juice, jelly, orange rind, and consommé. Cover and simmer for 1 hour, then add sherry, Tabasco and bitters. Season to taste with salt and Accent. Combine cornstarch with 3 tablespoons water; add to sauce, stirring. Cook until sauce is thickened and comes to a boil. Serve over duckling; garnish with Mandarin orange sections.

Serves 4.

LET'S NOT TALK TURKEY:
Recipes for Christmas by Allan McNab

Mr. McNab is another friend whom I lured into the *Bon Appétit* fold. He is an artist whose drawings are included in the permanent collections of the British Museum, the National Gallery and others and has been active in many fields of artistic endeavor both here and in England. At present he is Director of Administration of the Art Institute of Chicago. The most unusual thing about him, to my mind, is that he is an Englishman who can cook. He was enthusiastic about the idea of doing a piece on goose and pig for the Christmas issue of our little magazine and I wish that I had the space to reprint the entire article, since the gentleman writes as well as he draws and cooks.

Goose: How to Roast It and What to Stuff It With:

The authors of many of our cookbooks have a tendency to feel that they have discharged their obligation to the goose if they accord it the same treatment they advocate for the duck. This is not the way to respect the bird which was held sacred by the Romans because a wakeful goose had warned the city of the impending invasion of the Gauls. Distant descendants of these Gauls provide us with scores of recipes from Confit d'Oie to the delicious white goose pie of Poitou, but our present concern is with the traditional Christmas goose. It should be young and should weigh 10 to 12 lbs. A goose more than 18 months old should not be eaten but kept as a watchdog.

Preparations before cooking a goose are, in almost all cases, the same. Rub the bird well all over with at least a tablespoon of salt. Then prick it well with a sharp fork and spread at least a tablespoon of butter over the breast. Add a cup of boiling water to the roasting pan before you put it in the oven. Allow 25 minutes to the pound and keep the oven at 375 degrees. Baste it as often as possible. And drink a full-bodied Burgundy with it.

The best of the French stuffings — that used with the Oie de Dijon — is prepared by combining and cooking together for ½ to ¾ of an hour ½ lb. of chicken livers, the liver of the goose, a cup of Burgundy, 1 finely chopped onion, a clove of garlic, a bay leaf, a liberal amount of chopped chives and a pinch of basil. After cooking, strain and save the wine. Pass all the remainder through the meat grinder and combine with 2 cups of coarse breadcrumbs. Mix well, binding with the yolks of 2 eggs and 2 tablespoons of butter. The inside of the bird may be rubbed with garlic and moistened with Burgundy. This is optional. Stuff the bird with the mixture. Don't pack too tightly. Then combine the wine with the unstrained juice of 3 or 4 oranges and use this to baste the goose.

The French also use an apple stuffing which is less rich and is made by peeling and quartering eight or ten apples and cooking them in ½ cup water until tender. After they have been cooled, add 2 tablespoons of brown sugar, 2 cups coarse breadcrumbs, 2 tablespoons of melted butter and yolks of 2 eggs. This method of preparation calls for giblet gravy, which should be made with Burgundy as a base.

[I must now, in the interests of allowable space, skip Mr. McNab's un-
flattering remarks about the traditional English goose dinner and proceed
with his German Christmas goose — P. H.]:

Start by soaking a pound of prunes overnight in enough port wine to
cover. Next day cook them slowly until the stones can be easily removed.
To the prunes and what is left of the wine add ½ cup of coarse breadcrumbs, 6 apples peeled and chopped fine, 2 tablespoons of brown sugar
and 1 tablespoon of butter. Mix well together. Before stuffing, moisten the
inside of the goose with port wine. Then stuff and roast as usual. You must
serve a sauce with this goose, so put 2 cups of port wine into a double
boiler. Add a full half of one of the standard size pots of imported French
mustard, the grated rind of an orange and that of 2 lemons, pepper and salt.
Cook, over simmering water, until hot. The sauce is usually thick enough,
but, if you like, it may be thickened in the usual way. [NOTE: the best way
to do this is to dissolve 1 tablespoon of arrowroot flour or cornstarch in ¼
cup of cold water and stir into the sauce. — P. H.]
The goose is served with thinly sliced cucumbers that have been lightly
sautéed in butter.

[After pointing out the difficulties of finding a real market where you can
order a suckling pig (being sure that it is not more than 3 weeks old) and
a real butcher who knows how to truss it and prepare it for roasting, and
after announcing that a properly roasted piglet is so delicious that little
else is necessary in the way of stuffing or sauces, my friend proceeds to give
several mouth-watering recipes for dressing it up. I pass on to you four of
these — P. H.]:

Suckling Pig: How to Roast It and What to Stuff It With:

The traditional Spanish method of preparing Cochinillo Asado (Suckling
Pig) is simple and presents no problem for the average city dweller. Scrub
the pig thoroughly and dry it with a cloth. With a sharp knife, make a
series of long shallow cuts in the skin of the back and the sides. In a mixing
bowl, prepare a paste of 3 or 4 tablespoons lard, 1 or 2 ounces of finely
chopped parsley, a pinch of bouquet garni or sage, salt and pepper. Mix
thoroughly and rub into the incisions and over the back. The pig should be

put into a hot oven to sear, then cooked slowly at 250 degrees for 2 to 3 hours, depending on size. Paper or foil should be used to protect ears and legs from over-browning. Remove from the oven and brush over the back and sides with a cup of thick cream and return to the oven for another half hour. The perfect drink to accompany this noble dish is a mellow sherry.

To prepare English forcemeat as it has been done since long before Dickens wrote a single line, slice 1 lb. of onions and place in cold water, and boil for 5 minutes. In a medium size skillet, melt ¼ lb. of butter. Strain and dry the onions, and fry them in the butter until they are golden brown. Add 2 cups of coarse bread crumbs, 2 teaspoons of chopped sage (fresh if you can find it), salt, pepper and a little nutmeg. Mix well in stuffing but do not pack too tightly.

There are several excellent French stuffings. The main difference lies in the choice of ground veal, chopped liver or pork sausage as the basic ingredient. All are excellent and the method of preparing is the same in each case. To 2 or 3 cups of coarse breadcrumbs (more or less depending on the amount of stuffing that you have to make), add 1 large apple, finely chopped, 2 tabespoons chopped parsley, and ½ lb. of whatever basic ingredient you select: veal, liver or pork sausage. Add 1 clove of mashed garlic, ½ of an onion, finely chopped, nutmeg, salt and pepper. Combine with 2 well-beaten eggs. Before stuffing, moisten the inside of the pig with brandy.

The German stuffing, naturally, begins with sauerkraut and caraway seed. The method is to mix 1½ lbs. of sauerkraut, 1 chopped onion, 2 chopped apples, 4 small pork sausages thinly sliced, 1 teaspoon of caraway seed, and a pinch of pepper. Add salt and sauté with ¼ lb. butter. When well blended, stuff the suckling pig. If you try the German method, put a piece of wood in the pig's mouth before you put it in the oven and remove the plug of wood and substitute it with a small red apple before serving.

Whatever stuffing you select, serve the pig whole and carve it at table. Whether you decide to put a red apple in its mouth, or be a little Chinese and have a red flower on its head, the pig should appear on a large platter on a bed of watercress.

SWEET AND SOUR PORK FROM
MA HAWLEY'S KITCHEN

In the same letter with the recipe for Ma Hawley's Codfish Balls, my friend sent this along with the following comment: "If you like Chinese food, try this." The same to you.

Cut 2 lbs. fresh pork tenderloin into strips approximately 1½″ by 1″.

Beat 1 egg, add salt, 1 cup water, 1 tablespoon salad oil, 1 cup sifted flour and beat until smooth. Dip meat in this mixture and fry in deep, hot fat (375 degrees). Drain on absorbent paper. Keep warm.

Cook 2 seeded green peppers cut in strips like the meat, 4 slices canned pineapple cut in wedges, 1 cup mixed sweet pickles in a little water for 5 minutes. Add to this 1 cup tomato catsup, 2 tablespoons vinegar, 1 cup sugar and salt to taste. Heat and add meat. Serve *hot* with rice.

This is supposed to serve four but it is marvelous so don't count on its doing so.

LOIN OF PORK KARTER

Responsible for this recipe is a Swiss gentleman named Egon Karter, operatic tenor, director of the successful Komödie Theater in Basle and an amateur chef of some renown. He made his first trip to this country not so long ago in order to be present at the wedding of his son and a young cousin of mine. He and I were introduced as chef and cookbook-writer, respectively, and when the time came to sit down and compare notes, our conversation centered about cooking. I think that I benefited most from the encounter, because I came away with this excellent recipe for pork cooked with whisky.

Put a 6-chop loin pork roast in a deep dish with about a pint of milk and refrigerate overnight, turning the meat occasionally. Next day remove the meat and discard the milk. Wash the dish and put the meat back with 1 medium onion, sliced, and 2 tablespoons Scotch whisky. Marinate, at room temperature, for an hour or more, turning occasionally.

Remove the meat and pat it dry with paper towels. Brown it quickly, on top of the stove, in 2 tablespoons olive oil. Discard the oil and add 2 tablespoons butter. Reduce heat and brown slowly, covered, for 15 minutes. Turn the meat a couple of times. Each time you turn it, sprinkle it with granulated sugar and whisky (1 tablespoon whisky). Put the skillet in a preheated 325-degree oven and cook for 1½ hours, uncovered, basting now and then.

Garnish the roast with crushed canned pineapple which has been chilled, strained and spiked with whisky to taste. Serve with puréed spinach. Serves 3-4.

SMALL ROAST LAMB

Avis DeVoto, who is as expert at cooking and editing cookbooks as her late husband, Bernard, was at writing about the Dry Martini (and many other things), tossed me the general idea for this recipe once, as we were going over a manuscript of mine. My scribbled notes were "boned 4 or 5 chop loin of lamb, tied up. Marinate in olive oil, lemon juice, rosemary. Roast not as long. All fat removed except ⅛ inch thick." Obviously, this is culinary shorthand from one cook to another. The following recipe is what I worked out:

For 4 people, have the butcher bone and roll an 8-chop loin of lamb and tie it up. All fat should be removed from the inside of the roll and a ⅛″ layer should be left on the outside. Put the roll in a deep dish and pour over it the juice of 1 lemon and ½ cup olive oil. Sprinkle with fresh or dried rosemary. Let marinate overnight, turning the meat occasionally. Remove from refrigerator at least 1 hour before cooking.

Preheat the oven to 450 degrees. Remove the meat from the marinade and rub it with Lawry's Seasoned Salt and freshly ground black pepper. Put on a rack in a shallow pan and sear it for 20 minutes turning so that all sides may brown. When this has been accomplished (you may have to keep the heat at 450 degrees for a little longer because the meat *must* brown) lower heat to 350 degrees. Cook, basting and turning occasionally, for 20-30 minutes depending on the color you wish the lamb to be. A meat thermometer will register 170 degrees for pink. Lacking a meat thermometer, cut a very small but deep slit in the meat using a sharp, narrow knife and see what color the meat is. Do this 10 minutes after lowering heat. Turn off the oven, open the door and let the roast rest for 15 minutes before carving. Since it will cook a little more during this time, do this while the meat is still a bit rarer than you wish.

Note: The recipe works equally well with pork, but the cooking time should be 1½ to 2 hours.

CHARLES MORTON'S CANADIAN BACON POT ROAST

About two years ago a distinguished gentleman sent me a recipe with the following remarks: "Here is a recipe which you might try, and attribute to me if you care to include it in your next book." I'm sure that Mr. Morton, associate editor of the *Atlantic Monthly* and guiding light of the Accent on Living department in that magazine, had no idea that my next book would be published by the Atlantic Monthly Press. I hope that this will surprise and please him. I tried the recipe and do like it, and here it is. It serves six unless one of them is my son, in which case I'd say it serves three.

Peel and slice, as for scalloped, a desired number of potatoes. Arrange these in a saucepan so as to make a nest around an 8-inch section of Canadian bacon. I do this in the vertical plane, standing the bacon on end, using a somewhat cylindrical aluminum saucepan that has a tight-fitting lid. [NOTE: Heavy aluminum I find is best. — P. H.]

Add about a quart of milk or enough to cover the contents and cover tightly. Simmer until potatoes are soft. That's all.

This dish is wonderfully good the next day, cold.

ARNI PSITO (Roast Lamb Greek Style)

Travel in other countries serves to strengthen, rather than diminish, Marilyn Kaytor's love for Greece and its islands. Again and again she returns to her favorite vacation spot to enjoy its beauty, savor its food and renew old friendships. Since food is her business and cooking is her hobby, she collects recipes wherever she goes and, due to her interest in Greece, there are many recipes from that country in her files. Lamb is a great favorite with the Greeks and roast lamb is the traditional Easter dish. This recipe came from a Greek family and is a typically Greek way of treating lamb. The "hind half" is not as big as it sounds and can be cooked on a broiler rack in any oven large enough to hold two legs of lamb. This is a spectacular and delicious way in which to serve lamb to a sizable group.

Clean for roasting the hind half of a lamb (which is the 2 hind legs together in one piece, shanks cut off) weighing about 13 pounds total. Insert 5 small cloves garlic, cut into ¼-inch-thick strips, into slits cut in meat with point of sharp knife. Rub meat well with pulpy lemon juice, thyme, oregano, salt and freshly ground black pepper. Let stand 1 hour. Place on roasting rack in pan. Roast 15 minutes at 450 degrees F. Reduce heat to 325 degrees F. Roast 2 hours, basting occasionally with melted butter and lemon juice. Put about ½ cup water into the roasting pan; add 12-18 peeled, medium-sized potatoes sprinkled well with salt, pepper and oregano. Roast 1½ hours more, or until done, basting again with melted butter and lemon juice. Stand meat on large copper tray, or platter, on bed of lemon or other green leaves. Turn oven high to brown potatoes, turning them in pan juices. Insert long skewer, stuck with small tomatoes and lemon halves, through backbone of meat. Let stand for 10 minutes. Surround with potatoes. Carve meat.

Serves 12-14.

From Marilyn Kaytor, Food Editor, LOOK Magazine.

BAHAMIAN LEG OF LAMB

The origin of this recipe escapes me. Whether it actually originated in the Bahamas or whether the gourmet who had the idea of combining lamb with pineapple and lime simply christened it thus, I do not know. Somehow it found its way into my notebook, however, and it is excellent.

5-6 lb. leg of lamb, boned for
   stuffing
1 cup crushed fresh pineapple
½ clove garlic
1 tablespoon scraped onion
2 tablespoons chopped parsley

2 tablespoons melted butter
2 cups toasted breadcrumbs
Salt, pepper
1 lime
Worcestershire Sauce

Rub the lamb inside and out with salt and pepper. Mix the pineapple, onion, parsley, butter and breadcrumbs together and either add the garlic minced, or put the half clove through a garlic press so that you just get the juice. Stuff the leg of lamb, sew or skewer the opening and rub the meat with the cut lime. Sear in a 450-degree oven until brown. Reduce the heat to 300 degrees and roast for 20 minutes to the pound. Baste occasionally with a combination of Worcestershire Sauce and water, using about 1 tablespoon Worcestershire to a cup of water.

Serves 6.

DIONE LUCAS'S GIGOT EN CROÛTE

1 small leg of lamb weighing not
   more than 5-6 lbs.
Salt, freshly ground black pepper,
   crushed clove garlic
1 lb. finely ground veal
2 egg whites
1 cup light cream
2 tablespoons finely chopped shallot

1 teaspoon finely chopped garlic
2 tablespoons finely chopped parsley
1 tablespoon finely chopped dill
⅛ teaspoon nutmeg
1 lb. bacon
Red wine, water
Pastry
Demi-glaze sauce

Bone the leg of lamb, remove fat, season well inside and out with salt, pepper and crushed garlic. Put ground veal in a mixer, add raw egg whites and mix well. Slowly beat in cream. Add chopped shallot, garlic, parsley, dill. Season with nutmeg and salt and pepper to taste. Stuff leg of lamb with this mixture. Wrap leg with bacon slices, tying each slice securely with string. Put in a roaster and pour a little red wine and some water in the bottom of the pan. Roast at 375 degrees for 20 minutes and baste often, adding 2 tablespoons red wine or water each time. Remove, cool. When cool, wrap in the following pastry:

Sift 4 cups flour and 2 teaspoons salt into a large bowl. Work up to a firm dough quickly with 1½ cups ice water. Roll out into a large square on a floured board. Place 1 lb. salt butter, which should be the same consistency as the dough, in the center and fold up like a package. Wrap in Saran Wrap and then in a cloth. Put in the refrigerator for ½ hour. Remove and roll out in a long strip. Fold in three. Wrap as before and chill for ½ hour. Remove and repeat the process — two rollings and two foldings. Put back in the refrigerator for ½ hour. Remove and repeat two rollings and two foldings. Chill for 2 hours. Remove, roll out ½ inch thick and line a large deep mold, such as a small, deep roasting pan. The mold should be large enough for the lamb to fit snugly. Place lamb in lined mold. Roll out remaining pastry ¾ inch thick and cover the mold carefully. Brush the edges of the covered mold with beaten egg. Brush the top with beaten egg and decorate with scraps of pastry rolled out and cut into shapes. Brush decoration with beaten egg, chill well and bake in a 425-degree oven for 25 minutes. Remove and serve on a hot platter with demi-glaze sauce:

For sauce:

2 chicken livers	¼ cup red wine
3 tablespoons butter	1¼ cups chicken stock
2 tablespoons brandy	2 teaspoons red currant jelly
1 teaspoon each: tomato paste, meat glaze	Pepper
2 teaspoons potato flour	1 small truffle, finely chopped

Brown chicken livers in 2 teaspoons butter. Flame with brandy. Remove livers and add 2 tablespoons butter to the pan. Stir in, off the fire, the tomato paste, meat glaze and flour. Mix in wine, stock and jelly. Stir over fire until boiling point is reached. Season with pepper and strain. Add chopped truffle and finely diced chicken livers.

Serves 8.

ESCALOPES DE VEAU FARCIES
À L'ESPAGNOLE

A globe-trotting friend fetched me this recipe from Spain. It takes a bit of uncomplicated doing but it's worth it, not only because it is so good but because your efforts can be seen. In the case of many dishes you slave all day, and the end result, while excellent in taste, gives no indication of the meticulous preparations that went into it. This one does. Serve it hot or cold. It's a toss-up as to which is better.

2 thick veal cutlets, 10 oz. each	½ pint dry white wine
3 eggs	½ pint water
14 oz. green olives	Pepper, olive oil
4 slices lean raw ham cut ⅛″ thick	½ cup flour
2 green peppers	

Have the butcher slice each cutlet lengthwise but not quite through. Flatten out into large cutlets.

Hard-boil the eggs and cut them in quarters. Cut the fat off the ham and cut it into strips ½″ wide. Put the peppers, whole, in a 450-degree oven for 10 minutes. Remove them, peel and seed them and cut them into strips. Stone the olives and cut ¼ of them in halves. (The others will be cooked whole in the sauce.)

Spread lengthwise on each cutlet alternate rows of ham, olives, egg, and peppers. Roll the cutlets up gently and tie them with string. Dust them with flour.

Heat 2 tablespoons of oil in an iron casserole and brown the cutlets on all sides over medium heat. Sprinkle with a tablespoon of flour. Add the remaining olives, the wine and the water. Sprinkle lightly with salt and pepper. Bring to a boil and cover, but not tightly. Lower the heat and cook for 45 minutes. To serve, remove the strings, slice the rolls ½″ thick and garnish with the olives. Serve the sauce separately.

Serves 4.

JIM BEARD'S VITELLO TONNATO

3½ to 4 lbs. lean leg of veal, boned, rolled and firmly tied
1 large onion sliced
1 small can anchovies
1 7-oz. can tuna fish in oil (olive oil if possible)
2-3 stalks celery cut in chunks
1-2 carrots sliced
½ sour pickle
Few sprigs parsley
Pinch thyme
Few peppercorns
2 cloves garlic
1 pint dry white wine
1 pint rich chicken stock
1½ to 2 cups mayonnaise
Salt, freshly ground pepper, lemon juice
3 cups cooked, cold rice
Chopped parsley, capers

The day before you plan to serve Vitello Tonnato, put the veal in a large heavy skillet with a tight-fitting cover. Add the onion, anchovies and their oil, tuna fish and oil, the celery, carrots, pickle, parsley, thyme, peppercorns and garlic. Pour in the white wine and chicken stock and bring to a boil. Lower the heat, cover the skillet and simmer until the veal is tender. Turn the meat 2 or 3 times as it cooks. Cool in the stock. Put meat and stock, in the skillet, in the refrigerator to chill overnight.

The next day, remove the meat, roll it in foil and return to the refrigerator. Cook the stock, over high heat, until reduced to 1 pint. Chill.

Place a cup of mayonnaise in an electric blender and add a little of the chilled stock. Blend until the sauce is a smooth mixture, not too thick and firm. It should have just enough body to cling to sliced veal. (You will probably use a cup of stock and 1½ to 2 cups mayonnaise. Add lemon juice and seasonings to taste.)

To serve, heap the cold rice on a large platter, piling it high in the center. Sprinkle with chopped parsley. Cut the veal into thin slices and arrange them overlapping down the center of the rice. Spoon some of the sauce over the meat and garnish with chopped capers. Serve the rest of the sauce separately.

Serves 12 generously.

MY BEEF WELLINGTON, PÉRIGUEUX SAUCE

There are many versions of this famous party recipe. Some are easier than this and some are more complicated; some are more expensive and some, less so. I have tried them all, adopting an idea here and there. Although this could be called a middle-of-the-road version, no short cuts in price or effort are discernible. It is a superlative dish. Serve it with a purée of peas or Celery Amandine and drink a fine Burgundy.

1¼ lbs. mushrooms, very finely minced
5 shallots or green onions, very finely minced
Butter and shortening
3 tablespoons minced parsley
1½ cups clear beef consommé
1 tablespoon arrowroot flour or cornstarch

1 cup Madeira
3 chopped truffles
Salt, freshly ground black pepper
6 cups all-purpose flour
1 whole beef filet weighing 3 lbs., trimmed of all fat
5-oz. can pâté de foie gras
1 egg

A good deal of the preparation for this dinner can be done the day before. First, cook the mushrooms and shallots or onions in 4 ounces butter until all moisture has cooked away. Add the minced parsley toward the end. Cool the mixture, cover and refrigerate.

Next, make a Périgueux sauce by heating the beef consommé with 1¼ tablespoons of butter, adding the arrowroot flour or cornstarch dissolved in ⅓ cup Madeira and stirring over low heat until thick. Add the truffles. Season with salt and pepper and store in the refrigerator.

Thirdly, make the pastry. Blend the flour and 2½ cups half soft butter and half other shortening, with the fingers, until a sandy mass has been obtained. Add 1 cup cold water gradually, mixing slowly and working the dough into a ball. The less water used the better. Wrap in waxed paper and refrigerate.

On the day of the dinner remove the duxelles (mushroom mixture) from the refrigerator. Also remove the meat and bring it to room temperature.

Reprinted from *House and Garden:* Copyright © 1962 by The Conde Nast Publications, Inc.

Fold the tip back and tie it securely. Tie the other end, too, if necessary. Season the beef with salt and freshly ground black pepper.

Melt 4 ounces butter in a shallow pan which is long enough to hold the filet but as narrow as possible. Braise the meat on top of the range for 35 minutes, turning it often with spoons. Moisten with Madeira, using about ⅔ cup, from time to time. Allow the meat to cool but not in the refrigerator.

Add the pâté de foie gras to the duxelles, mix well and add 1 teaspoon of the Périgueux sauce. Taste for seasoning.

Roll out the pastry in a rectangular shape about 14″ x 9″ and ¼″ thick —large enough to envelop the filet. Spread the duxelles over the pastry, leaving a border uncovered. Place the meat in the center with that side down which you want eventually to be up. Fold the pastry over the meat and seal the seam and ends with water. Place, seam-side down, on a cookie sheet and brush the top and sides with the egg, well-beaten and mixed with a little water or cream. Prick thoroughly with a fork in a crisscross design. Bake in a preheated oven for 30 minutes. Serve sliced with the Périgueux sauce, hot, on the side. (Slice very thin — this is a rich dish.)

Serves 8-10.

DIONE LUCAS'S BEEF STROGANOV AND GNOCCHIS VORENIKIS

2 lbs. tail end filet of beef	1 teaspoon meat glaze, BV or Bovril
2 tb. salt butter	1 teaspoon tomato paste
3 tb. brandy	2 tb. flour
½ oz. dried mushrooms softened in ¼ cup water	1½ cups beef stock
	Freshly cracked black pepper
1 teaspoon finely chopped yellow onion	1 cup sour cream
	2 tb. chopped fresh dill
1 teaspoon finely chopped garlic	

Trim off all fat from beef filet and cut the meat into long strips ½ to ¾ inch thick, cutting with the grain of the meat. Heat butter in a deep heavy pan. When very hot brown meat, a few pieces at a time. Be sure the pieces do not touch and that the heat of the pan remains constant. Sear the meat

Reprinted from *House and Garden:* Copyright © 1960 by The Conde Nast Publications, Inc.

all over very quickly. Remove and set aside. Heat brandy, pour into the pan and stir with a wooden spoon to lift up all the glaze. Drain the mushrooms, reserving the liquid. Chop them very finely and add to the pan with the onions and garlic. Cook over a very slow fire for 2-3 minutes, then stir in, off the fire, the meat glaze, tomato paste and flour. When smooth, stir in the strained mushroom liquid and the beef stock. Season with pepper. Stir over the fire until thickened, then slowly and carefully stir in the sour cream. Add the dill. Just before serving, put back the meat and stir it into the hot sauce off the fire — the meat should not cook any more, just reheat the sauce. Serve with:

Gnocchis Vorenikis

1 lb. cottage cheese	Salt, cayenne pepper
½ lb. cream cheese	6 oz. sweet butter
2 eggs, beaten	½ cup fresh grated Parmesan cheese
Flour	

Strain cottage and cream cheeses through a fine strainer. Put into a bowl and slowly mix in the beaten eggs. Add just enough flour to bind, approximately 2 level tablespoons. Season with salt and cayenne pepper to taste. Cover bowl and chill in the refrigerator for at least ½ hour. Have ready a large pan of boiling salted water. Reduce the heat to a slow simmer. Put in the cheese mixture in small teaspoonfuls and allow to poach without boiling for 20 minutes or until they come up to the surface of the water and are firm to the touch. (Gnocchis may be made in advance, left in the cooled water and gently reheated without boiling.) Slowly dissolve the butter and season it with salt and pepper. Brush the bottom of an au gratin dish with a little of the butter. Carefully drain the gnocchis and place in the dish. Sprinkle them well with the Parmesan cheese and the rest of the butter.

Serves 8.

MAURICE MOORE-BETTY'S STEAK AND KIDNEY PIE

Maurice Moore-Betty, who has recently established a successful one-man catering operation in New York City, is singularly well-equipped for his chosen profession; his interest in cooking stems from his childhood, he has had excellent professional training, and he has an open and inquiring mind. He began, at the age of nine, to cook the fish and game that he and his brother and sister caught, shot or trapped in the streams and forests surrounding his home in England. (When I asked if they poached, he answered, "To the hilt!") As a young man he lived all over the world, growing cotton in the Sudan and tobacco in Rhodesia, among other things. Settled in London after the last war, he found that servants were unobtainable and restaurant food indifferent, so he decided to learn to cook professionally and worked for a year in the kitchens of the Ritz Hotel. He started at the bottom, helping to stoke the four banks of coal stoves, chopping and stirring. The chef at that time was one M. Avignon, a cousin of the famous Louis Diat, and a man of great dignity and charm. He took a liking to Maurice and when something out of the ordinary was being prepared he would summon him from his menial duties so that he could watch what was going on. He also gave the younger man keys to his library and access to his files, and from two until five every day, Maurice studied. This year of apprenticeship was followed by other culinary experiences including owning and operating a small restaurant and finally, in the early fifties, his present occupation in New York. Another recipe of Mr. Moore-Betty's appears a little further on. This is the pie:

1½ lbs. rump of beef sliced very thin	1 egg yolk
1 dozen oysters and their juice	Salt, pepper
½ lb. beef kidney, all fat removed	Flour
Puff pastry for a 9-10 inch pie, your own, or a purchased, uncooked crust	

Cut the beef into slices 3 inches long and dust them with seasoned flour. Cut the oysters in half and roll each half in a piece of beef. Split the kidney in half and remove all membrane and white veins. Cut in 1″ cubes and dust with seasoned flour.

Select a deep pie dish of a size that will just barely manage to hold the meat. It will probably be about 9″ or 10″ in diameter. When filled the dish must be piled well above the level of the edge.

Fill the dish with alternate layers of oysters rolled in beef and pieces of kidney. Pour in the oyster juice. If there is not enough liquid to fill this to ⅔ of its capacity, add water.

Cover with a pastry crust and thoroughly seal it to the edges of the dish by painting the dough and the edge of the dish with beaten egg and pressing the dough down firmly. Pastry crusts may be bought in pastry shops in many large cities. If you make your own, follow a good recipe for puff paste and use ⅔ as much butter as flour. Do not make any slits in this crust. At the start of the cooking it will look dismally flat, but as the meat begins to cook and steam, it rises to a lovely height. Mr. Moore-Betty follows this procedure for any kind of pie that calls for a complete crust: chicken, fish or fruit.

Serves 4 generously.

ROULADES DE BOEUF: LES POMMES VAPEUR

This recipe was culled from the little French magazine *Cuisine et Vins de France,* which, by the way, bears the subtitle *Confort et Bien-Etre au Foyer* — a nice thought: comfort and well-being at the hearth.

12 thin rectangular slices of round steak	Salt, pepper, nutmeg
¾ lb. pork sausage meat	1 pint red wine
2 shallots or spring onions	1 cup beef bouillon
1 sprig parsley	1 tablespoon flour
¼ lb. cooked ham	Scant ½ cup butter
2 eggs	2 teaspoons oil
	Thyme, marjoram, bay leaf

Mince the shallots, or spring onions, the parsley and the ham. Put them in a bowl and add the sausage meat and eggs. Mix lightly with a fork. Taste for seasoning and add salt and pepper.

Spread the slices of meat, which have been flattened by the butcher, on a board. Salt and pepper them lightly and distribute the stuffing among them. Roll the slices up crosswise and tie them with fine string, fastening the open ends securely.

Melt the butter in an iron or earthenware cocotte and add the oil. When the fat is hot, add the rolls and brown, over fairly high heat, turning them so that they brown on all sides. Remove them and set aside.

Add the flour to the cocotte, stir, and cook over medium heat until the roux is golden. Add, gradually, the bouillon and wine. Add pinches of thyme and marjoram, a crumbled bay leaf and a dash of nutmeg. Put the meat back in the cocotte and cook, covered, for 2 hours. Have a look from time to time, to see that the rolls are not sticking to the bottom of the pan. Stir quickly, at these times, being careful that the lid is not off the cocotte for too long so that the sauce does not evaporate. Add a little hot bouillon if the sauce reduces too much. Keep the heat medium and steady throughout the cooking. Remove strings.

Serve with Les Pommes Vapeur (steamed potatoes).

[NOTE: This is the very best way to cook small, new potatoes. They may be garnished for other dishes with chopped parsley, melted butter, chives or in whatever you wish. For the Roulades, however, serve them just as they are. The sauce will be sufficient garnish. You must have a steamer to make these potatoes. There is a perforated, collapsible gadget on the market which has adjustable feet to keep it out of the water and will fit any size pot. — P. H.]

Choose new potatoes about the size of an average egg (all exactly the same size, if possible.) Put them in the steamer over simmering water, cover and cook for ½ hour.

Serves six.

POTATO PURÉE (Purée de Pommes de Terre)

There is as much difference between our mashed potatoes, good as they are, and the French purée as there is between a sirloin butt steak and a Chateaubriand. The secret of this creamy dish is two-fold; first, the potatoes must be old and floury and second, they must be dried out after the initial boiling. The drier they are, the more milk they absorb and the creamier they become. I found to me what seems the perfect recipe in the little French magazine *Cuisine et Vins de France.* This is it:

2½ lbs. old Idaho potatoes	2½ tablespoons butter
½ onion, peeled	1 cup milk or more
Salt, nutmeg	

Peel and quarter the potatoes. Cook them in salted water with the onion until they are soft but not mushy and waterlogged. Heat the milk with the butter while the potatoes are cooking. Drain the potatoes thoroughly and put them through a ricer into the same pan in which they were cooked but which you have wiped dry. Put the pan over very low heat and add the milk and butter mixture gradually, beating with a wooden spatula or spoon. Season to taste with salt and nutmeg. The purée can be kept warm in a double boiler but should be beaten at intervals with the wooden spoon. More hot milk may be added, if necessary, to give the potatoes the desired consistency, which is that of heavy cream. This will serve 6 to 8.

BILL GROSVENOR'S CURRIED ONIONS

One swallow may not make a summer but one dish can make a meal memorable. An excellent Thanksgiving dinner at Pam and Bill Grosvenor's in Pelham, New York, a while back, would have been just another excellent Thanksgiving dinner, enhanced, I admit, by charming hosts and delightful guests, had it not been for these onions. Anyone who has tried knows how difficult it is to dream up something different for that ever-so-traditional feast — something delicious to taste and delightful to look at; and that is what was accomplished with this dish. The onions were uniform in size, not quite as large as ping-pong balls, and the sauce, which was the color of a field of mustard in the spring, not only tasted wonderful but looked beautiful, flanked by the deep orange of yams, the good green of the beans and the dark brown and creamy tan of the sliced turkey. Take plenty of time with the sauce so that it will be delicate and without a hint of starchy taste and, if possible, have the onions all the same size, whether larger or smaller than Bill's.

For six:

18 white onions, about 1½ lbs.	½ cup light cream
2 tablespoons butter	½ teaspoon thyme, ½ teaspoon
3 tablespoons curry powder	marjoram
2 tablespoons flour	Salt, white pepper
2 cups milk, scalded	

Cook the onions in their skins in boiling salted water until tender. This will take between 15 and 20 minutes depending on the size of the onions. Drain and slip off the skins.

Melt the butter in an iron saucepan and stir in the flour and curry powder, using a wooden spoon. Cook for 5 minutes or more over low heat. Add the hot milk, stirring constantly, and cook until smooth. Continue to cook, over low heat, until reduced by half, stirring occasionally. (The use of the iron pan makes constant stirring unnecessary.) Season to taste with salt, pepper and the herbs. Thin with the cream to the desired consistency. Combine with the onions and heat together.

MY SPECIAL COLESLAW

I venture to say that coleslaw is the most popular salad in America. In one form or another, it is to be found on the menu of practically every restaurant in the country, from short order luncheonettes to the Pavillon. I'm sure that I'm in the minority, but until this version was served to me by friends, some years ago, I never liked it. On that occasion it accompanied a large pink slice of hot roast beef — a great combination. Even if you think you prefer another kind of dressing, try this.

1 tablespoon butter
1 tablespoon flour
1 teaspoon sugar
1 teaspoon salt
1 teaspoon dry mustard
Dash of freshly ground pepper

2 beaten eggs
½ pint light cream
2 tablespoons vinegar
Fine chopped cabbage

Cream butter with flour, sugar, salt, mustard and pepper. Add beaten eggs. Mix well. Add the cream. Heat vinegar, add to the first mixture and cook, over medium heat, until thick. Cool and mix with the cabbage, allowing ½ cup dressing to 2 cups cabbage.

CHESTNUTS WITH DRIED GRAPES
A Postilion Recipe

This is a specialty at Mme. Kuony's restaurant in Fond du Lac, Wisconsin.

1 lb. shelled fresh chestnuts or 1 lb. dried chestnuts which will have soaked overnight
Chicken stock
3 tablespoons rendered beef kidney fat
1 cup fine sweet port
½ cup dark brown sugar
2 teaspoons salt
A couple turns of the black pepper mill

3 pieces crystallized ginger, chopped very fine
¾ cup washed, dried grapes (the ones you purchase during the holidays that look very much like a long triangular bunch of grapes, which they are — always wrapped in cellophane). Do not seed these. The seed adds to the flavor and texture, just as in *grappe* cheese.

Put the chestnuts in a heavy-bottomed pan and cover them amply with chicken stock and bring them to a very slow simmer. Simmer for as long as it will take to have them become tender. (That depends on when the chestnuts were harvested.) It is essential to let them cook very slowly and when they begin to show transparency, add the kidney fat, the port, brown sugar, salt, black pepper, and ginger, and let this simmer together until the last ingredients added form a glaze as the chestnuts begin to release their natural chestnut flavor. Then add the washed, dried grapes.

Continue simmering until the chestnuts are transparent and when a fork is inserted they look very much like a well-boiled potato. Adjust seasoning.

The chestnuts should be whole or part whole. The sauce should be opaque and have the consistency of a light Béchamel of a rich brown color.

Serve with turkey, any other fowl, game. Also good with goose. Do not get discouraged. This takes a long time to prepare and is better re-heated the next day. Compensate with chicken stock if this should be necessary to prolong the cooking.

SAUCE GUSTAV FOR SEAFOOD

Who is Gustav? What is he? I regret to say that I cannot remember, but this pale green sauce is equally elegant both to look at and to taste. Serve it with shrimp, lobster, crabmeat or cold salmon.

½ cup parsley clusters
½ cup watercress leaves
1 shallot, scallion or small onion, peeled or sliced
1 clove garlic, peeled and sliced
1 teaspoon dry mustard
1 egg yolk

1 scant tablespoon tarragon vinegar
Juice of ½ lemon
¼ teaspoon salt
1 cup Hellmann's mayonnaise (or homemade)
½ cup sour cream

Put first 9 ingredients in an electric blender. Blend for a minute. (Remove top, turn off motor and push greens down into blades if necessary; continue blending.) Add mayonnaise and sour cream and blend a few seconds longer. Chill.

This is enough sauce for 3 lbs. seafood.

SAUCE WES-MAR FOR STEAK

Wesley Ruggles and his French wife, Marcelle, who divide their time between Paris, Deauville and Los Angeles, gave me this un-French-sounding sauce for steak. Don't decide to eliminate the sugar before trying the sauce. It is not noticeable as such but lends an indefinable flavor.

Melt a piece of butter the size of an egg. Stir in a 10½ oz. can of clear beef consommé. Mix 1 scant tablespoon of arrowroot flour or cornstarch with ½ cup cold water and add to simmering consommé. Stir until thick and clear. Add salt and pepper to taste and 1 lump sugar. Add ¾ cup black currants that have been soaked in cognac for 3 hours. Add 5 oz. Madeira. Simmer for 3 minutes.

COLD CUCUMBER SAUCE FOR BROILED CHICKEN

Once again, the source is obscure. The ingredients are odd and the fact that the sauce is cold is odd, but the contrast in flavor and temperature with simply seasoned, crisp broiled chicken is something really special.

Mix together:

1 teaspoon Gulden's mustard
1 teaspoon tarragon vinegar
¼ cup pickled grated horseradish

1 teaspoon confectioner's sugar
½ medium cucumber, peeled, seeded and chopped

Fold in 1 cup whipped cream and chill. This is enough for 2 broilers or four portions.

SAUCE ÉLÉGANTE FOR ROAST LAMB

This sauce was invented for, and served at a dinner given by the Confrérie des Chevaliers du Tastevin in Chicago in January 1964. It accompanied roast rack of lamb. It may be strained or not, but the consensus is that it has more zip and looks better unstrained.

Heat together:

¼ lb. butter
¾ cup currant jelly
¼ cup chopped fresh mint or dried mint

¼ cup tomato catsup
¼ cup red Burgundy
1 tablespoon grated orange rind

Makes about 1¾ cup sauce.

CURRIED SALAD DRESSING

If the main dish of a light meal has been a chicken, corn or clam chowder I like to depart from my usual vinaigrette salad dressing. Sometimes a Caesar salad fills the bill, but more often I dress romaine lettuce with this unusual mixture:

Combine:

1 teaspoon dry mustard	1 teaspoon (or more) curry powder
2 tablespoons lemon juice	1 clove of garlic, put through the
1 teaspoon salt	press
1 teaspoon freshly ground black	1 dash Worcestershire Sauce
pepper	1 cup olive oil

Mix well and chill.

HELEN McCULLY'S APPLE SLICES BAKED IN BUTTER

Take 4 to 5 greenings; pare, core, and slice very thin. Arrange in neat rows, overlapping slightly, in a flat baking dish that can go to the table. Sprinkle lightly with salt, fairly generously with sugar, add the juice of 1 lemon and pour melted butter over all. Place in a preheated 300-degree F., or moderate, oven and bake, basting occasionally, for about 25 minutes or until apple slices are tender. This can be done ahead of time, if you wish.

Just before you are ready to serve, sprinkle with granulated sugar and dot all over with butter. Slide under the broiler until the edges of the apples have turned golden. Serve immediately with pork, goose, duck or game. In fact, any place you'd usually serve apple sauce.

HEAVENLY CHEESE PIE

You may have noticed, if you have ever perused the yellowed pages of someone's grandmother's handwritten recipes, that this sort of name was often given to their favorite dishes. This is an heirloom recipe from a Chicago friend and it fully lives up to its quaint title. In fact, it is a little too heavenly — that is to say, a little too sweet — for many tastes. Since I have found the score to be about fifty-fifty, I feel that I must present the recipe in its original form and leave the alterations up to you. My suggestion would be, if you plan to cut down on the sugar, to do so in the chocolate mixture rather than in the crust or the meringue. The recipe makes two "heavenly" 9″ pies and is well worth experimenting with.

¾ lb. graham cracker crumbs
½ cup light brown sugar, firmly packed

¼ teaspoon nutmeg
⅔ cup melted butter

¾ lb. semi-sweet chocolate bits
1 lb. cream cheese, softened
1 cup light brown sugar, firmly packed

¼ tsp. salt
4 egg yolks

4 egg whites
¼ cup light brown sugar, firmly packed

1 pint heavy cream
2 tsp. vanilla

1. Combine crumbs, brown sugar, nutmeg and butter. Blend thoroughly.

2. Reserve ¼ of mixture for topping. Divide remainder between two 9″ pans; press firmly against bottom and sides, using an 8″ pan to press crumbs into shape. Chill thoroughly.

3. Melt chocolate over hot but not boiling water. Cook 10 minutes.

4. Blend cream cheese, sugar and salt. Add egg yolks, beaten separately, one at a time. Beat after each addition. Add cooled chocolate.

5. Beat egg whites until stiff but not dry. Add the last amount of sugar gradually, beating until stiff and glossy.

6. Fold chocolate mixture into meringue. Whip cream until thick and shiny. Add vanilla. Fold into filling. Pour into pie shells. Sprinkle top with reserved crumbs. Decorate with whipped cream from pastry tube if desired.

Chill several hours or overnight.

MOCHA MOUSSE, SAUCE TIA MARIA

The origin of the mousse is lost. All I know is that I did not invent it, although I did develop the sauce. It is important that the latter be thickened with arrowroot flour because, in that way, it is crystal clear and one can see the pale beige mousse underneath it. It is a light dessert, as beautiful to look at as it is to taste. This recipe will serve ten.

6 egg yolks	2 envelopes gelatin
¾ cup granulated sugar	1½ pints heavy cream
1½ cups strong coffee	

Make a soft custard with the egg yolks, sugar and coffee. Add the gelatin, which has been softened in ½ cup cold water. Stir and cool. Whip the cream and fold it in. Pour into a 2-quart melon-shaped mold and chill. Unmold and pour Sauce Tia Maria over the mousse before serving.

Sauce Tia Maria

3 cups strong coffee	2 tablespoons arrowroot flour
1½ cups sugar	2 oz. Tia Maria liqueur

Heat the coffee with the sugar. Stir the arrowroot into ¼ cup cold water and add. Simmer and stir until thickened. Add Tia Maria and chill.

Note: Whenever a sauce should be crystal clear, as in this case, arrowroot flour is preferable to cornstarch. Cornstarch may be substituted, however, if arrowroot is not available. Kahlua may also be substituted for Tia Maria.

SWEET POTATO PIE

This is another recipe from Avery Island.

Boil 6 large yams until tender. Peel and mash. Put them in an electric mixer with 2 cups sugar, 2 eggs, ½ lb. melted butter, 1 cup bourbon whisky and 1 teaspoon nutmeg. Pour into 2 unbaked 9″ pie shells and bake at 400 degrees for 30 minutes. Serve with sweetened whipped cream laced with bourbon.

NID D'HIRONDELLE

This is a version of the famous Mont Blanc as served by Max Guggiari at the Imperial House in Chicago. If you do not want to go to the trouble of shelling chestnuts, and no matter what anyone says, there is no really easy way to do this, buy them shelled but uncooked. If you cannot find these, buy a can of unsweetened chestnut purée, add vanilla to taste and proceed with the second paragraph of the recipe.

Cook 1 lb. shelled chestnuts in sweetened, vanilla-flavored milk. Cool, strain and purée them.

Add powdered sugar to taste, ½ lb. softened sweet butter, 1 tablespoon of light cream and 2 oz. Grand Marnier. Mix thoroughly. Using a pastry tube with a very small round opening, pipe the purée around the edge of a round platter. The result should look like a ring of vermicelli spaghetti. Chill thoroughly. Fill the center of the ring with faintly sweetened whipped cream. If desired, pipe a border of whipped cream around the outside of the purée.

Serves 6.

JUNE PLATT'S ICED PLUM PUDDING

Mrs. Platt found this recipe in an early American cookbook. She suggests that it might be the forefather of our present day Tutti-Frutti Ice Cream. To me, it is much more interesting.

1 doz. bitter almonds, blanched	¼ cup granulated sugar
1 doz. sweet almonds, blanched	½ cup milk
⅜ cup dried currants, picked over, washed and dried	1 pint heavy cream
	2 teaspoons rosewater

⅓ cup seeded raisins, cut in half with scissors

¼ cup citron, cut in tiny cubes

½ vanilla bean split and cut in 1″ pieces

3 slices preserved lime cut fine

½ cup apricot jam

1½ tb. flour

Yolks of 4 eggs

2 1 lb. cans peeled whole apricots, pitted

½ cup apricot brandy

Blanch the almonds by putting them in a pan of cold water and bringing to a boil. Drain, allowing cold water to run over them, and pinch off the skins. Soak in cold water while you prepare the above ingredients. Add the vanilla bean to the milk, bring gently to the boiling point, remove from the fire and let stand. Pound the sweet and bitter almonds to a paste in a mortar or a sturdy bowl, using a pestle or wooden potato masher, moistening them as you work with the rosewater, a few drops at a time. This prevents oiling.

Mix raisins, currants, citron and lime in a bowl, sprinkle with flour and toss lightly to coat evenly. Strain the scalded milk through a fine sieve, pressing on the bean to get all the benefit of the black parts. Add 1 cup heavy cream to the milk, sweeten with granulated sugar, add the almond paste, stir well and flavor with ¼ cup apricot brandy. Place in top part of enamel double boiler, with the egg yolks, and cook over boiling water stirring constantly until thickened or for about 2-3 minutes. Do not overcook. Add floured fruits and continue cooking for just a few seconds, stirring well. Remove from the fire and cool completely. When cold, stir in ½ cup apricot jam. Beat 1 cup heavy cream until stiff and fold it into the mixture. Place in a 1 quart melon mold, adjust lid and place in the freezing compartment of the refrigerator to freeze solid. This will take at least 8 hours. When ready to serve, remove the lid, run a knife carefully around the edge. Spread a cloth wrung out in very hot water over the mold for a second or two to loosen, and invert it onto an ice cold oval serving platter. Garnish quickly with 2 cans pitted and peeled apricots, well-drained of their juice and flavored with ¼ cup apricot brandy. Serve at once.

For 6.

REEVE'S APPLES

An unusual apple dessert from a friend named Reeve.

9 large cooking apples	Dash lemon juice
3 cups water	4 cups granulated sugar

Peel and core the apples and leave them whole. Dissolve the sugar in the water, add the lemon juice and apples and simmer, uncovered, for 2 hours. Place in a glass bowl and chill thoroughly.

Serve with this sauce:

1 pint milk	4 egg yolks
5 tablespoons granulated sugar	

Beat the milk, sugar and egg yolks together. Cook, stirring often, in a double boiler over simmering water until slightly thick. Serve hot or cold. Serves 6.

JANUARY PUDDING

This is another recipe from my English friend, Maurice Moore-Betty. It is a steamed pudding but has the distinction of being as light as air and, for some reason — perhaps the chemical interaction of brown sugar, jam and baking soda — an unmistakably nutty flavor. Mr. Moore-Betty told me that the pudding was a family specialty, that he had never seen the recipe for it in any cookbook and that it was always — and only — served in January, at his home in Hunts. For that reason we decided to call it January Pudding.

¼ lb. butter	3 tablespoons raspberry jam
¼ lb. flour	2 beaten eggs
2 oz. dark brown sugar	½ teaspoon baking soda

Cream the butter, preferably in an electric mixer. Beat in the flour, jam, sugar, eggs and baking soda, beating well between each addition. Pour into a greased 2 quart bowl or mold and steam for 2 hours. Serve with a purée of raspberries, whipped cream or a mixture of the two. Crème Fraîche, of which you have heard elsewhere in this book, should be delicious with this, flavored or not with raspberry purée.

Serves 6.

CARROT CAKE

A genial lady named Jenella cooks for friends of mine in Winchester, Kentucky. Even if I did not enjoy going to the Keenland Summer Sales or the spring and fall race meetings, I would enjoy visiting at Bwamazon Farm on account of Jenella's cooking. This cake is one of her specialties, and don't let the fact that it is made out of carrots put you off. One would never know that a single carrot had been involved in the making of this dark and spicy confection. Serve it for dessert all by itself; it is too rich and important to be an accompaniment to anything else.

2 cups all-purpose flour	2 cups shredded carrots
2 teaspoons cinnamon	2 cups granulated sugar
2 teaspoons baking soda	1 cup Wesson oil
2 teaspoons double acting baking powder	4 unbeaten eggs
1 teaspoon salt	1 cup chopped pecans

Sift dry ingredients, except sugar, together. Mix sugar with oil in an electric mixer. Add dry ingredients alternately with the eggs to the sugar and oil, mixing after each addition. Add carrots and nuts. Bake at 350 degrees for 1 hour in a 9″ tube pan with the bottom greased.

Icing:

¼ lb. butter	1 box confectioner's sugar
8 oz. Philadelphia cream cheese	2 teaspoons vanilla extract

Allow butter and cheese to soften. Mix together and blend in the sugar. Add the vanilla.

[NOTE: This makes a very generous amount of icing. If you would prefer not to have a good half inch of it, cut the recipe down by a third. — P. H.]

CHOCOLATE PASTRY CAKE

The recipe for the fabulous chocolate cake served at La Fonda del Sol, the beautiful Spanish restaurant in New York's Time and Life Building, is a closely guarded secret. This is as near an approximation of the confection as the General Foods Test Kitchens were able to evolve. A friend connected with General Foods gave it to me when she heard that I was trying to acquire the recipe for this book. I have tried it and recommend it to you.

1 cup Baker's semi-sweet (6 oz. package) glazed chocolate chips
½ cup granulated sugar
½ cup water
¼ teaspoon ground cinnamon

2 teaspoons vanilla extract
1 package (9 or 10 oz.) pie crust mix or homemade pie crust
2 cups whipping cream

Place chocolate chips, sugar, water and cinnamon in small saucepan. Set over low heat and stir frequently until chips are melted and mixture is smooth. Remove from heat, add vanilla and cool to room temperature.

Blend ¾ cup chocolate sauce into pie crust mix. Divide crust mixture into 4 parts. Press or spread each part over the bottom of an inverted 8″ round or square cake pan to within ¼″ of the edge. Bake all four in hot oven (425 degrees F.) 8 to 10 minutes, or until pastry is firm. Remove from oven. If necessary, trim edges with a sharp knife. Cool pastry layers; then run the tip of a knife under edges of layers to loosen them from pans. Lift layers very carefully as they are very fragile.

Whip the cream until it just begins to hold soft peaks. Fold in the remaining chocolate sauce. Spread between torte layers and over the top. Chill at least 8 hours. If desired, garnish with additional chocolate chips before serving. Makes 9 to 12 servings.

Homemade pie crust: Combine 2¼ cups sifted flour and 1 teaspoon salt. Cut in ½ cup shortening until mixture resembles coarse meal. Cut in an additional ¼ cup shortening until mixture is the size of large peas.

Index of Sources

Index of Recipes

Index of Recipes

Index of Recipes